C-122   CAREER EXAMINATION SERIES

This is your
PASSBOOK for...

Car Maintainer, Group A

Test Preparation Study Guide
Questions & Answers

COPYRIGHT NOTICE

This book is SOLELY intended for, is sold ONLY to, and its use is RESTRICTED to individual, bona fide applicants or candidates who qualify by virtue of having seriously filed applications for appropriate license, certificate, professional and/or promotional advancement, higher school matriculation, scholarship, or other legitimate requirements of education and/or governmental authorities.

This book is NOT intended for use, class instruction, tutoring, training, duplication, copying, reprinting, excerption, or adaptation, etc., by:

1) Other publishers
2) Proprietors and/or Instructors of "Coaching" and/or Preparatory Courses
3) Personnel and/or Training Divisions of commercial, industrial, and governmental organizations
4) Schools, colleges, or universities and/or their departments and staffs, including teachers and other personnel
5) Testing Agencies or Bureaus
6) Study groups which seek by the purchase of a single volume to copy and/or duplicate and/or adapt this material for use by the group as a whole without having purchased individual volumes for each of the members of the group
7) Et al.

Such persons would be in violation of appropriate Federal and State statutes.

PROVISION OF LICENSING AGREEMENTS – Recognized educational, commercial, industrial, and governmental institutions and organizations, and others legitimately engaged in educational pursuits, including training, testing, and measurement activities, may address request for a licensing agreement to the copyright owners, who will determine whether, and under what conditions, including fees and charges, the materials in this book may be used them. In other words, a licensing facility exists for the legitimate use of the material in this book on other than an individual basis. However, it is asseverated and affirmed here that the material in this book CANNOT be used without the receipt of the express permission of such a licensing agreement from the Publishers. Inquiries re licensing should be addressed to the company, attention rights and permissions department.

All rights reserved, including the right of reproduction in whole or in part, in any form or by any means, electronic or mechanical, including photocopying, recording, or by any information storage and retrieval system, without permission in writing from the Publisher.

Copyright © 2024 by
National Learning Corporation

212 Michael Drive, Syosset, NY 11791
(516) 921-8888 • www.passbooks.com
E-mail: info@passbooks.com

PUBLISHED IN THE UNITED STATES OF AMERICA

PASSBOOK® SERIES

THE *PASSBOOK® SERIES* has been created to prepare applicants and candidates for the ultimate academic battlefield – the examination room.

At some time in our lives, each and every one of us may be required to take an examination – for validation, matriculation, admission, qualification, registration, certification, or licensure.

Based on the assumption that every applicant or candidate has met the basic formal educational standards, has taken the required number of courses, and read the necessary texts, the *PASSBOOK® SERIES* furnishes the one special preparation which may assure passing with confidence, instead of failing with insecurity. Examination questions – together with answers – are furnished as the basic vehicle for study so that the mysteries of the examination and its compounding difficulties may be eliminated or diminished by a sure method.

This book is meant to help you pass your examination provided that you qualify and are serious in your objective.

The entire field is reviewed through the huge store of content information which is succinctly presented through a provocative and challenging approach – the question-and-answer method.

A climate of success is established by furnishing the correct answers at the end of each test.

You soon learn to recognize types of questions, forms of questions, and patterns of questioning. You may even begin to anticipate expected outcomes.

You perceive that many questions are repeated or adapted so that you can gain acute insights, which may enable you to score many sure points.

You learn how to confront new questions, or types of questions, and to attack them confidently and work out the correct answers.

You note objectives and emphases, and recognize pitfalls and dangers, so that you may make positive educational adjustments.

Moreover, you are kept fully informed in relation to new concepts, methods, practices, and directions in the field.

You discover that you are actually taking the examination all the time: you are preparing for the examination by "taking" an examination, not by reading extraneous and/or supererogatory textbooks.

In short, this PASSBOOK®, used directedly, should be an important factor in helping you to pass your test.

CAR MAINTAINER—GROUP A

JOB DESCRIPTION
Maintains and repairs subways car bodies by performing the necessary welding, cutting, burning, brazing, sheet metal work, forge work and carpentry work. Performs such other duties as the Transit Authority is authorized by law to prescribe in its regulations.

EXAMPLES OF TYPICAL TASKS
Repairs or replaces the metal interior and exterior panels of subway car bodies. Removes and replaces air conditioners and their component parts. Removes and replaces generators, motors, draft gears, electrical boxes, converters, knife switches, fuse boxes and draw bar couplers. Removes and replaces seats and seat backs, glass panels, stanchions, flooring and light fixtures. Repairs pantograph gates and springs, door operators and mechanical linkages. Strips and dresses subway cars. Unhooks hoses and linkages. On the road, works on subway cars involved in collisions and derailments.

TEST DESCRIPTION
The written test will be of the multiple-choice type and may include questions on: procedures used in the fabrication of steel and heavy metal enclosures, assemblies and shapes, including the use of proper tools and equipment; the proper use of welding techniques, including the use of proper welding tools and equipment; job-related mathematics; the reading and interpretation of drawings and sketches; the bending, rolling and cutting of sheet metal; the use of various measuring devices, such as vernier calipers, dial indicators, rulers and gauges; safe work practices and procedures; other work related areas.

HOW TO TAKE A TEST

I. YOU MUST PASS AN EXAMINATION

A. *WHAT EVERY CANDIDATE SHOULD KNOW*

Examination applicants often ask us for help in preparing for the written test. What can I study in advance? What kinds of questions will be asked? How will the test be given? How will the papers be graded?

As an applicant for a civil service examination, you may be wondering about some of these things. Our purpose here is to suggest effective methods of advance study and to describe civil service examinations.

Your chances for success on this examination can be increased if you know how to prepare. Those "pre-examination jitters" can be reduced if you know what to expect. You can even experience an adventure in good citizenship if you know why civil service exams are given.

B. *WHY ARE CIVIL SERVICE EXAMINATIONS GIVEN?*

Civil service examinations are important to you in two ways. As a citizen, you want public jobs filled by employees who know how to do their work. As a job seeker, you want a fair chance to compete for that job on an equal footing with other candidates. The best-known means of accomplishing this two-fold goal is the competitive examination.

Exams are widely publicized throughout the nation. They may be administered for jobs in federal, state, city, municipal, town or village governments or agencies.

Any citizen may apply, with some limitations, such as the age or residence of applicants. Your experience and education may be reviewed to see whether you meet the requirements for the particular examination. When these requirements exist, they are reasonable and applied consistently to all applicants. Thus, a competitive examination may cause you some uneasiness now, but it is your privilege and safeguard.

C. *HOW ARE CIVIL SERVICE EXAMS DEVELOPED?*

Examinations are carefully written by trained technicians who are specialists in the field known as "psychological measurement," in consultation with recognized authorities in the field of work that the test will cover. These experts recommend the subject matter areas or skills to be tested; only those knowledges or skills important to your success on the job are included. The most reliable books and source materials available are used as references. Together, the experts and technicians judge the difficulty level of the questions.

Test technicians know how to phrase questions so that the problem is clearly stated. Their ethics do not permit "trick" or "catch" questions. Questions may have been tried out on sample groups, or subjected to statistical analysis, to determine their usefulness.

Written tests are often used in combination with performance tests, ratings of training and experience, and oral interviews. All of these measures combine to form the best-known means of finding the right person for the right job.

II. HOW TO PASS THE WRITTEN TEST

A. NATURE OF THE EXAMINATION

To prepare intelligently for civil service examinations, you should know how they differ from school examinations you have taken. In school you were assigned certain definite pages to read or subjects to cover. The examination questions were quite detailed and usually emphasized memory. Civil service exams, on the other hand, try to discover your present ability to perform the duties of a position, plus your potentiality to learn these duties. In other words, a civil service exam attempts to predict how successful you will be. Questions cover such a broad area that they cannot be as minute and detailed as school exam questions.

In the public service similar kinds of work, or positions, are grouped together in one "class." This process is known as *position-classification*. All the positions in a class are paid according to the salary range for that class. One class title covers all of these positions, and they are all tested by the same examination.

B. FOUR BASIC STEPS

1) Study the announcement

How, then, can you know what subjects to study? Our best answer is: "Learn as much as possible about the class of positions for which you've applied." The exam will test the knowledge, skills and abilities needed to do the work.

Your most valuable source of information about the position you want is the official exam announcement. This announcement lists the training and experience qualifications. Check these standards and apply only if you come reasonably close to meeting them.

The brief description of the position in the examination announcement offers some clues to the subjects which will be tested. Think about the job itself. Review the duties in your mind. Can you perform them, or are there some in which you are rusty? Fill in the blank spots in your preparation.

Many jurisdictions preview the written test in the exam announcement by including a section called "Knowledge and Abilities Required," "Scope of the Examination," or some similar heading. Here you will find out specifically what fields will be tested.

2) Review your own background

Once you learn in general what the position is all about, and what you need to know to do the work, ask yourself which subjects you already know fairly well and which need improvement. You may wonder whether to concentrate on improving your strong areas or on building some background in your fields of weakness. When the announcement has specified "some knowledge" or "considerable knowledge," or has used adjectives like "beginning principles of..." or "advanced ... methods," you can get a clue as to the number and difficulty of questions to be asked in any given field. More questions, and hence broader coverage, would be included for those subjects which are more important in the work. Now weigh your strengths and weaknesses against the job requirements and prepare accordingly.

3) Determine the level of the position

Another way to tell how intensively you should prepare is to understand the level of the job for which you are applying. Is it the entering level? In other words, is this the position in which beginners in a field of work are hired? Or is it an intermediate or advanced level? Sometimes this is indicated by such words as "Junior" or "Senior" in the class title. Other jurisdictions use Roman numerals to designate the level – Clerk I, Clerk II, for example. The word "Supervisor" sometimes appears in the title. If the level is not indicated by the title, check the description of duties. Will you be working under very close supervision, or will you have responsibility for independent decisions in this work?

4) Choose appropriate study materials

Now that you know the subjects to be examined and the relative amount of each subject to be covered, you can choose suitable study materials. For beginning level jobs, or even advanced ones, if you have a pronounced weakness in some aspect of your training, read a modern, standard textbook in that field. Be sure it is up to date and has general coverage. Such books are normally available at your library, and the librarian will be glad to help you locate one. For entry-level positions, questions of appropriate difficulty are chosen – neither highly advanced questions, nor those too simple. Such questions require careful thought but not advanced training.

If the position for which you are applying is technical or advanced, you will read more advanced, specialized material. If you are already familiar with the basic principles of your field, elementary textbooks would waste your time. Concentrate on advanced textbooks and technical periodicals. Think through the concepts and review difficult problems in your field.

These are all general sources. You can get more ideas on your own initiative, following these leads. For example, training manuals and publications of the government agency which employs workers in your field can be useful, particularly for technical and professional positions. A letter or visit to the government department involved may result in more specific study suggestions, and certainly will provide you with a more definite idea of the exact nature of the position you are seeking.

III. KINDS OF TESTS

Tests are used for purposes other than measuring knowledge and ability to perform specified duties. For some positions, it is equally important to test ability to make adjustments to new situations or to profit from training. In others, basic mental abilities not dependent on information are essential. Questions which test these things may not appear as pertinent to the duties of the position as those which test for knowledge and information. Yet they are often highly important parts of a fair examination. For very general questions, it is almost impossible to help you direct your study efforts. What we can do is to point out some of the more common of these general abilities needed in public service positions and describe some typical questions.

1) General information

Broad, general information has been found useful for predicting job success in some kinds of work. This is tested in a variety of ways, from vocabulary lists to questions about current events. Basic background in some field of work, such as sociology or economics, may be sampled in a group of questions. Often these are principles which have become familiar to most persons through exposure rather than through formal training. It is difficult to advise you how to study for these questions; being alert to the world around you is our best suggestion.

2) Verbal ability

An example of an ability needed in many positions is verbal or language ability. Verbal ability is, in brief, the ability to use and understand words. Vocabulary and grammar tests are typical measures of this ability. Reading comprehension or paragraph interpretation questions are common in many kinds of civil service tests. You are given a paragraph of written material and asked to find its central meaning.

3) Numerical ability

Number skills can be tested by the familiar arithmetic problem, by checking paired lists of numbers to see which are alike and which are different, or by interpreting charts and graphs. In the latter test, a graph may be printed in the test booklet which you are asked to use as the basis for answering questions.

4) Observation

A popular test for law-enforcement positions is the observation test. A picture is shown to you for several minutes, then taken away. Questions about the picture test your ability to observe both details and larger elements.

5) Following directions

In many positions in the public service, the employee must be able to carry out written instructions dependably and accurately. You may be given a chart with several columns, each column listing a variety of information. The questions require you to carry out directions involving the information given in the chart.

6) Skills and aptitudes

Performance tests effectively measure some manual skills and aptitudes. When the skill is one in which you are trained, such as typing or shorthand, you can practice. These tests are often very much like those given in business school or high school courses. For many of the other skills and aptitudes, however, no short-time preparation can be made. Skills and abilities natural to you or that you have developed throughout your lifetime are being tested.

Many of the general questions just described provide all the data needed to answer the questions and ask you to use your reasoning ability to find the answers. Your best preparation for these tests, as well as for tests of facts and ideas, is to be at your physical and mental best. You, no doubt, have your own methods of getting into an exam-taking mood and keeping "in shape." The next section lists some ideas on this subject.

IV. KINDS OF QUESTIONS

Only rarely is the "essay" question, which you answer in narrative form, used in civil service tests. Civil service tests are usually of the short-answer type. Full instructions for answering these questions will be given to you at the examination. But in case this is your first experience with short-answer questions and separate answer sheets, here is what you need to know:

1) Multiple-choice Questions

Most popular of the short-answer questions is the "multiple choice" or "best answer" question. It can be used, for example, to test for factual knowledge, ability to solve problems or judgment in meeting situations found at work.

A multiple-choice question is normally one of three types—
- It can begin with an incomplete statement followed by several possible endings. You are to find the one ending which *best* completes the statement, although some of the others may not be entirely wrong.
- It can also be a complete statement in the form of a question which is answered by choosing one of the statements listed.

- It can be in the form of a problem – again you select the best answer.

Here is an example of a multiple-choice question with a discussion which should give you some clues as to the method for choosing the right answer:

When an employee has a complaint about his assignment, the action which will *best* help him overcome his difficulty is to
- A. discuss his difficulty with his coworkers
- B. take the problem to the head of the organization
- C. take the problem to the person who gave him the assignment
- D. say nothing to anyone about his complaint

In answering this question, you should study each of the choices to find which is best. Consider choice "A" – Certainly an employee may discuss his complaint with fellow employees, but no change or improvement can result, and the complaint remains unresolved. Choice "B" is a poor choice since the head of the organization probably does not know what assignment you have been given, and taking your problem to him is known as "going over the head" of the supervisor. The supervisor, or person who made the assignment, is the person who can clarify it or correct any injustice. Choice "C" is, therefore, correct. To say nothing, as in choice "D," is unwise. Supervisors have and interest in knowing the problems employees are facing, and the employee is seeking a solution to his problem.

2) True/False Questions

The "true/false" or "right/wrong" form of question is sometimes used. Here a complete statement is given. Your job is to decide whether the statement is right or wrong.

SAMPLE: A roaming cell-phone call to a nearby city costs less than a non-roaming call to a distant city.

This statement is wrong, or false, since roaming calls are more expensive.

This is not a complete list of all possible question forms, although most of the others are variations of these common types. You will always get complete directions for answering questions. Be sure you understand *how* to mark your answers – ask questions until you do.

V. RECORDING YOUR ANSWERS

Computer terminals are used more and more today for many different kinds of exams.
For an examination with very few applicants, you may be told to record your answers in the test booklet itself. Separate answer sheets are much more common. If this separate answer sheet is to be scored by machine – and this is often the case – it is highly important that you mark your answers correctly in order to get credit.
An electronic scoring machine is often used in civil service offices because of the speed with which papers can be scored. Machine-scored answer sheets must be marked with a pencil, which will be given to you. This pencil has a high graphite content which responds to the electronic scoring machine. As a matter of fact, stray dots may register as answers, so do not let your pencil rest on the answer sheet while you are pondering the correct answer. Also, if your pencil lead breaks or is otherwise defective, ask for another.

Since the answer sheet will be dropped in a slot in the scoring machine, be careful not to bend the corners or get the paper crumpled.

The answer sheet normally has five vertical columns of numbers, with 30 numbers to a column. These numbers correspond to the question numbers in your test booklet. After each number, going across the page are four or five pairs of dotted lines. These short dotted lines have small letters or numbers above them. The first two pairs may also have a "T" or "F" above the letters. This indicates that the first two pairs only are to be used if the questions are of the true-false type. If the questions are multiple choice, disregard the "T" and "F" and pay attention only to the small letters or numbers.

Answer your questions in the manner of the sample that follows:

32. The largest city in the United States is
    A. Washington, D.C.
    B. New York City
    C. Chicago
    D. Detroit
    E. San Francisco

1) Choose the answer you think is best. (New York City is the largest, so "B" is correct.)
2) Find the row of dotted lines numbered the same as the question you are answering. (Find row number 32)
3) Find the pair of dotted lines corresponding to the answer. (Find the pair of lines under the mark "B.")
4) Make a solid black mark between the dotted lines.

VI. BEFORE THE TEST

Common sense will help you find procedures to follow to get ready for an examination. Too many of us, however, overlook these sensible measures. Indeed, nervousness and fatigue have been found to be the most serious reasons why applicants fail to do their best on civil service tests. Here is a list of reminders:

- Begin your preparation early – Don't wait until the last minute to go scurrying around for books and materials or to find out what the position is all about.
- Prepare continuously – An hour a night for a week is better than an all-night cram session. This has been definitely established. What is more, a night a week for a month will return better dividends than crowding your study into a shorter period of time.
- Locate the place of the exam – You have been sent a notice telling you when and where to report for the examination. If the location is in a different town or otherwise unfamiliar to you, it would be well to inquire the best route and learn something about the building.
- Relax the night before the test – Allow your mind to rest. Do not study at all that night. Plan some mild recreation or diversion; then go to bed early and get a good night's sleep.
- Get up early enough to make a leisurely trip to the place for the test – This way unforeseen events, traffic snarls, unfamiliar buildings, etc. will not upset you.
- Dress comfortably – A written test is not a fashion show. You will be known by number and not by name, so wear something comfortable.

- Leave excess paraphernalia at home – Shopping bags and odd bundles will get in your way. You need bring only the items mentioned in the official notice you received; usually everything you need is provided. Do not bring reference books to the exam. They will only confuse those last minutes and be taken away from you when in the test room.
- Arrive somewhat ahead of time – If because of transportation schedules you must get there very early, bring a newspaper or magazine to take your mind off yourself while waiting.
- Locate the examination room – When you have found the proper room, you will be directed to the seat or part of the room where you will sit. Sometimes you are given a sheet of instructions to read while you are waiting. Do not fill out any forms until you are told to do so; just read them and be prepared.
- Relax and prepare to listen to the instructions
- If you have any physical problem that may keep you from doing your best, be sure to tell the test administrator. If you are sick or in poor health, you really cannot do your best on the exam. You can come back and take the test some other time.

VII. AT THE TEST

The day of the test is here and you have the test booklet in your hand. The temptation to get going is very strong. Caution! There is more to success than knowing the right answers. You must know how to identify your papers and understand variations in the type of short-answer question used in this particular examination. Follow these suggestions for maximum results from your efforts:

1) Cooperate with the monitor

The test administrator has a duty to create a situation in which you can be as much at ease as possible. He will give instructions, tell you when to begin, check to see that you are marking your answer sheet correctly, and so on. He is not there to guard you, although he will see that your competitors do not take unfair advantage. He wants to help you do your best.

2) Listen to all instructions

Don't jump the gun! Wait until you understand all directions. In most civil service tests you get more time than you need to answer the questions. So don't be in a hurry. Read each word of instructions until you clearly understand the meaning. Study the examples, listen to all announcements and follow directions. Ask questions if you do not understand what to do.

3) Identify your papers

Civil service exams are usually identified by number only. You will be assigned a number; you must not put your name on your test papers. Be sure to copy your number correctly. Since more than one exam may be given, copy your exact examination title.

4) Plan your time

Unless you are told that a test is a "speed" or "rate of work" test, speed itself is usually not important. Time enough to answer all the questions will be provided, but this does not mean that you have all day. An overall time limit has been set. Divide the total time (in minutes) by the number of questions to determine the approximate time you have for each question.

5) Do not linger over difficult questions

If you come across a difficult question, mark it with a paper clip (useful to have along) and come back to it when you have been through the booklet. One caution if you do this – be sure to skip a number on your answer sheet as well. Check often to be sure that you have not lost your place and that you are marking in the row numbered the same as the question you are answering.

6) Read the questions

Be sure you know what the question asks! Many capable people are unsuccessful because they failed to *read* the questions correctly.

7) Answer all questions

Unless you have been instructed that a penalty will be deducted for incorrect answers, it is better to guess than to omit a question.

8) Speed tests

It is often better NOT to guess on speed tests. It has been found that on timed tests people are tempted to spend the last few seconds before time is called in marking answers at random – without even reading them – in the hope of picking up a few extra points. To discourage this practice, the instructions may warn you that your score will be "corrected" for guessing. That is, a penalty will be applied. The incorrect answers will be deducted from the correct ones, or some other penalty formula will be used.

9) Review your answers

If you finish before time is called, go back to the questions you guessed or omitted to give them further thought. Review other answers if you have time.

10) Return your test materials

If you are ready to leave before others have finished or time is called, take ALL your materials to the monitor and leave quietly. Never take any test material with you. The monitor can discover whose papers are not complete, and taking a test booklet may be grounds for disqualification.

VIII. EXAMINATION TECHNIQUES

1) Read the general instructions carefully. These are usually printed on the first page of the exam booklet. As a rule, these instructions refer to the timing of the examination; the fact that you should not start work until the signal and must stop work at a signal, etc. If there are any *special* instructions, such as a choice of questions to be answered, make sure that you note this instruction carefully.

2) When you are ready to start work on the examination, that is as soon as the signal has been given, read the instructions to each question booklet, underline any key words or phrases, such as *least, best, outline, describe* and the like. In this way you will tend to answer as requested rather than discover on reviewing your paper that you *listed without describing*, that you selected the *worst* choice rather than the *best* choice, etc.

3) If the examination is of the objective or multiple-choice type – that is, each question will also give a series of possible answers: A, B, C or D, and you are called upon to select the best answer and write the letter next to that answer on your answer paper – it is advisable to start answering each question in turn. There may be anywhere from 50 to 100 such questions in the three or four hours allotted and you can see how much time would be taken if you read through all the questions before beginning to answer any. Furthermore, if you come across a question or group of questions which you know would be difficult to answer, it would undoubtedly affect your handling of all the other questions.

4) If the examination is of the essay type and contains but a few questions, it is a moot point as to whether you should read all the questions before starting to answer any one. Of course, if you are given a choice – say five out of seven and the like – then it is essential to read all the questions so you can eliminate the two that are most difficult. If, however, you are asked to answer all the questions, there may be danger in trying to answer the easiest one first because you may find that you will spend too much time on it. The best technique is to answer the first question, then proceed to the second, etc.

5) Time your answers. Before the exam begins, write down the time it started, then add the time allowed for the examination and write down the time it must be completed, then divide the time available somewhat as follows:
    - If 3-1/2 hours are allowed, that would be 210 minutes. If you have 80 objective-type questions, that would be an average of 2-1/2 minutes per question. Allow yourself no more than 2 minutes per question, or a total of 160 minutes, which will permit about 50 minutes to review.
    - If for the time allotment of 210 minutes there are 7 essay questions to answer, that would average about 30 minutes a question. Give yourself only 25 minutes per question so that you have about 35 minutes to review.

6) The most important instruction is to *read each question* and make sure you know what is wanted. The second most important instruction is to *time yourself properly* so that you answer every question. The third most important instruction is to *answer every question*. Guess if you have to but include something for each question. Remember that you will receive no credit for a blank and will probably receive some credit if you write something in answer to an essay question. If you guess a letter – say "B" for a multiple-choice question – you may have guessed right. If you leave a blank as an answer to a multiple-choice question, the examiners may respect your feelings but it will not add a point to your score. Some exams may penalize you for wrong answers, so in such cases *only*, you may not want to guess unless you have some basis for your answer.

7) Suggestions
    a. Objective-type questions
        1. Examine the question booklet for proper sequence of pages and questions
        2. Read all instructions carefully
        3. Skip any question which seems too difficult; return to it after all other questions have been answered
        4. Apportion your time properly; do not spend too much time on any single question or group of questions

5. Note and underline key words – *all, most, fewest, least, best, worst, same, opposite,* etc.
6. Pay particular attention to negatives
7. Note unusual option, e.g., unduly long, short, complex, different or similar in content to the body of the question
8. Observe the use of "hedging" words – *probably, may, most likely,* etc.
9. Make sure that your answer is put next to the same number as the question
10. Do not second-guess unless you have good reason to believe the second answer is definitely more correct
11. Cross out original answer if you decide another answer is more accurate; do not erase until you are ready to hand your paper in
12. Answer all questions; guess unless instructed otherwise
13. Leave time for review

   b. Essay questions
      1. Read each question carefully
      2. Determine exactly what is wanted. Underline key words or phrases.
      3. Decide on outline or paragraph answer
      4. Include many different points and elements unless asked to develop any one or two points or elements
      5. Show impartiality by giving pros and cons unless directed to select one side only
      6. Make and write down any assumptions you find necessary to answer the questions
      7. Watch your English, grammar, punctuation and choice of words
      8. Time your answers; don't crowd material

8) Answering the essay question

Most essay questions can be answered by framing the specific response around several key words or ideas. Here are a few such key words or ideas:

M's: manpower, materials, methods, money, management
P's: purpose, program, policy, plan, procedure, practice, problems, pitfalls, personnel, public relations

   a. Six basic steps in handling problems:
      1. Preliminary plan and background development
      2. Collect information, data and facts
      3. Analyze and interpret information, data and facts
      4. Analyze and develop solutions as well as make recommendations
      5. Prepare report and sell recommendations
      6. Install recommendations and follow up effectiveness

   b. Pitfalls to avoid
      1. *Taking things for granted* – A statement of the situation does not necessarily imply that each of the elements is necessarily true; for example, a complaint may be invalid and biased so that all that can be taken for granted is that a complaint has been registered

2. *Considering only one side of a situation* – Wherever possible, indicate several alternatives and then point out the reasons you selected the best one
3. *Failing to indicate follow up* – Whenever your answer indicates action on your part, make certain that you will take proper follow-up action to see how successful your recommendations, procedures or actions turn out to be
4. *Taking too long in answering any single question* – Remember to time your answers properly

IX. AFTER THE TEST

Scoring procedures differ in detail among civil service jurisdictions although the general principles are the same. Whether the papers are hand-scored or graded by machine we have described, they are nearly always graded by number. That is, the person who marks the paper knows only the number – never the name – of the applicant. Not until all the papers have been graded will they be matched with names. If other tests, such as training and experience or oral interview ratings have been given, scores will be combined. Different parts of the examination usually have different weights. For example, the written test might count 60 percent of the final grade, and a rating of training and experience 40 percent. In many jurisdictions, veterans will have a certain number of points added to their grades.

After the final grade has been determined, the names are placed in grade order and an eligible list is established. There are various methods for resolving ties between those who get the same final grade – probably the most common is to place first the name of the person whose application was received first. Job offers are made from the eligible list in the order the names appear on it. You will be notified of your grade and your rank as soon as all these computations have been made. This will be done as rapidly as possible.

People who are found to meet the requirements in the announcement are called "eligibles." Their names are put on a list of eligible candidates. An eligible's chances of getting a job depend on how high he stands on this list and how fast agencies are filling jobs from the list.

When a job is to be filled from a list of eligibles, the agency asks for the names of people on the list of eligibles for that job. When the civil service commission receives this request, it sends to the agency the names of the three people highest on this list. Or, if the job to be filled has specialized requirements, the office sends the agency the names of the top three persons who meet these requirements from the general list.

The appointing officer makes a choice from among the three people whose names were sent to him. If the selected person accepts the appointment, the names of the others are put back on the list to be considered for future openings.

That is the rule in hiring from all kinds of eligible lists, whether they are for typist, carpenter, chemist, or something else. For every vacancy, the appointing officer has his choice of any one of the top three eligibles on the list. This explains why the person whose name is on top of the list sometimes does not get an appointment when some of the persons lower on the list do. If the appointing officer chooses the second or third eligible, the No. 1 eligible does not get a job at once, but stays on the list until he is appointed or the list is terminated.

X. HOW TO PASS THE INTERVIEW TEST

The examination for which you applied requires an oral interview test. You have already taken the written test and you are now being called for the interview test – the final part of the formal examination.

You may think that it is not possible to prepare for an interview test and that there are no procedures to follow during an interview. Our purpose is to point out some things you can do in advance that will help you and some good rules to follow and pitfalls to avoid while you are being interviewed.

What is an interview supposed to test?

The written examination is designed to test the technical knowledge and competence of the candidate; the oral is designed to evaluate intangible qualities, not readily measured otherwise, and to establish a list showing the relative fitness of each candidate – as measured against his competitors – for the position sought. Scoring is not on the basis of "right" and "wrong," but on a sliding scale of values ranging from "not passable" to "outstanding." As a matter of fact, it is possible to achieve a relatively low score without a single "incorrect" answer because of evident weakness in the qualities being measured.

Occasionally, an examination may consist entirely of an oral test – either an individual or a group oral. In such cases, information is sought concerning the technical knowledges and abilities of the candidate, since there has been no written examination for this purpose. More commonly, however, an oral test is used to supplement a written examination.

Who conducts interviews?

The composition of oral boards varies among different jurisdictions. In nearly all, a representative of the personnel department serves as chairman. One of the members of the board may be a representative of the department in which the candidate would work. In some cases, "outside experts" are used, and, frequently, a businessman or some other representative of the general public is asked to serve. Labor and management or other special groups may be represented. The aim is to secure the services of experts in the appropriate field.

However the board is composed, it is a good idea (and not at all improper or unethical) to ascertain in advance of the interview who the members are and what groups they represent. When you are introduced to them, you will have some idea of their backgrounds and interests, and at least you will not stutter and stammer over their names.

What should be done before the interview?

While knowledge about the board members is useful and takes some of the surprise element out of the interview, there is other preparation which is more substantive. It *is* possible to prepare for an oral interview – in several ways:

1) Keep a copy of your application and review it carefully before the interview

This may be the only document before the oral board, and the starting point of the interview. Know what education and experience you have listed there, and the sequence and dates of all of it. Sometimes the board will ask you to review the highlights of your experience for them; you should not have to hem and haw doing it.

2) Study the class specification and the examination announcement

Usually, the oral board has one or both of these to guide them. The qualities, characteristics or knowledges required by the position sought are stated in these documents. They offer valuable clues as to the nature of the oral interview. For example, if the job involves supervisory responsibilities, the announcement will usually indicate that knowledge of modern supervisory methods and the qualifications of the candidate as a supervisor will be tested. If so, you can expect such questions, frequently in the form of a hypothetical situation which you are expected to solve. NEVER go into an oral without knowledge of the duties and responsibilities of the job you seek.

3) Think through each qualification required

Try to visualize the kind of questions you would ask if you were a board member. How well could you answer them? Try especially to appraise your own knowledge and background in each area, *measured against the job sought*, and identify any areas in which you are weak. Be critical and realistic – do not flatter yourself.

4) Do some general reading in areas in which you feel you may be weak

For example, if the job involves supervision and your past experience has NOT, some general reading in supervisory methods and practices, particularly in the field of human relations, might be useful. Do NOT study agency procedures or detailed manuals. The oral board will be testing your understanding and capacity, not your memory.

5) Get a good night's sleep and watch your general health and mental attitude

You will want a clear head at the interview. Take care of a cold or any other minor ailment, and of course, no hangovers.

What should be done on the day of the interview?

Now comes the day of the interview itself. Give yourself plenty of time to get there. Plan to arrive somewhat ahead of the scheduled time, particularly if your appointment is in the fore part of the day. If a previous candidate fails to appear, the board might be ready for you a bit early. By early afternoon an oral board is almost invariably behind schedule if there are many candidates, and you may have to wait. Take along a book or magazine to read, or your application to review, but leave any extraneous material in the waiting room when you go in for your interview. In any event, relax and compose yourself.

The matter of dress is important. The board is forming impressions about you – from your experience, your manners, your attitude, and your appearance. Give your personal appearance careful attention. Dress your best, but not your flashiest. Choose conservative, appropriate clothing, and be sure it is immaculate. This is a business interview, and your appearance should indicate that you regard it as such. Besides, being well groomed and properly dressed will help boost your confidence.

Sooner or later, someone will call your name and escort you into the interview room. *This is it.* From here on you are on your own. It is too late for any more preparation. But remember, you asked for this opportunity to prove your fitness, and you are here because your request was granted.

What happens when you go in?

The usual sequence of events will be as follows: The clerk (who is often the board stenographer) will introduce you to the chairman of the oral board, who will introduce you to the other members of the board. Acknowledge the introductions before you sit down. Do not be surprised if you find a microphone facing you or a stenotypist sitting by. Oral interviews are usually recorded in the event of an appeal or other review.

Usually the chairman of the board will open the interview by reviewing the highlights of your education and work experience from your application – primarily for the benefit of the other members of the board, as well as to get the material into the record. Do not interrupt or comment unless there is an error or significant misinterpretation; if that is the case, do not hesitate. But do not quibble about insignificant matters. Also, he will usually ask you some question about your education, experience or your present job – partly to get you to start talking and to establish the interviewing "rapport." He may start the actual questioning, or turn it over to one of the other members. Frequently, each member undertakes the questioning on a particular area, one in which he is perhaps most competent, so you can expect each member to participate in the examination. Because time is limited, you may also expect some rather abrupt switches in the direction the questioning takes, so do not be upset by it. Normally, a board member will not pursue a single line of questioning unless he discovers a particular strength or weakness.

After each member has participated, the chairman will usually ask whether any member has any further questions, then will ask you if you have anything you wish to add. Unless you are expecting this question, it may floor you. Worse, it may start you off on an extended, extemporaneous speech. The board is not usually seeking more information. The question is principally to offer you a last opportunity to present further qualifications or to indicate that you have nothing to add. So, if you feel that a significant qualification or characteristic has been overlooked, it is proper to point it out in a sentence or so. Do not compliment the board on the thoroughness of their examination – they have been sketchy, and you know it. If you wish, merely say, "No thank you, I have nothing further to add." This is a point where you can "talk yourself out" of a good impression or fail to present an important bit of information. Remember, *you close the interview yourself.*

The chairman will then say, "That is all, Mr. _____, thank you." Do not be startled; the interview is over, and quicker than you think. Thank him, gather your belongings and take your leave. Save your sigh of relief for the other side of the door.

How to put your best foot forward

Throughout this entire process, you may feel that the board individually and collectively is trying to pierce your defenses, seek out your hidden weaknesses and embarrass and confuse you. Actually, this is not true. They are obliged to make an appraisal of your qualifications for the job you are seeking, and they want to see you in your best light. Remember, they must interview all candidates and a non-cooperative candidate may become a failure in spite of their best efforts to bring out his qualifications. Here are 15 suggestions that will help you:

1) Be natural – Keep your attitude confident, not cocky

If you are not confident that you can do the job, do not expect the board to be. Do not apologize for your weaknesses, try to bring out your strong points. The board is interested in a positive, not negative, presentation. Cockiness will antagonize any board member and make him wonder if you are covering up a weakness by a false show of strength.

2) Get comfortable, but don't lounge or sprawl

Sit erectly but not stiffly. A careless posture may lead the board to conclude that you are careless in other things, or at least that you are not impressed by the importance of the occasion. Either conclusion is natural, even if incorrect. Do not fuss with your clothing, a pencil or an ashtray. Your hands may occasionally be useful to emphasize a point; do not let them become a point of distraction.

3) Do not wisecrack or make small talk

This is a serious situation, and your attitude should show that you consider it as such. Further, the time of the board is limited – they do not want to waste it, and neither should you.

4) Do not exaggerate your experience or abilities

In the first place, from information in the application or other interviews and sources, the board may know more about you than you think. Secondly, you probably will not get away with it. An experienced board is rather adept at spotting such a situation, so do not take the chance.

5) If you know a board member, do not make a point of it, yet do not hide it

Certainly you are not fooling him, and probably not the other members of the board. Do not try to take advantage of your acquaintanceship – it will probably do you little good.

6) Do not dominate the interview

Let the board do that. They will give you the clues – do not assume that you have to do all the talking. Realize that the board has a number of questions to ask you, and do not try to take up all the interview time by showing off your extensive knowledge of the answer to the first one.

7) Be attentive

You only have 20 minutes or so, and you should keep your attention at its sharpest throughout. When a member is addressing a problem or question to you, give him your undivided attention. Address your reply principally to him, but do not exclude the other board members.

8) Do not interrupt

A board member may be stating a problem for you to analyze. He will ask you a question when the time comes. Let him state the problem, and wait for the question.

9) Make sure you understand the question

Do not try to answer until you are sure what the question is. If it is not clear, restate it in your own words or ask the board member to clarify it for you. However, do not haggle about minor elements.

10) Reply promptly but not hastily

A common entry on oral board rating sheets is "candidate responded readily," or "candidate hesitated in replies." Respond as promptly and quickly as you can, but do not jump to a hasty, ill-considered answer.

11) Do not be peremptory in your answers

A brief answer is proper – but do not fire your answer back. That is a losing game from your point of view. The board member can probably ask questions much faster than you can answer them.

12) Do not try to create the answer you think the board member wants

He is interested in what kind of mind you have and how it works – not in playing games. Furthermore, he can usually spot this practice and will actually grade you down on it.

13) Do not switch sides in your reply merely to agree with a board member

Frequently, a member will take a contrary position merely to draw you out and to see if you are willing and able to defend your point of view. Do not start a debate, yet do not surrender a good position. If a position is worth taking, it is worth defending.

14) Do not be afraid to admit an error in judgment if you are shown to be wrong

The board knows that you are forced to reply without any opportunity for careful consideration. Your answer may be demonstrably wrong. If so, admit it and get on with the interview.

15) Do not dwell at length on your present job

The opening question may relate to your present assignment. Answer the question but do not go into an extended discussion. You are being examined for a *new* job, not your present one. As a matter of fact, try to phrase ALL your answers in terms of the job for which you are being examined.

Basis of Rating

Probably you will forget most of these "do's" and "don'ts" when you walk into the oral interview room. Even remembering them all will not ensure you a passing grade. Perhaps you did not have the qualifications in the first place. But remembering them will help you to put your best foot forward, without treading on the toes of the board members.

Rumor and popular opinion to the contrary notwithstanding, an oral board wants you to make the best appearance possible. They know you are under pressure – but they also want to see how you respond to it as a guide to what your reaction would be under the pressures of the job you seek. They will be influenced by the degree of poise you display, the personal traits you show and the manner in which you respond.

ABOUT THIS BOOK

This book contains tests divided into Examination Sections. Go through each test, answering every question in the margin. We have also attached a sample answer sheet at the back of the book that can be removed and used. At the end of each test look at the answer key and check your answers. On the ones you got wrong, look at the right answer choice and learn. Do not fill in the answers first. Do not memorize the questions and answers, but understand the answer and principles involved. On your test, the questions will likely be different from the samples. Questions are changed and new ones added. If you understand these past questions you should have success with any changes that arise. Tests may consist of several types of questions. We have additional books on each subject should more study be advisable or necessary for you. Finally, the more you study, the better prepared you will be. This book is intended to be the last thing you study before you walk into the examination room. Prior study of relevant texts is also recommended. NLC publishes some of these in our Fundamental Series. Knowledge and good sense are important factors in passing your exam. Good luck also helps. So now study this Passbook, absorb the material contained within and take that knowledge into the examination. Then do your best to pass that exam.

EXAMINATION SECTION

EXAMINATION SECTION
TEST 1

DIRECTIONS: Each question or incomplete statement is followed by several suggested answers or completions. Select the one that BEST answers the question or completes the Statement. *PRINT THE LETTER OF THE CORRECT ANSWER IN THE SPACE AT THE RIGHT.*

1. The piston of a hydraulic jack is operated by   1.____

    A. electricity   B. oil pressure
    C. a rotating thread   D. air pressure

2. The PROPER tool to use when tightening a nut on a large diameter bolt is a(n)   2.____

    A. brace and bit   B. gas pliers
    C. open end wrench   D. vise grip pliers

3. Employees are cautioned, as a safety measure, not to use water to extinguish fires near   3.____
the 600-volt third rail.
The MOST logical reason for this caution is that the water

    A. will cause a corrosive steam vapor to develop
    B. may damage the running gear of the subway car
    C. will cause the running rails to become slippery
    D. may transmit electrical shock to the user

4. When a piece of old equipment is taken apart, the fastening devices that are MOST likely   4.____
to be reused are the

    A. bolts   B. cotter pins   C. rivets   D. gaskets

5. The wrench which is LEAST likely to slip off a standard size nut is a _____ wrench.   5.____

    A. box   B. monkey
    C. Stillson   D. spanner

6. If a car maintainer lets oil fall on the floor, he should wipe it up right away because   6.____

    A. the oil will attract rats
    B. people may slip on the oil and fall
    C. the oil can be used again
    D. oil will cause corrosion

7. Old rags soaked with oil or grease can easily catch on fire.   7.____
They should be put into

    A. open steel drums
    B. metal cans with covers
    C. metal cans and soaked with water
    D. plastic cans with covers

8. When used in connection with a portable pneumatic drill, the term *old man* refers to a(n)   8.____

    A. experienced operator who works with a helper
    B. adjustable support which is clamped to a steel beam

C. special drill for soft materials
D. drill selection gage

9. A flexible shaft coupling SHOULD be used for the condition where _____ a motor shaft.

   A. the input shaft of a gear box is to be connected to
   B. a pulley wheel is to be mounted on
   C. a drill chuck is to be mounted on
   D. a grinding wheel is to be mounted on

10. The dimension of a machined shaft must be 2.000 ± .002". Of the four shafts tested, the one that is NOT acceptable measures

    A. 2.003"   B. 2.002"   C. 1.999"   D. 1.998"

11. Flat wheels on a subway car are MOST likely to result from

    A. loss of brake air
    B. passenger overload
    C. moving the car at high speeds
    D. moving the car with brakes locked

12. The metal which is MOST likely to crack when struck a heavy blow is

    A. cast iron   B. forged steel
    C. malleable iron   D. wrought iron

13. The MOST important reason for removing pressure from an air hose before breaking the hose connection to a pneumatic wrench is to avoid

    A. loss of air   B. damage to the wrench
    C. personal injury   D. overloading the compressor

14. The MOST important reason for wearing safety shoes when working under subway cars is to

    A. reduce fatigue   B. avoid injury
    C. save money   D. avoid criticism

15. Cotter pins are MOST generally used with _____ nuts.

    A. acorn   B. castellated
    C. knurled   D. wing

16. When putting out a fire with a hand extinguisher, it is BEST to direct the discharge at the _____ the fire.

    A. area behind   B. area in front of
    C. highest flames in   D. base of

17. Steel dowel pins are GENERALLY used to fit two steel parts together when it is necessary to

    A. secure additional strength and stiffness of the two parts
    B. secure exact placement of these parts with respect to each other
    C. maintain a loose fit between the parts
    D. maintain a flow of lubricant through the dowel pins

18. Of the following, the factor which is LEAST likely to make an employee accident prone is   18.____

   A. poor health
   B. seniority in his job
   C. *moonlighting* on a second job
   D. bad feelings toward his foreman

19. The process of calibrating wrenches applies MAINLY to   19.____

   A. socket wrenches
   B. offset wrenches
   C. impact wrenches
   D. long handled open-end wrenches

20. A practical method which is COMMONLY used to keep a nut from loosening on a bolt is to   20.____

   A. fill in the exposed threads on the bolt with solder
   B. use a centerpunch on the face of the nut at the threads
   C. bend the end of the bolt
   D. tape the end of the bolt

21. Backlash in a meshed pair of gears   21.____

   A. tends to reduce noise
   B. decrease with wear
   C. will cause the gears to jam
   D. is the *play* between the gear teeth

22. A pinion with 12 teeth engages a gear rack having 6 teeth per inch. When the rack has moved two inches, the pinion will have made _____ revolution(s).   22.____

   A. 1/4 of a
   B. 1/2 of a
   C. 1
   D. 2

23. If an 8" level indicates 16 quarts of oil in the tank shown, then the number of quarts of oil to be added to raise the level from 8" to 10" is _____ quarts.   23.____

   A. 2
   B. 4
   C. 6
   D. 8

24. Using only the sizes of washers shown, the least number of washers needed to exactly fill the 1 1/4" space is   24.____

   A. 2
   B. 3
   C. 4
   D. 5

25. The number of complete turns the handle must make to fully close the jaws of the vise shown is
    A. 4
    B. 8
    C. 16
    D. 20

26. In order to properly secure the three metal pieces shown in the sketch together by means of the single machine screw, a thread should be tapped in piece
    A. #2 and #3
    B. #3
    C. #2
    D. #1

27. *Lapping* is a shop process used on metal parts in order to produce a very smooth surface.
    Lapping would PROBABLY be used on a
    A. brake cylinder bore B. very fine steel thread
    C. dowel hole D. brake actuating pin

28. In order to obtain an interference fit of a rod in a machined hole, the rod
    A. diameter should be slightly smaller than the hole diameter
    B. diameter should be slightly larger than the hole diameter
    C. should be heated before inserting it in the hole
    D. should be cooled before inserting it in the hole

29. When grinding a flat chisel, it is good practice to keep the chisel moving across the face of the grinding wheel in order to
    A. prevent burning of the chisel tip
    B. reduce amount of sparks
    C. maintain a uniform wheel speed
    D. prevent grooving of the wheel

30. If a 4 1/16" shaft wears six thousandths of an inch on the diameter, the new diameter measures
    A. 4.0025"   B. 4.0565"   C. 4.0595"   D. 4.0619"

31. A drill gage is used for measuring drill
    A. diameter B. length
    C. hardness D. cutting speed

32. The reading shown on the micrometer is 32.____
    A. 0.203
    B. 0.227
    C. 0.228
    D. 0.247

33. Shortening the length of a bolt by cutting through the threaded portion damages the thread. 33.____
    The SIMPLEST procedure to reduce the difficulty of threading a nut on this bolt is to

    A. clean up the damaged thread with a 3-cornered file and then wire brush
    B. run a die on the bolt after cutting
    C. cut parallel to the threads in the groove of the thread
    D. turn on a nut past the cutting point prior to cutting and then back it off

34. The process of shaping metal by the application of heat and compressive forces is called 34.____

    A. forging   B. casting   C. broaching   D. piercing

35. Annealing and tempering are methods of 35.____

    A. forming metals   B. forming plastics
    C. heat treating metals   D. surfaces finishing of metals

36. The PROPER cross section of a fillet weld is, MOST NEARLY 36.____

    A. triangular   B. square
    C. rectangular   D. flat

37. A short weld deposit made to temporarily hold parts which are to be joined is called a _____ weld. 37.____

    A. bead   B. groove   C. seam   D. tack

38. The PRIMARY purpose of welding or brazing fluxes is to 38.____

    A. prevent formation of oxides on the welding joint
    B. improve the conductivity of the electrical circuit
    C. increase the number of voids in the joint
    D. prevent fusion and penetration throughout the joint

39. The practice of using cutting oil when drilling a hole in steel plates is 39.____

    A. *good;* without oil the drill would wobble
    B. *poor;* the oil could wash off the location markings
    C. *good;* the oil will cool the metal and preserve the cutting edge
    D. *poor;* the oil would help clog the drill with chips

40. If it is necessary for you to do some work with your hands under a piece of heavy equipment while a fellow worker lifts up and holds one end of it by means of a pinch bar, the MOST important safety precaution that should be taken is to 40.____

    A. wear work gloves
    B. work as fast as possible
    C. insert a temporary block to support the equipment
    D. watch the bar and be ready to get clear if it slips

KEY (CORRECT ANSWERS)

1. B	11. D	21. D	31. A
2. C	12. A	22. C	32. B
3. D	13. C	23. B	33. D
4. A	14. B	24. B	34. A
5. A	15. B	25. C	35. C
6. B	16. D	26. B	36. A
7. B	17. B	27. A	37. D
8. B	18. B	28. B	38. A
9. A	19. C	29. D	39. C
10. A	20. B	30. B	40. C

TEST 2

DIRECTIONS: Each question or incomplete statement is followed by several suggested answers or completions. Select the one that BEST answers the question or completes the statement. *PRINT THE LETTER OF THE CORRECT ANSWER IN THE SPACE AT THE RIGHT.*

1. Hammering the end of a rivet to form a head is known as   1.____
   A. peening   B. galling   C. stuffing   D. extracting

2. A material that is often used in journal bearings is   2.____
   A. stainless steel   B. babbitt
   C. ceramic   D. chromium

3. A type of closed end wrench is the _____ wrench.   3.____
   A. spanner   B. ratchet
   C. box   D. hollow set screw

4. The hammer which should NOT be used when there is danger of injuring a piece of work is a hammer with a head made of   4.____
   A. lead   B. rawhide   C. steel   D. babbitt

5. Worm and worm gear combinations are used PRIMARILY as   5.____
   A. speed increasers   B. speed reducers
   C. torque reducers   D. torque limiters

6. In an accident report, the information which is MOST useful in decreasing the recurrence of similar type accidents is the   6.____

   A. cause of the accident
   B. number of people involved
   C. time the accident happened
   D. extent of injuries sustained

7. If a main gear having 50 teeth is revolving at 250 RPM, then the speed of a 10 tooth pinion driving this gear is _____ RPM.   7.____
   A. 50   B. 500   C. 1250   D. 2500

8. The spiral flutes on a drill are provided to   8.____

   A. remove the chips
   B. form a clearance hole
   C. save material
   D. prevent binding on one side of the lip

9. When working with overhead cranes, the SAFEST way to lift a load is to lift the load   9.____

   A. at the fastest lift speed
   B. straight upward
   C. at a slight angle to the vertical
   D. with slings twisted

7

10. Hex nuts are MOST easily removed from a cylinder head with a _____ wrench.

    A. spanner   B. box   C. strap   D. Stillson

11. A fellow employee working in a confined space is seen to stagger and become unconscious because of gas fumes. The BEST immediate action to be taken is to

    A. call for an ambulance
    B. give him a stimulant
    C. rub his arms and legs
    D. get him into fresh air

12. A rubber air line hose will deteriorate MOST rapidly when in contact with

    A. tap water
    B. dirty water
    C. oil
    D. soapsuds

13. In order to prevent an adjustment nut from loosening due to subway car vibration, the MOST practical solution would be to use a

    A. lockwasher
    B. jamnut
    C. castellated nut
    D. cotter pin

14. The principal reason for NOT using your finger to align holes in two metal plates is that

    A. this is an unsafe practice
    B. this is not an accurate method
    C. your finger may be moist or greasy
    D. the holes are usually too small

15. If a 10-24 x 3/4 machine screw is not available, the screw which could be MOST easily modified to use in an emergency is a

    A. 12-24 x 1 1/2
    B. 12-24 x 3/4
    C. 10-24 x 1 1/2
    D. 10-24 x 1/2

16. Brass is an alloy of copper AND

    A. nickel   B. aluminum   C. iron   D. zinc

17. In order to cut thread into a blind hole in a cast housing, taps are used in the following order:

    A. Bottoming tap, taper tap, plug tap
    B. Plug tap, taper tap, bottoming tap
    C. Taper tap, plug tap, bottoming tap
    D. Plug tap, bottoming tap, taper tap

18. Goggles are NOT necessary when

    A. cutting angle iron with a torch
    B. grinding welded rails
    C. welding track
    D. removing an insulator from a transformer

19. When riveting a thin metal sheet to an angle iron it is good procedure to start riveting at the center of the joint, working out in both directions.
This procedure helps to prevent the sheet metal from

    A. buckling
    B. tearing
    C. stretching
    D. contracting

19.____

20. Small cuts or abrasions suffered by a car maintainer should be

    A. ignored, unless they are painful
    B. taken care of at the end of his tour
    C. ignored, because they are seldom important
    D. taken care of immediately, because infection may result

20.____

21. An accident victim with an injured spine should be

    A. immediately carried to a first aid station
    B. turned over on his stomach
    C. moved only if absolutely necessary
    D. given artificial respiration

21.____

22. One circular hole four inches in diameter is to be cut out of the center of a sheet of steel, 0.144" thick. A hole saw is not available in this size.
Of the following, the MOST practical method to use is to

    A. punch out the hole with a four inch punch and die
    B. drill out the hole with a four inch drill
    C. drill a small hole in the center and then ream out the hole to the proper diameter
    D. drill out a large number of small holes along the circumference and then knock out the disc

22.____

23. The MAIN reason for lubricating moving metal parts of a mechanism is to

    A. remove rust from the surface
    B. protect the chrome plated finish
    C. decrease the friction
    D. protect the paint finish

23.____

24. Electric arc welding is COMMONLY done by the use of _____ voltage and _____ amperage.

    A. low; high
    B. high; high
    C. low; low
    D. high; low

24.____

25. One of the strictest safety rules enforced in a rigging gang that is using a power crane is that only one man gives the movement signals to the operator of the crane and the rest of the gang follows the signals.
The only signal that anyone in the gang can properly give is a _____ signal.

    A. boom-up   B. hoist   C. swing   D. stop

25.____

26. Slack in cables or tie rods is USUALLY taken up by the use of 26.____

    A. clamps   B. Crosby slips   C. drift pins   D. turnbuckles

27. The safety device used on moving machinery to prevent overtravel is called a(n) 27.____

    A. governor   B. unloader
    C. overload relay   D. limit switch

28. A high level of friction is useful 28.____

    A. in the bearings of a motor
    B. between the wheels of a train and the rails
    C. between the piston and cylinder of a hydraulic brake actuator
    D. between rotor and stator of a motor

29. In reference to tools, the term *preventive maintenance* refers to 29.____

    A. carrying tools in such a manner that they cannot injure anyone
    B. a regular schedule of taking care of tools
    C. the immediate repair of tools when they are damaged
    D. permitting only trained men to use tools

30. Protective goggles should be worn when 30.____

    A. climbing a ladder   B. reading a gage
    C. using a chipping hammer   D. driving a hi-lo truck

31. In order to provide a close-fitting hole for a taper pin, the hole is drilled first and then the hole is 31.____

    A. reamed   B. broached   C. countersunk   D. filed

Questions 32-40.

DIRECTIONS: Questions 32 to 40 inclusive are based on the two views of the steel block shown on the next page. Consult this drawing when answering these questions.

32. Dimension R is
    A. 4 1/8"
    B. 4 5/8"
    C. 5"
    D. 5 1/2"

33. The depth of the 1/2" SLOT is
    A. 1/4"
    B. 5/8"
    C. 7/8"
    D. 3"

34. Dimension W is
    A. 3"
    B. 2 1/2"
    C. 2"
    D. 1 1/2"

35. Dimension Y is
    A. 3"
    B. 2 1/2"
    C. 2"
    D. 1 1/2"

36. The shortest length of any 1/4" hole is
    A. 4 5/8"
    B. 3 3/8"
    C. 5/8"
    D. 1/4"

37. The number of 1/4" holes 4" long is
    A. 4
    B. 3
    C. 2
    D. 1

38. Dimension T (width of CHANNEL) is
    A. 6"
    B. 4"
    C. 3 1/8"
    D. 1 1/2"

39. Dimension X is
    A. 1/4"
    B. 5/8"
    C. 7/8"
    D. 1"

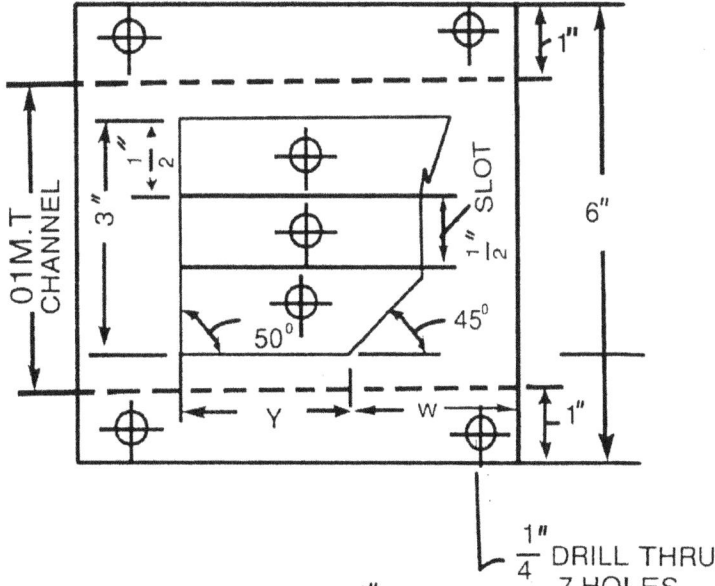

NOTE: 1. ALL HOLES ARE THROUGH HOLES.
2. NOT TO SCALE.

40. The greatest length of any 1/4" hole is 40._____
    A. 5 1/2"
    B. 4 5/8"
    C. 4 1/8"
    D. 4"

KEY (CORRECT ANSWERS)

1. A	11. D	21. C	31. A
2. B	12. C	22. D	32. D
3. C	13. B	23. C	33. B
4. C	14. A	24. A	34. B
5. B	15. C	25. D	35. C
6. A	16. D	26. D	36. B
7. C	17. C	27. D	37. C
8. A	18. D	28. B	38. B
9. B	19. A	29. B	39. C
10. B	20. D	30. C	40. B

EXAMINATION SECTION
TEST 1

DIRECTIONS: Each question or incomplete statement is followed by several suggested answers or completions. Select the one that BEST answers the question or completes the statement. *PRINT THE LETTER OF THE CORRECT ANSWER IN THE SPACE AT THE RIGHT.*

Questions 1-8.

DIRECTIONS: Questions 1 through 8, inclusive, are based on the paragraph JACKS shown below. When answering these questions, refer to this paragraph.

JACKS

When using a jack, a workman should cheek the capacity plate or other markings on the jack to make sure the device is heavy enough to support the load. Where there is no plate, capacity should be determined and painted on the side of the jack. The workman should see that jacks are well lubricated, but only at points where lubrication is specified, and should inspect them for broken teeth or faulty holding fixtures. A jack should never be thrown or dropped upon the floors such treatment may crack or distort the metal, thus causing the jack to break when a load is lifted. It is important that the floor or ground surface upon which the jack is placed be level and clean, and the safe limit of floor loading is not exceeded. If the surface is earth, the jack base should be set on heavy wood blocking, preferably hardwood, of sufficient size that the blocking will not turn over, shift, or sink. If the surface is not perfectly level, the jack may be set on blocking, which should be leveled by wedges securely placed so that they cannot be brushed or forced out of place. "Extenders" of wood or metal, intended to provide a higher rise where a jack cannot reach up to load or lift it high enough, should never be used. Instead, a larger jack should be obtained or higher blocking which is correspondingly wider and longer — should be placed under the jack. All lifts should be vertical with the jack correctly centered for the lift. The base of the jack should be on a perfectly level surface, and the jack head, with its hardwood shim, should bear against a perfectly level meeting surface.

1. To make sure the jack is heavy enough to support a certain load, the workman should

    A. lubricate the jack
    B. shim the jack
    C. check the capacity plate
    D. use a long handle

2. A jack should be lubricated

    A. after using
    B. before painting
    C. only at specified points
    D. to prevent slipping

3. The workman should inspect a jack for

    A. manufacturer's name
    B. broken teeth
    C. paint peeling
    D. broken wedges

4. Metal parts on a jack may crack if 4._____

   A. the jack is thrown on the floor
   B. the load is leveled
   C. blocking is used
   D. the handle is too short

5. It would NOT be a safe practice for a workman to 5._____

   A. center the jack under the load
   B. set the jack on a level surface
   C. use hardwood for blocking
   D. use *extenders* to reach up to the load

6. Wedges may safely be used to 6._____

   A. replace a broken tooth
   B. prevent the overloading of a jack
   C. level the blocking under a jack
   D. straighten distorted metal

7. Blocking should be 7._____

   A. made of a soft wood
   B. placed between the jack base and the earth surface
   C. well lubricated
   D. used to repair a broken tooth

8. A hardwood shim should be used 8._____

   A. between the head and its meeting surface
   B. under the jack
   C. as a filler
   D. to level a surface

9. When a long pipe is being carried, the front end should be held high and the rear end low. 9._____
   The MAIN reason for this is to

   A. prevent injury to others when turning blind corners
   B. make it easier to carry
   C. prevent injury to the man carrying the pipe
   D. prevent damage to the pipe

10. As a serviceman, you notice a condition in the shop which you believe to be dangerous, but is under the jurisdiction of another department. 10._____
    You should

    A. immediately notify your superior
    B. call the assistant general superintendent
    C. take no action, as your department is not involved
    D. send a letter to the department involved

11. All employees should regularly read the bulletin board at their job location MAINLY in order to

    A. learn what previously posted material has been removed
    B. show that they have an interest in the department
    C. see whether other employees have something for sale
    D. become familiar with new orders or procedures posted on it

12. The book of rules and regulations states that employees must give notice, in person or by telephone, at least one hour before they are scheduled to report for duty, of their intention to be absent from work.
    The LOGICAL reason for having this rule is that

    A. the employees' time can be recorded in advance
    B. a substitute can be provided
    C. it allows time to check the employees' record
    D. it reduces absenteeism

13. When tools are found in poor condition, the reason is MOST often because of

    A. misuse of tools
    B. their use by more than one person
    C. defects in the manufacture of tools
    D. their use in construction work

14. When lifting a heavy object, a man should NOT

    A. twist his body while lifting
    B. bend knees
    C. have secure footing
    D. take a firm grip on the object

15. The MAIN purpose of the periodic inspection of machines and equipment is to

    A. locate stolen property
    B. make the workmen more familiar with the equipment
    C. discover minor faults before they develop into more serious conditions
    D. encourage the workmen to take better care of their equipment

16. If a serviceman does not understand a verbal order given him by his foreman, he should

    A. do the best he can
    B. ask for a different assignment
    C. ask the foreman to explain it
    D. look it up in the book of rules

17. A rule prohibits indulgence in intoxicating liquor, or being under its influence, while on duty. This rule is rigidly enforced in order to

    A. prevent an employee from endangering himself or others
    B. help reduce littering
    C. eliminate absenteeism
    D. help promote temperance

18. As a newly appointed serviceman, your foreman would expect you to

    A. make many blunders
    B. repair car equipment
    C. study car maintenance on your own time
    D. follow his instructions closely

19. Your work will probably be MOST appreciated by your superior if you

    A. continually ask questions about your work
    B. keep him informed whenever you think someone has violated a rule
    C. continually come to him with suggestions for improving the job
    D. do your share by completing assigned tasks properly and on time

20. One of your fellow workers has to leave work a half-hour early and asks you to punch his time card for him.
    You should

    A. punch out for him, but be sure to tell your supervisor
    B. tell him that no one is allowed to punch out someone else's time card
    C. punch out for him because you know he would do the same for you
    D. tell him he must promise to stay an extra half-hour tomorrow before you punch out for him

21. As far as is practicable, fiber rope should not be allowed to become wet, as this hastens decay. The MOST logical conclusion to be drawn from this statement is that

    A. fiber rope is stronger than nylon rope
    B. shrinkage of wet rope is not a problem
    C. nylon rope is better than wire rope
    D. wet rope should be thoroughly dried before being stored away

22. The MAIN reason that gear cases are stacked on a pallet is to

    A. help servicemen find gear cases quickly
    B. help stockmen keep track of gear cases
    C. avoid hand-carrying of gear cases
    D. prevent damage to gear cases

23. If you are holding a heavy load by the pull rope on a block and tackle, your BEST procedure is to

    A. let the rope hang loose
    B. snub the rope around a fixed object
    C. pull sideways to jam the rope in the block
    D. stand on the rope and hold the end

24. Modern electric power tools such as electric drills come with a third conductor in the power cord, which is used to connect the case of the tool to a grounded part of the electric outlet.
    The reason for this additional electrical conductor is to

A. protect the user of the tool should the motor short out to the case
B. provide for continued operation of the tool should the regular grounded line-wire open
C. eliminate sparking between the tool and the material being worked upon
D. provide a spare wire for additional controls

25. When a long ladder is being used, a length of rope should be tied from its lowest rung to a fixed support in order to prevent   25.____

    A. breaking the rungs
    B. the ladder from slipping
    C. anyone from removing the ladder
    D. anyone from walking under the ladder

26. When the level of the liquid in a storage battery on a Hi-lo truck is too low, the proper liquid to add to bring the level up to normal is   26.____

    A. salt   B. alkaline solution
    C. acid solution   D. distilled water

27. The MOST important reason for servicemen to keep their work areas neat and clean is that it   27.____

    A. makes more room for storage
    B. makes for happier workers
    C. prevents tools from being broken
    D. decreases the chances of accidents to workmen

28. The one of the following which is the BEST example of a material that does NOT burn easily is   28.____

    A. canvas   B. paper   C. wood   D. asbestos

29. The CHIEF reason for not letting oily rags or dust cloths accumulate in storage closets is that they   29.____

    A. look dirty
    B. may start a fire by spontaneous combustion
    C. take up space which may be used for more important purposes
    D. may drip oil onto the floor

30. The MOST logical reason for a serviceman to blow out electrical and mechanical equipment under car bodies before they are worked on by maintainers is to   30.____

    A. cool the equipment for the maintainers
    B. prevent rusting of equipment and parts
    C. prevent the maintainers from getting dirty while working
    D. prevent fires caused by heavy accumulation of dust

31. The liquid in heavy duty hydraulic jacks used in the car shops is   31.____

    A. water   B. oil   C. mercury   D. alcohol

32. It is not considered good practice to paint portable wooden ladders. 32.____
    The MOST logical reason for this is that the paint

    A. would quickly wear off
    B. might hide serious defects
    C. might rub off on a supporting wall
    D. would dry out the rungs

33. In order to lift a loaded pallet overhead by means of a crane, it would be MOST desirable 33.____
    to use a

    A. single wire rope sling   B. long crowbar
    C. pallet sling   D. rope splice

34. Of the following methods, the one which is the BEST way to keep rust off metal tools is to 34.____

    A. keep them dry and oil them once in a while
    B. air blast them
    C. file or grind them often
    D. wash them carefully with warm water

35. A Hi-Lo truck delivering a compressor to a work area approaches a closed door. 35.____
    The proper procedure for the Hi-Lo operator to follow is to

    A. open the door while standing on the operating end of the Hi-Lo truck
    B. open the door with the platform of the Hi-Lo truck
    C. stop the Hi-Lo truck, wedge open the door, and then proceed
    D. make a detour and follow a different path

36. The path between the two yellow lines on a main shop floor is used for 36.____

    A. picking up and discharging workers that want a ride on a Hi-Lo
    B. parking area for forklifts
    C. the traffic path for Hi-Lo's and forklifts
    D. storage of materials unloaded from Hi-Lo's

37. While on the way to a storeroom, you notice that oil has dripped on the floor from a jour- 37.____
    nal box and created a slipping hazard.
    You should

    A. ignore it as it is not your doing
    B. get some *speedi-dry* nearby and spread it over the oil
    C. wait until you return from the storeroom to take care of it
    D. call the supervisor and tell him about it

38. An employee always obeys the safety rules of his department because it has become a 38.____
    habit to work by these rules. This is

    A. *good;* such a habit will get work done safely
    B. *bad;* it is hard to change a habit
    C. *good;* safety rules won't work if they have to be thought about
    D. *bad;* safety rules should always be thought about before doing anything and not
       allowed to become a habit

39. If *you* are working in an inspection shop and you notice a trolley bug on one contact shoe of a car, it will mean that   39.____

    A. all contact shoes of the car are *live*
    B. only that contact shoe, that the bug is on, is *live*
    C. only the contact shoes, on the same side of the car that the bug is on, are *live*
    D. only the contact shoes of the one truck are *live*

40. It is necessary for a serviceman to wear a respirator when he is   40.____

    A. climbing a ladder
    B. operating a chipping gun
    C. blowing out the equipment under a car
    D. lubricating gear cases

KEY (CORRECT ANSWERS)

1. C	11. D	21. D	31. B
2. C	12. B	22. C	32. B
3. B	13. A	23. B	33. C
4. A	14. A	24. A	34. A
5. D	15. C	25. B	35. C
6. C	16. C	26. D	36. C
7. B	17. A	27. D	37. B
8. A	18. D	28. D	38. A
9. A	19. D	29. B	39. A
10. A	20. B	30. D	40. C

TEST 2

DIRECTIONS: Each question or incomplete statement is followed by several suggested answers or completions. Select the one that BEST answers the question or completes the statement. *PRINT THE LETTER OF THE CORRECT ANSWER IN THE SPACE AT THE RIGHT.*

1. The type of fire extinguisher which you would NOT use to extinguish a fire around electrical circuits is

   A. carbon dioxide
   B. dry chemical
   C. water
   D. dry sand

   1.____

2. Artificial respiration is applied when an accident has caused

   A. breathing difficulties
   B. loss of blood
   C. broken ribs
   D. burns

   2.____

3. Workers must NOT wear clothes that are too big when they work near moving machinery because

   A. that kind of dress will attract attention
   B. some part of the clothes can catch in the machinery
   C. big clothes get dirtier
   D. big clothes are hard to replace

   3.____

4. The MOST likely reason why an employee should make out a report after using the contents of a first aid kit is that

   A. he will learn to write a good report
   B. unauthorized use may be prevented
   C. used material will be replaced
   D. a new seal may be provided

   4.____

5. A shop employee is involved in an accident and severely injures his ankle. If a tourniquet were used, it would be to

   A. keep the ankle warm
   B. prevent infection
   C. prevent the ankle from moving
   D. stop the loss of blood

   5.____

6. If a serviceman has frequent accidents, it is MOST likely that he is

   A. a man who works best by himself
   B. satisfied with his job
   C. violating too many safety rules
   D. simply one of those persons who is unlucky

   6.____

7. In treating a cut finger, the FIRST action should be to

   A. wash it
   B. bandage it
   C. request sick leave
   D. apply antiseptic

   7.____

8. When administering first aid to a person suffering from shock as a result of an accident, it is MOST important to

   8.____

A. keep him moving
B. prop him up in a sitting position
C. apply artificial respiration
D. cover the person and keep him warm

9. First aid instructions are given to some employees to

    A. eliminate the need for calling a doctor
    B. prepare them to give emergency aid
    C. collect blood for the blood bank
    D. reduce the number of accidents

10. The BEST reason for not using compressed air from an air hose for cleaning dust from clothing is that

    A. the clothing may be torn by the blast
    B. it is a dangerous practice
    C. this air contains too much moisture
    D. the air pressure will drop too low

11. Protective helmets give servicemen the MOST protection from

    A. falling objects   B. fire
    C. eye injuries   D. electric shock

12. Fuses are used in electric circuits

    A. so that electrical power tools cannot short circuit
    B. to burn out under an overload before electrical equipment is damaged
    C. to increase the amount of current that may be carried in the wires
    D. so that workmen can cut off the current without looking for the switch

13. The one of the following that is MOST effective in reducing the danger from hazardous vapors is

    A. immediate disposal of all wastes
    B. labeling all substances clearly
    C. maintaining good ventilation
    D. wearing proper clothing at all times

14. A serviceman should NEVER look into the arc from an electric welding torch.
    The BEST reason for this is that

    A. it can have a harmful effect on his eyes
    B. it will distract the welder from his work
    C. the serviceman is not allowed to operate a welding torch
    D. electric arc welding uses a large electrical current

15. The floors of 2 cars are to be painted with a special test paint. Assume that the floor area in each car is 600 square feet. A gallon of this paint will cover 400 square feet.
    The number of gallons of this paint that you should pick up at the storeroom to paint the 2 car floors would be

    A. 6   B. 5   C. 4   D. 3

16. Assume that you are sent to the storeroom for 1,000 of 600-volt contact tips which are to be distributed equally to 5 foremen, but you find that the storeroom can only supply you with 825.
    If you distribute these 825 tips equally to the 5 foremen, the number of tips that each foreman will receive is

    A. 165   B. 175   C. 190   D. 200

17. You are asked to fill six 5-gallon cans of oil from a full drum containing 52 gallons. When you have filled the six cans, the number of gallons of oil left in the drun will be MOST NEARLY

    A. 14   B. 16   C. 22   D. 30

18. A certain wire rope is made up of 6 strands, each strand containing 19 wires.
    The total number of wires in this wire rope is

    A. 25   B. 96   C. 114   D. 144

19. The hook should be the weakest part of any crane, hoist, or sling.
    According to this statement, if a particular hook has a rated capacity of 2 1/2 tons, then the MAXIMUM load thatshould be lifted with this hook is _____ pounds.

    A. 150   B. 3,000   C. 5,000   D. 5,500

20. Assume that 2 car wheels weigh 635 pounds each and are attached to an axle weighing 1,260 pounds.
    The total weight of this assembly is MOST NEARLY _____ pounds.

    A. 1,270   B. 1,520   C. 1,895   D. 2,530

21. If an employee authorizes his employer to deduct 4% of his $450 weekly salary for a savings bond, the MINIMUM number of weekly deductions required to get enough money to buy a bond costing $54 is

    A. 3   B. 6   C. 8   D. 9

22. In weighing out a truckful of scrap metal, the scale reads 21,496 lbs. If the empty truck weighs 9,879 lbs., the amount of scrap metal, in pounds, is MOST NEARLY

    A. 10,507   B. 10,602   C. 11,617   D. 12,617

23. Four trays of material are placed on the body of a delivery truck for delivery to the inspection shop. Each tray is 4 feet wide and 4 feet long.
    If these trays are placed side by side on the floor of the delivery truck, together they will cover an area of the floor MOST NEARLY _____ square feet.

    A. 32   B. 48   C. 64   D. 72

24. Assume that you are operating a degreasing tank and its tray holds 5 gear cases. It takes 40 minutes to clean one tray of gear cases.
    At the end of 6 hours of operation (excluding lunch break and loading and unloading time), the number of gear cases cleaned will be

    A. 30   B. 36   C. 45   D. 50

25. If a serviceman's weekly gross salary is $480, and 20% is deducted for taxes, his take-home pay is

    A. $360   B. $384   C. $420   D. $432

26. Two-thirds of 10 feet is MOST NEARLY

    A. 6'2"   B. 6'8"   C. 6'11"   D. 7'1"

27. You are directed to pick up a tray load of brake shoes.
    The combined weight of tray and brake shoes is 4,000 pounds. Assume that each brake shoe weighs 40 pounds and the tray weighs 240 pounds.
    The number of brake shoes in the tray is MOST NEARLY

    A. 88   B. 94   C. 100   D. 106

28. The one of the following materials that is used to protect equipment from rain is a

    A. sprinkler   B. tarpaulin
    C. compressor   D. templet

29. The use of wet rope near power lines and other electrical equipment is

    A. a dangerous practice
    B. sure to interrupt telephone service
    C. recommended as a safe practice
    D. common in the car shop but not in maintenance of way

Questions 30-34.

DIRECTIONS: Questions 30 through 34, inclusive, are based on the following paragraph, table, and floor plan. Each line in the table contains the name of a certain piece of car equipment together with its destination in the car shop. The floor plan shows a car shop divided into six areas, each with a different code number.

TABLE

NAME OF CAR EQUIPMENT	DESTINATION IN CAR SHOP
Journal boxes	Degreasing tanks
Door operators	Car body shop Main shipping Air brake shop
Air compressors	
Unit valves	Truck shop Degreasing tanks Main shipping Air brake shop
Wheels Gear assemblies	
Unit switches Variable load units	
Motor couplings	Degreasing tanks Truck shop Degreasing tanks Car body shop Main shipping Car body shop
Motors Brake linkage	
Fan motors Batteries	
Motor generators	

CAR SHOP FLOOR PLAN

Overhaul Shop	Air Brake Shop	Main Shipping
AREA 1	AREA 2	AREA 3
Degreasing Tanks	Truck Shop	
AREA 4	AREA 5	
Car Body Shop AREA 6		

In each of Questions 30 through 34, there are the names of four types of car equipment, and a code number for a destination in the car shop. In each question, select the CORRECT combination of equipment name and destination code number as determined by referring to the Table and Car Shop Floor Plan.

30. A. Motor generators: Area 6
    B. Fan motors: Area 5
    C. Motor couplings: Area 1
    D. Motor end housings: Area 2

30.____

31. A. Door operators: Area 3
    B. Air compressors: Area 5
    C. Brake linkage: Area 4
    D. Variable load units: Area 6

31.____

32. A. Batteries: Area 1
    B. Unit switches: Area 3
    C. Motor controllers: Area 2
    D. Fan motors: Area 4

32.____

33. A. Wheels: Area 2
    B. Motor end housings: Area 6
    C. Journal boxes: Area 3
    D. Unit valves: Area 2

33.____

34. A. Gear assemblies: Area 4
    B. Motor couplings: Area 3
    C. Variable load units: Area 6
    D. Unit valves: Area 5

34.____

35. The drawing at the right is an assembly sketch. Study the sketch and select the CORRECT assembly procedure.
    A. 3 onto 4, 2 onto 5, 1 onto 5, and tighten
    B. 4 onto 3, 1 onto 5, 5 through 4 and 3, tighten 2 onto 5
    C. 5 into 3, 2 and 1 onto 5, 4 into 3, and tighten
    D. 4 into 3, 5 through 3 and 4, 2 onto 5, 1 onto 5, and tighten

35.____

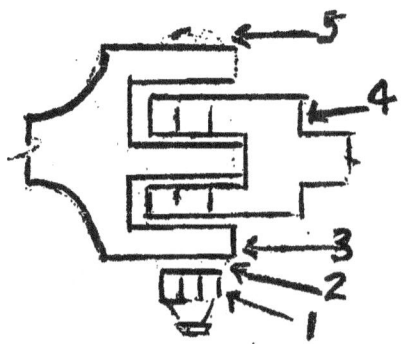

Questions 36-37.

DIRECTIONS: Questions 36 and 37 are based on the following data and sketch. When answering these questions, refer to this material.

The average clearance requirements for 2-ton, 3-ton, and 5-ton forklift trucks are shown in the following sketch. Dimensions are: R, the overall length including loads S, the overall widths T, the overall height; U, the minimum permissible width of aisle.

	2-Ton Truck	3-Ton Truck	5-Ton Truck
B	112	118	142
S	45	46	47
T	85	85	85
U	76	79	92

All dimensions are in inches.

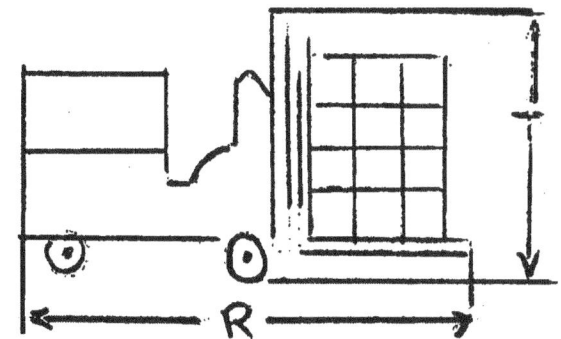

36. From the data given above, it can be seen that the overall length, including load, of a 3-ton truck is _____ inches.

    A. 85   B. 92   C. 118   D. 142

37. From the data given above, it can be seen that the overall height of a 2-ton truck is _____ inches.

    A. 47   B. 76   C. 79   D. 85

38.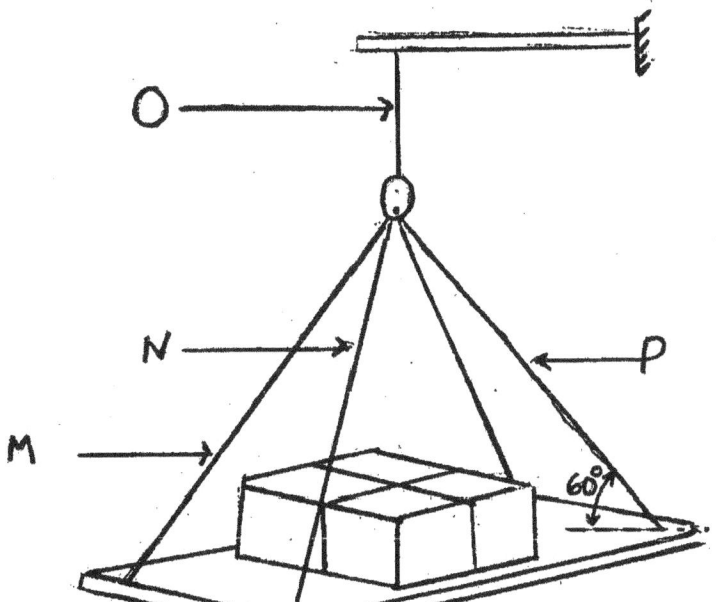

The above diagram shows a loaded sling suspended from a crane. The rope which carries the heaviest load is

A. M   B. N   C. O   D. P

39. If the tray shown in the diagram at the right is being pushed in the direction shown by the arrows, it is MOST likely to move in the direction of the arrow shown in

39._____

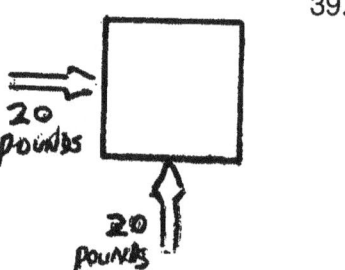

A.

B.

C.

D.

40.

40._____

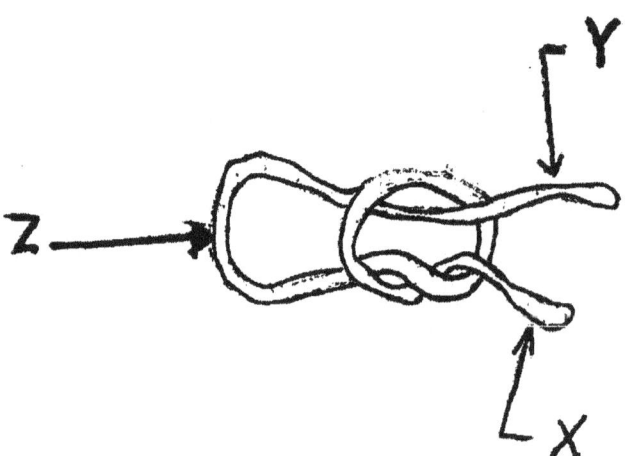

The above diagram shows a slip knot. The way this knot is nade, it would be CORRECT to say that the knot can be untied by pulling on line _____ while holding _____.

A. X; line Z
B. Y; line X
C. X and line Y together; line Z
D. Z; lines X and Y together

KEY (CORRECT ANSWERS)

1. C	11. A	21. A	31. C
2. A	12. B	22. C	32. B
3. B	13. C	23. C	33. D
4. C	14. A	24. C	34. A
5. D	15. D	25. B	35. D
6. C	16. A	26. B	36. C
7. A	17. C	27. B	37. D
8. D	18. C	28. B	38. C
9. B	19. C	29. A	39. B
10. B	20. D	30. A	40. B

EXAMINATION SECTION
TEST 1

DIRECTIONS: Each question or incomplete statement is followed by several suggested answers or completions. Select the one that BEST answers the question or completes the statement. *PRINT THE LETTER OF THE CORRECT ANSWER IN TE SPACE AT THE RIGHT.*

1. The hole size for a 1/2"-13" NC tapped hole maintaining a 65% thread height is

    A. 25/64"   B. 7/16"   C. 31/64"   D. 33/64"

2. A good flux for black iron is

    A. zinc chloride
    B. rosin
    C. resin
    D. sal ammoniac

3. The unified thread system which provides for an interchange of parts manufactured in the United States, Great Britain, and Canada is a combination of the _____ thread and the _____ thread.

    A. American national form; whitworth
    B. sharp V; acme
    C. American national form; acme
    D. American national form; sellers

4. The pan head of self-tapping screw, with a gimlet point, used for fastening light sheet metal, is referred to as type

    A. A   B. B   C. C   D. D

5. Terne plate is black iron coated with a mixture of

    A. lead and tin
    B. lead and zinc
    C. lead and nickel
    D. tin and zinc

6. The worm gear of a thread chasing dial is designed to mesh with the

    A. feed screw
    B. split nut
    C. lead screw
    D. gear rack

7. The taper per foot for an American standard taper pin is

    A. 1/16"   B. 1/8"   C. 3/32"   D. 1/4"

8. To give a cutting speed of 35 f.p.m., a 3/4" drill should be run at about _____ r.p.m.

    A. 70   B. 176   C. 280   D. 350

9. The kaws on a pair of combination snips are

    A. curved   B. serrated   C. notched   D. straight

10. The taper that MOST closely resembles the Morse taper is known as the

    A. Pratt and Whitney
    B. Sellers
    C. Jarno
    D. Brown and Sharpe

11. The gage used to set the threading tool in the lathe is called a(n) _____ gage.   11._____
    A. center   B. thread   C. pitch   D. angle

12. Ten-point steel has a carbon content of   12._____
    A. .010%   B. .10%   C. 1%   D. 10%

13. The conductor stake used in sheet metal work has   13._____
    A. a round, slender horn and a rectangular horn
    B. two tapered horns of different diameters
    C. one slender horn and two shanks
    D. two cylindrical horns of different diameters

14. When draw filing a piece of cold rolled steel 1/2" x 1/2" x 6", the BEST file to use is the   14._____
    A. vixon   B. XF
    C. mill   D. double cut smooth

15. Babbitt is an alloy of copper, tin, and   15._____
    A. antimony   B. zinc   C. aluminum   D. nickel

16. The hand reamer that lends itself BEST to reaming a pulley hole with a keyway is the _____ reamer.   16._____
    A. adjustable hand   B. straight tooth
    C. spiral tooth   D. increment cut

17. An acme thread has an included angle of   17._____
    A. 29°   B. 55°   C. 59 1/2°   D. 60°

18. The straight single depth of a 1/2"-13 American national form thread is   18._____
    A. .0375   B. .0423   C. .0499   D. .0562

19. A four inch cylinder made of 1 X tin, joined with a #4 grooved seam, should have a stock allowance for the seam equal to   19._____
    A. 2 1/2 times the width of the seam plus 4 times the thickness of the metal
    B. 3 times the width of the seam
    C. 3 1/2 times the width of the seam plus twice the thickness of the metal
    D. 3 times the width of the seam plus three times the thickness of the metal

20. The process of heating cold rolled steel, impregnating with a carbonaceous material, and quenching is known as   20._____
    A. normalizing   B. nitriding
    C. case-hardening   D. spherodizing

21. A solder made of 60% tin and 40% lead melts at _____ °F.   21._____
    A. 370   B. 415   C. 430   D. 461

22. A steel or wrought-iron block, other than the anvil, that is used for forge work is the _____ block.

    A. forming   B. vee   C. shaping   D. swage

23. A gate for a mold should always be shaped so that it

    A. is parallel to the drag surface
    B. slopes toward the mold
    C. slopes away from the mold
    D. connects with the heavy section of the pattern

24. Graphite is sometimes used in foundry practice as a

    A. binder for the sand
    B. binder for small cores
    C. mold facing
    D. material for making gaggers and chaplets

25. A newly developed structural steel that puts weather to work to protect itself and requires no painting is known as

    A. Stan-Steel   B. Ketos
    C. Cor-Ten   D. Armco

26. The process of heating and quenching tool steel from a temperature either within or above the critical temperature range is known as

    A. annealing   B. tempering
    C. hardening   D. normalizing

27. Of the following, the information that is NOT part of the manufacturer's grinding wheel marking symbols is

    A. grain size   B. grade
    C. wheel shape   D. structure

28. The rapid dulling of a twist drill, especially at the outer end of the lips (corners), is evidence that the

    A. drill has excessive lip clearance
    B. drill is revolving too rapidly
    C. point has been ground to an angle of less than 118°
    D. drill is riding on its *heel*

29. The size of a lathe mandrel or arbor is designated

    A. on the small end
    B. in accordance with standards set by individual manufacturers
    C. on the large end
    D. on both ends

30. The numbered lines on the barrel of a micrometer are in increments of 30._____

    A. .001"   B. .005"   C. .025"   D. .100"

KEY (CORRECT ANSWERS)

1.	B		16.	C
2.	A		17.	A
3.	A		18.	C
4.	A		19.	B
5.	A		20.	C
6.	C		21.	A
7.	D		22.	D
8.	B		23.	C
9.	D		24.	C
10.	C		25.	C
11.	A		26.	C
12.	B		27.	C
13.	D		28.	B
14.	C		29.	C
15.	A		30.	D

TEST 2

DIRECTIONS: Each question or incomplete statement is followed by several suggested answers or completions. Select the one that BEST answers the question or completes the statement. *PRINT THE LETTER OF THE CORRECT ANSWER IN THE SPACE AT THE RIGHT.*

1. To tap a hole for 1/8" standard pipe, one should use a tap designated 1/8 -   1.____

    A. 13 NSP   B. 20 NPT   C. 23 NTP   D. 27 NPT

2. A promising development in steel technology to produce BETTER steel more efficiently is   2.____

    A. modern blooming   B. continuous casting
    C. wet rolling   D. rapid ingot teaming

3. The spindle bore of an engine lathe is USUALLY equipped with a _____ taper.   3.____

    A. Morse   B. Brown and Sharpe
    C. Pratt and Whitney   D. Sellers

4. The space from the edge of the metal to the center of the rivet line should be AT LEAST _____ times the diameter of the rivet.   4.____

    A. 1 1/2   B. 2   C. 3   D. 4

5. A good forging heat for steel is   5.____

    A. cherry red (1375° F)   B. blood red (1075° F)
    C. light yellow (1975° F)   D. white (2200° F)

6. The tools BEST suited to forge a shoulder are the _____ and sledge.   6.____

    A. top fuller   B. bottom fuller
    C. set hammer   D. hardie

7. A base box is the unit of measure for tin plate and contains _____ sheets _____.   7.____

    A. 56; 18" x 20"   B. 100; 20" x 28"
    C. 112; 14" x 20"   D. 128; 18" x 20"

8. Of the following, the stake BEST suited for forming a common funnel is the   8.____

    A. creasing   B. blow horn
    C. beakhorn   D. candlemold

9. The body of sand used to form a recess or opening in a casting is called a   9.____

    A. core   B. core print
    C. fillet   D. cored hole

10. Tin plate with a light coating of tin is called _____ plate.   10.____

    A. coke tin   B. charcoal tin
    C. dairy   D. terne

11. The gage used to measure the thickness of iron and steel sheet metal is

    A. American
    B. United States standard
    C. Brown and Sharpe
    D. stubs

12. If a cross-feed screw on a lathe has eight threads per inch, and the micrometer dial is graduated so that a single division indicates a movement of one one-thousandth of an inch, the micrometer dial will have _____ equal divisions.

    A. 90 B. 100 C. 125 D. 250

13. Screws for use in metal, whose size is designated by a gage number indicating the diameter of the body of the screw, are called

    A. set screws
    B. machine bolts
    C. cap screws
    D. machine screws

14. An accurate method of checking the size of a twist drill would be to use a micrometer to measure the

    A. body of the drill
    B. point of the drill across the land
    C. point of the drill across the margin
    D. flute of the drill

15. If the cutting speed of steel is 75 feet per minute when using a high speed steel cutter to turn a 1 1/2" diameter piece of steel, the spindle speed of the lathe should be _____ RPM.

    A. 75 B. 186 C. 200 D. 340

16. In foundry, the process of making a mold in sand from a pattern with an irregular parting line USUALLY involves

    A. coping down
    B. a lost wax process
    C. a split pattern
    D. a sweep mold

17. The cutting action of a twist drill is aided by a *rake* action which is provided for on the drill by the

    A. web B. flute C. land D. margin

18. The included angle on the head of a standard flat-head machine screw is

    A. 60° B. 90° C. 82° D. 59°

19. The main alloying elements in monel metal are

    A. nickel, zinc, copper
    B. chrome, nickel, copper
    C. copper, zinc, tin
    D. nickel, copper

20. When turning a slender rod in a lathe, springing is minimized by using a

    A. compound rest
    B. follower rest
    C. cross rest
    D. draw-in bar

21. In foundry practice, a strike bar is used for 21.____

    A. loosening the pattern
    B. striking off flashing
    C. separating cope and drag
    D. making sand even with top of flask

22. The forge operation of enlarging the cross-sectional area of a bar is called 22.____

    A. upsetting   B. drawing out
    C. fullering   D. spreading

23. A screw thread that is NOT used much today is the 23.____

    A. acme   B. square
    C. American standard D. S.A.E.

24. One of the first men to produce carbide tools was 24.____

    A. Johannson   B. Metcalf   C. Jarno   D. Moissan

25. The twist drill that is exactly the same diameter as the letter E drill is 25.____

    A. 1/4"   B. #40   C. #1   D. 5/16"

26. The cross-sectional shape of a warding file is 26.____

    A. square
    B. tapered wedge
    C. rectangular (wide and thin)
    D. rectangular (wide and thick)

27. The steel that would lend itself BEST for making a center punch is 27.____

    A. high speed   B. 1020 machinery
    C. cold rolled   D. drill rod

28. One thousand 10 oz. rivets weigh about 28.____

    A. 1000 x 10 oz.   B. 10 oz.
    C. 1 lb.   D. 10 lbs.

29. A good flux for tin plate is 29.____

    A. zinc chloride   B. muriatic acid
    C. rosin   D. cut acid

30. The material that gives high-speed steel its hardness and ability to keep an edge is 30.____

    A. tungsten   B. vanadium   C. chromium   D. platinum

KEY (CORRECT ANSWERS)

1.	D	16.	A
2.	B	17.	B
3.	A	18.	C
4.	B	19.	D
5.	C	20.	B
6.	C	21.	D
7.	C	22.	A
8.	B	23.	B
9.	A	24.	D
10.	A	25.	A
11.	B	26.	C
12.	C	27.	D
13.	D	28.	B
14.	C	29.	C
15.	C	30.	B

TEST 3

DIRECTIONS: Each question or incomplete statement is followed by several suggested answers or completions. Select the one that BEST answers the question or completes the statement. *PRINT THE LETTER OF THE CORRECT ANSWER IN THE SPACE AT THE RIGHT.*

1. A metal that has a coating of zinc is known as a(n) _____ metal. 1._____
   - A. nitrided
   - B. anodized
   - C. galvanized
   - D. normalized

2. A set of hand taps includes _____ taps. 2._____
   - A. machine, plug, and bottom
   - B. taper, plug, and machine
   - C. taper, machine, and bottom
   - D. taper, plug, and bottom

3. The pitch of the threads in a micrometer sleeve is _____ threads per inch. 3._____
   - A. 25
   - B. 40
   - C. 100
   - D. 1,000

4. The motion of the shaper ram is. 4._____
   - A. circular
   - B. rotary
   - C. reciprocating
   - D. semi-circular

5. A split die 5._____
   - A. is damaged beyond repair
   - B. can be adjusted
   - C. requires two wrenches to operate
   - D. contains two separate cutters

6. The diameter of a twist drill is measured across the 6._____
   - A. margin
   - B. web
   - C. flutes
   - D. shank

7. A template is a 7._____
   - A. type of hand shears
   - B. metal cutting saw
   - C. pattern
   - D. type of pin punch

8. The tool post is mounted in the clapper box in a 8._____
   - A. lathe
   - B. drill press
   - C. milling machine
   - D. shaper

9. To remove a taper shank drill from a drill press, use a 9._____
   - A. drift punch
   - B. pin punch
   - C. pipe wrench
   - D. chuck key

10. One complete turn of the handle on the index head of a milling machine will turn the work 10._____
    - A. 180°
    - B. 9°
    - C. 40°
    - D. 90°

11. Offsetting the tailstock on the lathe will

    A. facilitate boring
    B. enable threads to be cut accurately
    C. center-drill without oil
    D. produce a taper

12. A rack and pinion on a lathe give movement to the

    A. carriage   B. tailstock
    C. headstock   D. compound rest

13. A knurling tool is used in a

    A. milling machine   B. shaper
    C. lathe   D. drill press

14. The dead center in a lathe is found in the

    A. headstock   B. compound rest
    C. cross slide   D. tailstock

15. Lathe tool bits are made of _____ steel.

    A. low carbon   B. high speed
    C. machine   D. case hardened

16. The products of the blast furnace are

    A. waste gases, steel, and slag
    B. coke, slag, and pig iron
    C. waste gases, pig iron, and slag
    D. waste gases, coke, and slag

17. Solder is composed of _____ and lead.

    A. zinc   B. tin   C. copper   D. spelter

18. On a double thread, the lead is equal to

    A. the pitch   B. one-half the pitch
    C. twice the pitch   D. diameter

19. A vernier scale can be found on a

    A. height gage   B. surface plate
    C. dial indicator   D. telescope gage

20. The lines on the sleeve of a micrometer are _____ of an inch apart.

    A. .075   B. .025   C. .100   D. .001

21. An Allen head screw is tightened with a

    A. regular screwdriver
    B. spanner wrench
    C. cross-shaped screwdriver
    D. hexagon-shaped wrench

22. The handle of a file fits on the

　　A.　tang　　　　B.　heel　　　　C.　tail　　　　D.　sole

23. Countersinks for flat head screws have an included angle of

　　A.　60°　　　　B.　75°　　　　C.　82°　　　　D.　90°

24. A hand groover is used to

　　A.　remove chips from a groove or keyway
　　B.　lock a seam
　　C.　fold over a wired edge
　　D.　shape soft metal on a lathe

25. An example of a ferrous metal is

　　A.　brass　　　　B.　aluminum　　　　C.　iron　　　　D.　copper

26. The cold chisel commonly used to shape a keyway is a

　　A.　cape chisel　　　　　　　B.　flat chisel
　　C.　round chisel　　　　　　D.　diamond point

27. A foundry flask is used to

　　A.　analyze the sand　　　　B.　clean the pattern
　　C.　support the sand　　　　D.　clean the casting

28. A sprue pin is used to

　　A.　ram a pattern
　　B.　provide a hole through which the metal is poured
　　C.　locate the two halves of a split pattern
　　D.　clean the slag off molten metal

29. The sand used to separate the cope from the drag is _____ sand.

　　A.　parting　　　　B.　green　　　　C.　core　　　　D.　tempered

30. Fillets are used to

　　A.　simplify construction of the mold
　　B.　strengthen the casting
　　C.　strengthen the pattern
　　D.　support sand cores

KEY (CORRECT ANSWERS)

1.	C	16.	C
2.	D	17.	B
3.	B	18.	C
4.	C	19.	A
5.	B	20.	B
6.	A	21.	D
7.	C	22.	A
8.	D	23.	C
9.	A	24.	B
10.	B	25.	C
11.	D	26.	A
12.	A	27.	C
13.	C	28.	B
14.	D	29.	A
15.	B	30.	B

TEST 4

DIRECTIONS: Each question or incomplete statement is followed by several suggested answers or completions. Select the one that BEST answers the question or completes the statement. *PRINT THE LETTER OF THE CORRECT ANSWER IN THE SPACE AT THE RIGHT.*

1. The suggested cutting speed for high-speed drills when drilling steel is APPROXIMATELY _____ surface feet per minute. 1._____

    A. 200-250 B. 150-200 C. 100-150 D. 50-100

2. When a strong joint is needed to connect the bottom of a sheet-metal container to the body, the BEST joint to use is a 2._____

    A. burr or flange B. single seam
    C. double seam D. dovetail seam

3. The candle-mould stake 3._____

    A. is used for shaping sheet-metal candlestick holders
    B. has a slender horn for tube forming
    C. is used mainly for corner seam closing
    D. is used for wiring and beading

4. Left-hand aviation snips are designed to 4._____

    A. cut a curve to the left
    B. be used by left-handed people
    C. cut a curve to the right
    D. cut aluminum airplane parts

5. Ammonium chloride is also known as 5._____

    A. sal ammoniac
    B. bauxite
    C. amino acid
    D. a good electro-plating electrolyte

6. As the percentage of lead in soft solder increases, the 6._____

    A. melting point becomes higher
    B. melting point becomes lower
    C. strength of the joint decreases
    D. percentage of zinc decreases

7. To improve the machinability and resistance to corrosion of aluminum, the alloying metal is 7._____

    A. silicon B. copper C. manganese D. magnesium

8. Borax can be used 8._____

    A. as a flux in brazing
    B. for pickling silver

C. as an adhesive in copper enameling
D. as a cutting compound

9. A 42-tooth driving gear rotating at 400 RPM in a clockwise direction is connected to a 14-tooth gear by means of an idler gear.
   The speed and direction of rotation of the (14-tooth) driven gear is

   A. 1200 RPM and rotating clockwise
   B. 1200 RPM and rotating counter-clockwise
   C. 133 1/3 RPM and rotating counter-clockwise
   D. 133 1/3 RPM and rotating clockwise

10. Rouge used in metal polishing is made of

    A. decomposed shale   B. iron oxide
    C. powdered lava   D. silicon carbide

11. The BEST thickness of copper for doing repousse projects is _____ gauge.

    A. 14   B. 18   C. 24   D. 36

12. Copper is often pickled with

    A. a solution of sulphuric acid and water
    B. a solution of ammonium sulphide
    C. powdered tragacenth and alcohol
    D. kasenit

13. Liver of sulphur is also known as

    A. ferric sulphide   B. hyposulphite of soda
    C. potassium sulphide   D. sulphur dioxide

14. *German Silver* is USUALLY made of about

    A. 92% tin, 6% antimony, and 2% copper
    B. 64% copper, 18% nickel, and 18% zinc
    C. 925 parts of silver and 75 parts of copper
    D. 85% copper and 15% zinc

15. Blowholes in castings can be avoided by the use of

    A. a gate   B. vents
    C. a sprue pin   D. a core print

16. Chaplets are used

    A. with match-plate patterns
    B. to support cores
    C. in investment casting
    D. in shell mold casting

17. Muriatic acid is the same as

    A. hydrochloric acid   B. nitric acid
    C. sulphuric acid   D. aqua regia

18. Most of the steel made today is made in a(n).

    A. open-hearth furnace
    B. Bessemer converter
    C. electric furnace
    D. blast furnace

19. Nitriding is a process used for hardening

    A. special steel alloys by using ammonia gas
    B. low carbon steels
    C. steel parts requiring shallow surface hardness
    D. steel by exposing it while heated to a carbonaceous material

20. An aluminum oxide abrasive wheel is intended especially for grinding

    A. brass   B. iron   C. aluminum   D. steel

21. A scleroscope is used to

    A. examine crystalline structure
    B. determine hardness
    C. measure with extreme accuracy
    D. identify metal

22. The United States Standard (USS) gauge is used for measuring

    A. drills from #1 to #80
    B. steel wire, sheets, and plates
    C. copper, brass, and aluminum
    D. machine screw sizes #0 to #12

23. Back gears are USUALLY used on a lathe when

    A. knurling
    B. boring a hole
    C. reversing the feed
    D. high spindle speed is needed

24. The axes of spur gears are aligned so that they GENERALLY

    A. intersect at right angles
    B. intersect at acute angles
    C. intersect at obtuse angles
    D. are parallel to each other

25. The BEST file for filing steel on the lathe is a _____ file.

    A. vixen
    B. double-cut warding
    C. second-cut pillar
    D. long angle single-cut mill

26. In lathe work, the formula to use to determine the correct spindle speed when V = cutting speed in feet per minute, and D = diameter of workpiece in inches, is:

    A. $RPM = \dfrac{12\pi}{VD}$ B. $RPM = \dfrac{12V}{\pi D}$ C. $RPM = \dfrac{\pi D}{12V}$ D. $RPM = \dfrac{\pi V}{12D}$

27. The CORRECT sequence of drill sizes from smallest to largest is:

    A. #60, #30, 7/32", M
    B. #7, #50, 1/4", F
    C. #14, #2, Q, 1/8"
    D. B, R, 3/8", #12

28. The taper per foot on a part 2 5/16" in length and with a 15/16" diameter at one end and 11/16" at the other end, is

    A. .578"   B. .770"   C. .925"   D. 1.297"

29. The MAJOR diameter of a 5-40 NC machine screw is

    A. .125"   B. .140"   C. .155"   D. .170"

30. The usual amount left for removal with a reamer is

    A. 1/8" to 1/16"
    B. 1/16" to 1/32"
    C. 1/32" to 1/64"
    D. 1/64" to .005"

KEY (CORRECT ANSWERS)

1.	D	16.	B
2.	C	17.	A
3.	B	18.	A
4.	C	19.	A
5.	A	20.	D
6.	A	21.	B
7.	D	22.	B
8.	A	23.	A
9.	A	24.	A
10.	B	25.	D
11.	D	26.	B
12.	A	27.	A
13.	C	28.	D
14.	B	29.	A
15.	B	30.	D

EXAMINATION SECTION
TEST 1

DIRECTIONS: Each question or incomplete statement is followed by several suggested answers or completions. Select the one that BEST answers the question or completes the statement. *PRINT THE LETTER OF THE CORRECT ANSWER IN THE SPACE AT THE RIGHT.*

1. The hole diameter required for a 1 lb. tinners' rivet is MOST NEARLY 1.____

    A. 1/16"   B. 1/8"   C. 3/16"   D. 1/4"

Questions 2-3.

DIRECTIONS: Questions 2 and 3 refer to the sketch of the pipe shown below.

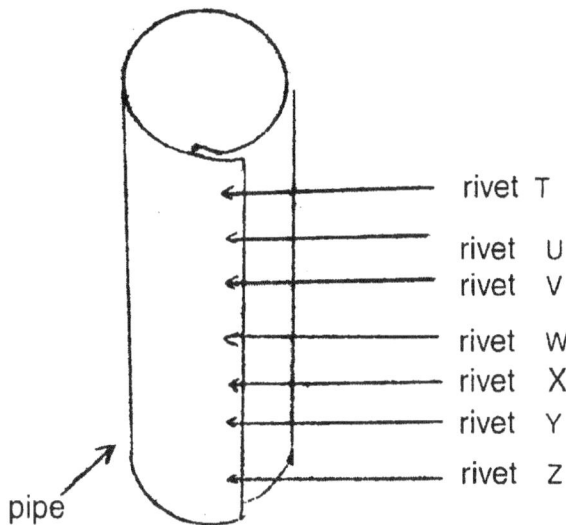

2. In riveting the seam shown above, the FIRST set of rivets that should be inserted in their holes is the set of rivets 2.____

    A. T and Z   B. U and Y   C. T and Y   D. U and Z

3. In riveting the seam shown above, the FIRST rivet that should be completely headed is rivet 3.____

    A. T   B. Z   C. U   D. W

4. Fire dampers in ductwork are generally held open by 4.____

    A. cotter pins   B. fusible links
    C. double-throw switches   D. coiled springs

45

5. The sketch shown above represents a sheet metal corner lap seam.
   The space that should be allowed for clearance when using 26 gage sheet metal is MOST NEARLY

   A. 7/16"   B. 5/16"   C. 3/16"   D. 1/16"

6. The MAIN reason for wiring the top edge of a large sheet metal can is to

   A. decrease the expansion of the can due to heat
   B. improve the appearance of the can
   C. increase the strength of the top of the can
   D. make it easier to form the rolled edge of the can

7. Short sections of pipe used to change the direction of ductwork in heating systems are known as

   A. tailpieces   B. fittings
   C. headpieces   D. neckpieces

8. Of the following tinners' rivet sizes, the one that should be used to rivet together two sheets of 26-gage sheet metal is _____ lb.

   A. 1   B. 2   C. 2 1/2   D. 3

9. Of the following types of seams, the one that is a dovetailed seam used in sheet metal work is the _____ seam.

   A. chamfered   B. beaded   C. dadoed   D. lapped

10. The tip of a soldering iron should be covered with solder before being used. The process of applying this solder to the tip is known as

    A. capping   B. skinning   C. tipping   D. tinning

11. The corner seam shown in the sketch at the right is a
    A. Pittsburgh lock
    B. concealed lock
    C. flange dovetail
    D. beaded dovetail

12. To prevent slippage of the sheet metal, seams are MOST often locked by using a

    A. rivet punch   B. Hilti-gun
    C. center punch and hammer   D. needle-nose pliers

13. In figuring the allowance for additional sheet metal needed to make a wired edge on 26-gage sheet metal, the diameter of the wire should be multiplied by   13.____

    A. 1 1/2   B. 2 1/2   C. 3 1/2   D. 4 1/2

14. Small openings around filters, cooling coils, and heating coils are frequently closed with galvanized sheet steel. This practice is known as   14.____

    A. safing   B. sounding   C. saddling   D. dunning

15. A hold-down clamp is a part normally found on a power-driven   15.____

    A. forming machine   B. drill
    C. squaring shear   D. oil-stone grinder

16. The stake that should be used for hand-forming a small sheet metal cone is a _____ stake.   16.____

    A. hatchet   B. bottom
    C. solid mandrel   D. blowhorn

17. A connection between a sheet metal duct and a fan should USUALLY be made by means of a   17.____

    A. Dresser coupling   B. corrugated expansion joint
    C. labyrinth ring   D. flexible collar

18. A bench plate is MOST often used to   18.____

    A. hold stakes   B. sharpen tools
    C. make moldings   D. bend steel rods

19. Of the following machines, the one that should be used to form the round edge that receives the wire used for a wired edge is a _____ machine.   19.____

    A. grooving   B. turning   C. beading   D. wiring

20.   20.____

    The sheet metal bead shown in the sketch above is a(n) _____ bead.

    A. single   B. ogee   C. cavetto   D. ragel

KEY (CORRECT ANSWERS)

1. B
2. A
3. D
4. B
5. C

6. C
7. B
8. A
9. B
10. D

11. A
12. C
13. B
14. A
15. C

16. D
17. D
18. A
19. B
20. B

TEST 2

DIRECTIONS: Each question or incomplete statement is followed by several suggested answers or completions. Select the one that BEST answers the question or completes the statement. *PRINT THE LETTER OF THE CORRECT ANSWER IN THE SPACE AT THE RIGHT.*

1. Of the following, the part that must be tightened on a drill press to properly secure a straight shank drill is the 1._____

    A. chuck
    B. lock quill
    C. collar
    D. gib head

2. Of the following gage designations, the one that is used for aluminum sheet metal is 2._____

    A. W & M B. B & S C. USSG D. G & M

3. Of the following types of pliers, the BEST one to use to clamp down sheet metal to the top of a work bench is the 3._____

    A. channel-lock
    B. vise grip
    C. slip-joint
    D. duck bill

4. The CORRECT machine to use to corrugate the end of a sheet metal pipe so that it can be fitted into another sheet metal pipe of the same diameter is the _____ machine, 4._____

    A. setting down
    B. burring
    C. elbow edge
    D. crimping

5. The wall and ceiling units that distribute air into a room are known as 5._____

    A. spreaders B. diffusers C. headers D. baffles

6. Of the following, the BEST flux to use for soldering galvanized iron is 6._____

    A. raw muriatic acid
    B. rosin
    C. sal ammoniac
    D. zinc chloride

7. Angle brackets for supporting ductwork are commonly anchored to concrete walls by means of _____ bolts. 7._____

    A. carriage B. J- C. expansion D. foot

8. Of the following bolts, the one that should be used when attaching a hanger to a wooden joist is a _____ bolt. 8._____

    A. dead B. lag C. dardalet D. toggle

9. Transite hoods that are used to handle chemical exhausts are made from cement and 9._____

    A. asbestos
    B. fiberglass
    C. lucite
    D. bauxite

10. Of the following sheet metals, the one that is MOST resistant to corrosion is 10._____

    A. copper
    B. aluminum
    C. monel
    D. galvanized steel

11. When bending sheet metal by hand, the BEST tool to use is a

   A. hand groover
   B. hand seamer
   C. hand ball tooler
   D. hand plier

12. Electric soldering irons are rated according to

   A. weight   B. wattage   C. length   D. resistance

13. An example of a hand sheet metal punch is the _____ punch.

   A. Whitney   B. revolving   C. arch   D. drive

14. Copper known as 16 oz. copper weighs 16 oz. per

   A. square foot
   B. square yard
   C. roofing square
   D. running foot of parapet wall

15. The melting point of half-and-half tin-lead solder is _____ the melting point of _____.

   A. greater than; tin
   B. equal to; lead
   C. less than; tin
   D. equal to one-half; lead

16. Of the following types of steel rivets of the same size, the STRONGEST is the _____ rivet.

   A. tinners'
   B. flathead
   C. roundhead
   D. countersunk

17. Of the following snips, the one that can cut relatively thick sheet metal with the LEAST effort is _____ snips.

   A. straight   B. aviation   C. duck bill   D. hawk bill

18. Of the following metals, the one that expands the MOST upon being heated is

   A. steel   B. tin   C. copper   D. aluminum

19. The stake shown in the sketch at the right is a _____ stake.
   A. hatchet
   B. conductor
   C. solid mandrel
   D. beak horn

20. When a circle is too large to be drawn with a pair of dividers, the PROPER tool to use is a

   A. trammel
   B. protractor
   C. combination set
   D. flexible curve

KEY (CORRECT ANSWERS)

1. A
2. B
3. B
4. D
5. B

6. A
7. C
8. B
9. A
10. C

11. B
12. B
13. A
14. A
15. C

16. C
17. B
18. D
19. A
20. A

EXAMINATION SECTION
TEST 1

DIRECTIONS: Each question or incomplete statement is followed by several suggested answers or completions. Select the one that BEST answers the question or completes the statement. *PRINT THE LETTER OF THE CORRECT ANSWER IN THE SPACE AT THE RIGHT.*

1. When sheet metal pipe with the seam on the inside is desired in order to have an unbroken outside surface, this will require a _____ seam.

    A. countersunk grooved B. folded
    C. regular grooved D. Pittsburgh

2. The process of forming sheet metal balls is called

    A. mushrooming or malleting
    B. raising or bumping
    C. drawing or rounding
    D. braking or blocking

3. If an uncoated 20-gauge metal sheet gauges 20 on a U.S. standard gauge, a 20-gauge galvanized metal sheet, when tested on the same gauge, will

    A. actually gauge 18 B. actually gauge 19
    C. also gauge 20 D. actually gauge 21

4. When the bottom of a large sheet metal container is to be joined to the body, it should be done by means of a _____ seam.

    A. simple lap B. grooved lock
    C. common lock D. double lock

5. The size designation of tinners' rivets is based on the

    A. number of rivets per pound
    B. rivet diameter only
    C. weight per thousand rivets
    D. length and diameter of the rivet

6. The decimal equivalent of 27/32 is MOST NEARLY

    A. 0.813   B. 0.828   C. 0.844   D. 0.859

7. When a suitable machine is not available, sheet metal can be formed to a variety of shapes by the use of

    A. bending slabs B. flatters
    C. bench stakes D. swage blocks

8. If a riveted sheet metal seam is also soldered, this is MOST likely done in order to

    A. strengthen the joint
    B. provide a fillet for appearance
    C. help set the rivets
    D. make the seam watertight

9. When circular and semicircular bends must be made in sheet metal, it is necessary to use

   A. a *hold-down* attachment
   B. a cornice brake
   C. circular shears
   D. a setting-down machine

10. Small interior circles are MOST easily cut in sheet metal with _____ snips.

    A. straight
    B. combination
    C. bulldog
    D. hawksbill

11. When a pattern must be developed for a cylindrically-shaped intersected ventilation pipe to be used on a slanting roof, the method of development should be the _____ method.

    A. parallel line
    B. radial line
    C. angular
    D. triangular

12. In order to prevent thin sheet metal from buckling when riveting it to an angle iron, the BEST procedure to follow is to

    A. start riveting at one end of the sheet and work towards the other end
    B. start riveting at both ends of the sheet and work in towards the center
    C. install alternate rivets, working in one direction, and then fill in the remaining rivets working in the other direction
    D. start riveting in the center of the joint, working out in both directions

13. A man being instructed in the proper technique of cutting sheet metal with a hammer and chisel on a bench vise should be told that the BEST results will be obtained if he keeps his eye on the

    A. head of the hammer
    B. head of the chisel
    C. cutting edge of the chisel
    D. cutting line just ahead of the chisel

14. Of the following methods, the one that is NOT suitable for reinforcing the tops of sheet metal articles is

    A. hemming
    B. wiring
    C. riveting with band iron
    D. beveling

15. Condensation will MOST likely form on the inside surface of a skylight during _____ weather when the air inside the building is _____.

    A. cold; warm
    B. warm; warm
    C. cold; cold
    D. warm; cold

16. Two branch ventilating ducts, one 5 inches square and the other 12 inches square, are to connect to a square main duct. In order for the main duct to have the same cross-sectional area as the two branch ducts combined, the dimension of the main duct should be _____ inches square.

    A. 13
    B. 15
    C. 17
    D. 21

17. In sheet metal layout work, the flat steel square would MOST likely be used for constructing _____ from a base line. 17.____

    A. 45° and 90° angles
    B. angles other than 45° or 90°
    C. right angles and parallel lines
    D. right angles but not parallel lines

18. In order to form a rounded flange on the circular edge of a sheet metal cylinder so that it can receive a wire, it is necessary to use a _____ machine. 18.____

    A. wiring   B. turning
    C. burring   D. setting down

19. Rosin is used as the flux when soldering 19.____

    A. tin plate   B. aluminum
    C. galvanized iron   D. zinc

20. If the width of the lock called for in a grooved seam is 1/2", then the allowance to be added to each edge to be joined is 20.____

    A. 1/2"   B. 3/4"   C. 1"   D. 1 1/2"

KEY (CORRECT ANSWERS)

1.	A	11.	A
2.	B	12.	D
3.	B	13.	C
4.	D	14.	D
5.	C	15.	A
6.	C	16.	A
7.	C	17.	C
8.	D	18.	B
9.	B	19.	A
10.	D	20.	B

TEST 2

DIRECTIONS: Each question or incomplete statement is followed by several suggested answers or completions. Select the one that BEST answers the question or completes the statement. *PRINT THE LETTER OF THE CORRECT ANSWER IN THE SPACE AT THE RIGHT.*

1. Sheet metal of 0.025" thickness is to be riveted to a 1" x 1" x 1/8" angle iron, using 3/16" diameter rivets.
   If a length of rivet equal to 1 1/2 rivet diameters is needed to form a proper rivet head, then the rivets used for this job should have a shank length MOST NEARLY of

   A. 11/32"   B. 7/16"   C. 23/32"   D. 1 5/16"

2. It is the function of a soldering flux to

   A. prevent the metals being soldered from overheating
   B. keep the soldering process from proceeding too rapidly for good metal fusion
   C. prevent oxidation from interfering with the soldering process
   D. keep the soldering process chemically neutral

3. A 10" square ventilating duct is connected to a 5" square ventilating duct by a 20" long reducer. If air is flowing in the 10" duct at a speed of 1 foot per second, we can assume that it is flowing in the 5" duct at

   A. a faster speed
   B. a slower speed
   C. the same speed
   D. a faster or slower speed, depending on its temperature

4. The distinction between sheet metal and metal plate is based upon _____ of material.

   A. type   B. flexibility
   C. thickness   D. density

5. By comparison with the melting temperatures of the metals to be joined by soldering, the melting temperature of the solder used

   A. must be lower
   B. must be higher
   C. must be about the same
   D. may be either lower or higher, depending on which metals are being soldered

6. When soldering the underside of a piece, it is normally good practice to tin and use only the working surface of the soldering copper instead of tinning all of its surfaces because, *otherwise,*

   A. the solder will be too hot for a good job
   B. the solder will have a tendency to flow away from the work
   C. the solder will be too cold for a good job
   D. too much solder will accumulate on the piece

7. A metal sheet 4'6" long is to have holes for spot welding drilled on a line parallel to the sheet. The holes are to be spaced 3 1/2" between centers, and the centers of the two end holes are to be 2 1/2" from the ends of the sheet. The number of holes to be drilled is

   A. 13　　　B. 14　　　C. 15　　　D. 16

8. If a scaled measurement of 1'3" on the drawing of a sheet metal layout represents an actual length of 10"0", then the drawing has been made to a scale of _____ inch to the foot.

   A. 3/4　　　B. 1 1/4　　　C. 1 1/2　　　D. 1 3/4

9. Light finishing work on the outside of a crowned sheet metal surface would usually be done with a _____ hammer.

   A. bumping
   B. machinist's
   C. dinging
   D. setting

10. A common flux for sheet metal is prepared by adding

    A. zinc to hydrochloric acid
    B. copper to sulfuric acid
    C. tin to nitric acid
    D. lead to acetic acid

11. When sheet metal is to be riveted, a rivet set is used to

    A. draw and upset the rivets but not head them
    B. upset and head the rivets but not draw them
    C. draw and head the rivets but not upset them
    D. draw, upset, and head the rivets

12. Assuming that it is desirable to have a minimum distance of at least 3 rivet diameters between centers of adjacent rivets and of at least 2 rivet diameters from the center of a rivet to the adjacent edge of a sheet, we could REASONABLY expect that an ordinary lap seam made with a single row of 5 rivets of 3/16" diameter would have a lap of _____ and a length of _____.

    A. 3/8"; 2 5/8"
    B. 3/8"; 3"
    C. 3/4"; 2 5/8"
    D. 3/4"; 3"

13. A tool that can be used both for scribing regular arcs and also transferring dimensions is the

    A. trammel
    B. protractor
    C. scriber
    D. combination square

14. The devices for clamping sheet metal in place on a squaring shear are the

    A. clamps
    B. hold-downs
    C. guides
    D. squares

15. When a hacksaw is used to cut sheet metal, the BEST blade to use is one with _____ teeth per inch.

    A. 14　　　B. 18　　　C. 24　　　D. 32

16. A tool which may be attached to a drill press and used to cut circles of 2 1/2 inch diameter or larger in sheet metal is the   16._____

    A. twist drill
    B. circular saw
    C. reamer
    D. hole saw

17. A versatile hand tool that can be used for a variety of sheet metalwork jobs such as bucking up rivet heads, straightening kinks in formed metal, forming seams, etc., is the   17._____

    A. hand dolly
    B. universal iron worker
    C. cupping tool
    D. set hammer

18. The gage of sheet metal is a measure of its   18._____

    A. thickness   B. area   C. length   D. width

19. A sheet metal plate has been cut in the form of a right triangle with sides of 5, 12, and 13 inches. The area of this plate is, in square inches,   19._____

    A. 30   B. 32 1/2   C. 60   D. 78

20. Of the following, the BEST reason for sheeting a sewer trench is to prevent   20._____

    A. the sewer from being covered with earth until after the final inspection
    B. water from seeping into the excavation
    C. the sides of the excavation from caving in during construction
    D. the sewer pipes being crushed

KEY (CORRECT ANSWERS)

1.	B	11.	C
2.	C	12.	D
3.	A	13.	A
4.	C	14.	B
5.	A	15.	D
6.	B	16.	D
7.	C	17.	A
8.	C	18.	A
9.	C	19.	A
10.	A	20.	C

EXAMINATION SECTION
TEST 1

DIRECTIONS: Each question or incomplete statement is followed by several suggested answers or completions. Select the one that BEST answers the question or completes the statement. *PRINT THE LETTER OF THE CORRECT ANSWER IN THE SPACE AT THE RIGHT.*

1. Stress relieving would MOST likely be used on welds of _____ carbon steel.   1._____

    A. low
    B. medium
    C. high
    D. low and medium

2. The steel used to make a chain would ordinarily be _____ steel.   2._____

    A. low carbon
    B. medium carbon
    C. high carbon
    D. alloy

3. Of the following steels, the MOST readily welded steel is _____ carbon steel.   3._____

    A. low B. medium C. high D. very high

4. The property known as *red hardness* would MOST likely be found in a steel used for making   4._____

    A. nails
    B. structural shapes
    C. rivets
    D. taps and dies

5. Wrought iron is superior to low carbon steel where the PRIMARY consideration is   5._____

    A. high strength
    B. ductility
    C. resistance to corrosion
    D. machineability

6. Of the following metals, the one that is NOT easily spot welded is   6._____

    A. low carbon steel
    B. nickel alloys
    C. stainless steel
    D. aluminum

7. The slag from a coated electrode   7._____

    A. serves no useful purpose
    B. helps produce a more ductile weld
    C. must be removed while the weld is still hot
    D. helps oxides form in the weld

8. When using the oxyacetylene torch to cut steel, the flame should   8._____

    A. contain an excess of acetylene
    B. contain an excess of oxygen
    C. have just enough oxygen to unite completely with the acetylene
    D. strike the steel at a flat angle

9. The amount of filler metal required for a 3/8-inch fillet weld is equal to the amount required for a J-inch fillet weld multiplied by   9._____

    A. 1 1/2   B. 1 3/4   C. 2   D. 2 1/4

59

10. A steel designated as SAE 1035

    A. contains 0.30% to 0.40% carbon
    B. is an alloy steel
    C. is a low carbon steel
    D. is a high carbon steel

11. Assume that the coupling of an oxygen hose has been smeared with a clean grease. This is

    A. *good* because it prevents rust
    B. *bad* because the hose will be hard to handle
    C. *good* because the grease is a preservative for the hose material
    D. *bad* because it could result in an explosion

12. Assume that a welder cracks the valves of the oxygen cylinder and the acetylene cylinder slightly and then closes them before he attached the regulators.
    He does this to

    A. blow away dirt in the valve
    B. identify the gas in the cylinder
    C. make sure that there is pressure in the cylinder
    D. make sure the valve is in operating condition

13. After connecting the regulator to the oxygen cylinder, the next step is to

    A. open the cylinder valve
    B. tighten the regulator pressure-adjusting screw
    C. loosen the regulator pressure-adjusting screw
    D. set the regulator pressure-adjusting screw to the desired working pressure

14. In oxyacetylene cutting, an excessive *drag* or *lag* is

    A. helpful in all cases
    B. more troublesome on straight cuts
    C. more troublesome on curved cuts
    D. helpful on level cuts

15. A respirator would MOST likely be worn when welding

    A. cast iron   B. galvanized iron
    C. low carbon steel   D. aluminum

16. The BEST material for backing bars is

    A. copper   B. steel
    C. cast iron   D. tin

17. Assume that oxyacetylene cutting must be performed in a room with a wood floor. The BEST precaution to take is to

    A. sweep the floor thoroughly
    B. wet the floor down with water
    C. place sheet steel on the floor in the vicinity of the cutting
    D. have one man act as a fire watchman

18. The feature which distinguishes resistance welding from other types of welding using electricity is concerned with

   A. voltage B. current C. electrode D. pressure

19. Assume that a fillet weld has an undercut.
    Prevention of undercutting on a similar weld can probably be BEST accomplished by

   A. using a higher welding current
   B. using a smaller electrode diameter
   C. keeping a larger molten weld puddle
   D. increasing the weaving motion of the electrode

20. An objection to shotblasting of a weld before visual examination of the weld for flaws is that shotblasting

   A. removes slag which indicates flaws
   B. does not clean the weld thoroughly
   C. does not remove oxide films
   D. may seal surface cracks

21. The *term boxing* refers to _____ welds.

   A. plug B. butt C. spot D. fillet

22. Incomplete penetration of a groove weld is MOST likely due to

   A. welding speed too slow
   B. gap at base of weld too narrow
   C. electrode diameter too small
   D. welding current too large

23. After a flashback in an oxyacetylene torch, the welder should

   A. relight the torch immediately
   B. shut off the oxygen and acetylene valves of the torch and allow the torch to cool before relighting
   C. shut off the oxygen valve of the torch and relight
   D. increase the oxygen pressure at the regulator to clear out the clogged orifice

24. A spark test is made to identify a metal. With proper pressure exerted, the length of the stream of sparks is about six feet.
    The metal is MOST probably

   A. low carbon steel   B. stainless steel
   C. nickel   D. aluminum

25. The BEST way to prevent the formation of a crater at the end of a weld is to

   A. break the arc with a sharp upward motion as soon as the end of the weld is reached
   B. move the electrode back over the completed weld and break the arc a few inches from the end of the weld
   C. pause at the end of the weld and then slowly withdraw the electrode until the arc breaks
   D. increase the voltage as the electrode nears the end of the weld

Questions 26-30.

DIRECTIONS: Questions 26 through 30 refer to the weld symbols shown below.

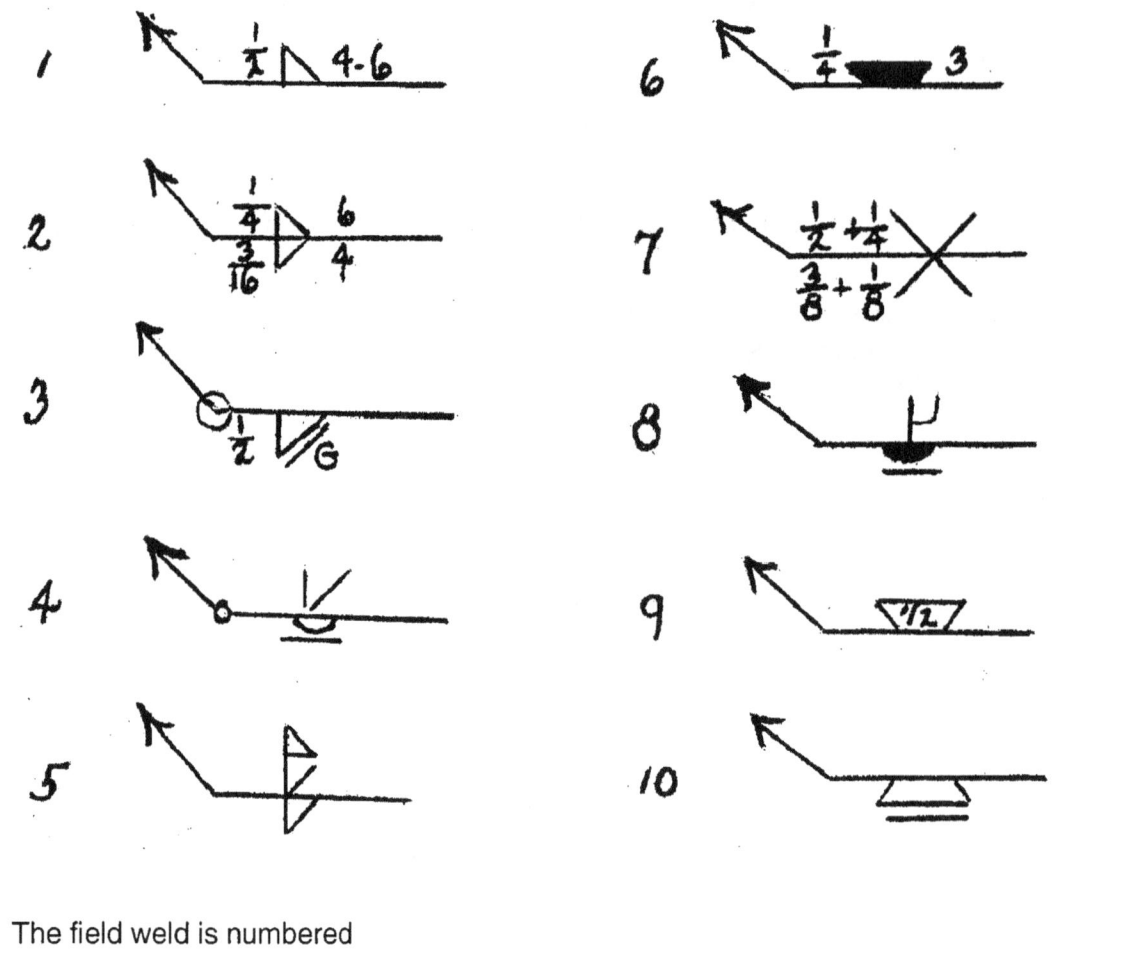

26. The field weld is numbered

    A. 3   B. 4   C. 6   D. 8

27. The weld which extends all around the joint is numbered

    A. 2   B. 3   C. 5   D. 7

28. The intermittent fillet weld is numbered

    A. 1   B. 2   C. 3   D. 5

29. The plug weld which is NOT filled completely is numbered

    A. 6   B. 8   C. 9   D. 10

30. The groove weld which is a melt-thru weld is numbered

    A. 4   B. 5   C. 6   D. 8

31. The cost of arc welding is increased by

   A. use of smaller diameter electrodes
   B. careful fit-up
   C. use of positioning fixtures
   D. use of setting-up fixtures

32. An electrode stub should be discarded when its length becomes _____ inch(es),

   A. 4   B. 2   C. 1   D. 1/2

33. It is GOOD welding practice to

   A. have a powerful fan blow air directly at the welder if he is working in a closed room
   B. weld material which is lying on a concrete floor
   C. ventilate a closed space such as a tank with oxygen "before welding inside the space or tank
   D. leave oxygen and acetylene cylinders outside a tank that is to be welded from the inside

34. When an oxygen cylinder is to be raised by a chain hoist, the hook of the hoist should be attached to

   A. the valve protection cap
   B. a rope sling around the cylinder
   C. a wire sling around the cylinder
   D. a cradle carrying the cylinder

35.

   The flame shown above, as seen with welder's goggles, is

   A. oxidizing   B. reducing
   C. neutral   D. stabilizing

36. A back step sequence of welding is MOST often used to

   A. reduce distortion
   B. increase strength of weld
   C. trap out slag
   D. eliminate undercutting

37. Welding results in the hardening of some metals. This can USUALLY be avoided by

   A. quenching   B. normalizing
   C. slow cooling   D. carburizing

38. The MAIN reason for the use of flux is to 38.____
    A. help the filler metal to adhere to the base metal
    B. remove oxides
    C. prevent overheating of the base metal
    D. replace carbon lost from the base metal during the welding process

39. One of the difficulties encountered in the oxyacetylene welding of aluminum is that aluminum 39.____
    A. does not readily form an oxide coating
    B. melts without changing color
    C. welding requires larger torch tips than those required for welding other metals
    D. must be preheated before it can be properly welded

40. The principle advantage of using an oxyhydrogen flame instead of an oxyacetylene flame for the welding of aluminum is that 40.____
    A. the lower temperature of the oxyhydrogen flame permits better control of the molten metal
    B. less flux is required with the oxyhydrogen since the flame is not as highly oxidizing as the oxyacetylene
    C. use of the oxyhydrogen flame permits making a weld with less filler rod because of better heat transfer
    D. the oxyhydrogen flame provides better shielding of the molten metal than the oxyacetylene flame

KEY (CORRECT ANSWERS)

1.	C	11.	D	21.	D	31.	A
2.	A	12.	A	22.	B	32.	B
3.	A	13.	C	23.	B	33.	D
4.	D	14.	C	24.	A	34.	D
5.	C	15.	B	25.	C	35.	B
6.	D	16.	A	26.	B	36.	A
7.	B	17.	C	27.	B	37.	C
8.	B	18.	D	28.	A	38.	B
9.	D	19.	B	29.	C	39.	B
10.	A	20.	D	30.	D	40.	A

TEST 2

DIRECTIONS: Each question or incomplete statement is followed by several suggested answers or completions. Select the one that BEST answers the question or completes the statement. *PRINT THE LETTER OF THE CORRECT ANSWER IN THE SPACE AT THE RIGHT.*

1. At 77°F, the oxygen pressure in a full cylinder of the type used by welders is MOST NEARLY _____ lbs./sq.in. 1._____

    A. 700 B. 1200 C. 1700 D. 2200

2. Acetylene cylinders should always be used in an upright position. 2._____
The MAIN reason for not using them when they are lying down is that in this position

    A. it is difficult to control discharge pressure
    B. pressure gages are more easily damaged
    C. cylinders can roll, becoming a safety hazard
    D. acetone will be withdrawn with the acetylene

3. The one of the following methods that is NOT commonly used to correct arc blow is to 3._____

    A. reduce the current
    B. increase the arc voltage
    C. weld toward a heavy tack
    D. *back step* on long welds

4. Shrinkage in non-preheated welded products can be reduced to a minimum by 4._____

    A. decreasing the size of each pass and increasing the number of passes
    B. avoiding the use of intermittent welds
    C. peening of welds in the cold state, except root and face-layers
    D. increasing the finished thickness of the weld

5. It is MOST important to take precautions to avoid residual stresses when welding 5._____

    A. wrought iron   B. mild steel
    C. cast iron   D. low carbon steel

6. When welding steel by the atomic hydrogen welding process, heat for the welding process is produced by the electric arc between 6._____

    A. two tungsten electrodes
    B. a steel electrode and the work piece
    C. two carbon electrodes
    D. a tungsten electrode and the work piece

7. Of the following, the MOST important characteristic of the submerged arc welding process is that the 7._____

    A. flux is a solid coating on the electrode
    B. arc is not visible while welding
    C. speed of welding is slower than with shielded metal arc welding
    D. process is fully automatic and cannot be used manually

8. Assume that a welding machine is rated for a 60% duty cycle. This means that the

   A. machine can be used only for welding pieces that are 60% of the thickness of a standard piece
   B. generator can be run only 60% of the time during a day
   C. arc can be on for no more than 6 minutes in a 10 minute period
   D. machine cannot supply adequate voltage if more than 60% of the electrode is consumed

9. Rectifier type welding machines are used PRIMARILY to obtain

   A. steady voltage A.C. regardless of length of arc
   B. B.C. current without use of a motor-generator
   C. an initial high voltage A.C. starting arc
   D. adequate D.C. voltage from a low voltage D.C. line

10. With well-designed electrode holders, overheating of the holder will MOST often result from

    A. a poor connection between the cable and the holder
    B. use of excessively long electrodes
    C. welding overhead instead of positioning flat
    D. improper grounding

11. Of the following, the electrode that would be classified as *low hydrogen* is

    A. E-6010   B. E-6012   C. E-6014   D. E-6016

12. The ductility of a metal is its ability to

    A. be welded without preheat
    B. stretch without cracking
    C. absorb alloys during the welding process
    D. retain its strength at all temperatures

13. *Freezing* of the electrode is MOST often caused by

    A. improper grounding of the work
    B. excessive current setting on the welding machine
    C. inability to strike the arc fast enough
    D. wrong electrode for type of work

14. The temperature at which iron melts is MOST NEARLY

    A. 2800°F   B. 4800°F   C. 6800°F   D. 8800°F

15. The oxidizing of aluminum is MOST similar to the

    A. enameling of magnesium   B. annealing of copper
    C. plating of steel   D. rusting of iron

16. Of the following, the metal that is MOST difficult to weld to other metals is

    A. nickel   B. magnesium   C. bronze   D. copper

17. Of the following methods of welding steel, the one for which a flux is NOT generally required is

    A. vapor shielded
    B. submerged arc
    C. electroslag
    D. TIG

18. A specific carbon-steel welding electrode is designated by a four digit number. The positions in which this electrode can be used is indicated by the _____ digit.

    A. 1st   B. 2nd   C. 3rd   D. 4th

19. The E-6013 electrode is MOST suitable for welding

    A. where deep penetration is required
    B. thin sheet steel
    C. under poor fit-up conditions
    D. when underbead cracking is a problem

20. The PRINCIPAL hardening agent in steel is

    A. carbon   B. silicon   C. phosphorus   D. sulphur

21. Internal stresses in a hardened steel are BEST relieved by

    A. normalizing
    B. quenching
    C. tempering
    D. carburizing

22. *Crater cracks* are caused MAINLY by

    A. slag inclusions
    B. improper joint preparation
    C. hot shrinkage
    D. improper angle of electrode

23. Slag inclusions are MOST common in welds made in the _____ position.

    A. flat
    B. horizontal
    C. vertical
    D. overhead

24. When welding structural steel outdoors in freezing weather, it is poor practice to strike the arc on the base metal at a point outside of the groove MAINLY because

    A. cracks would tend to start at this point
    B. the resulting weld would be unsightly
    C. it is difficult to hold the arc and transfer it to the groove
    D. weld spatter becomes more of a problem

25. A good rule to follow when welding very high carbon (over 1% carbon) steels is to

    A. get as much penetration as possible
    B. weld at a fairly high speed
    C. coat the surfacing of the parent metal with a stainless electrode first
    D. make flat beads

26. Of the following, the MOST important cause of underbead cracking is 26._____

    A. hardening of the surface of the parent metal
    B. excessive preheat
    C. too slow cooling of the weld
    D. running stringer beads instead of weaving

27. With respect to groove welding of alloy steel, the one of the following statements that is 27._____
    CORRECT is:
    Cracks in the root bead can

    A. be burnt out by deep penetration on the second pass
    B. be repaired by post heating on the second pass
    C. be corrected by increasing the interpass temperature
    D. not be melted out on the second pass

28. Of the following methods, grooving of cast iron prior to arc welding is BEST done by 28._____

    A. sawing   B. flame cutting
    C. arc cutting   D. grinding

29. Of the following types of cast iron, the one for which welding is NOT generally recom- 29._____
    mended is _____ iron.

    A. white cast   B. gray cast
    C. malleable   D. nodular

30. The one of the following metals that is NOT hardened by cold working is 30._____

    A. copper   B. steel   C. tin   D. aluminum

31. Copper is BEST annealed by 31._____

    A. heating and quenching in water
    B. cold working
    C. precipitation aging
    D. drawing

32. The one of the following that is a common hard surfacing alloy is 32._____

    A. chromium nickel   B. silicon oxide
    C. sintered manganese   D. tungsten carbide

33. Deep penetration should be avoided when arc welding cast iron MAINLY in order to 33._____

    A. reduce carbon pick-up from the parent metal
    B. eliminate the necessity of preheating
    C. speed up cooling of the metal
    D. prevent tempering of the base metal

34. Of the following types of electrodes, the BEST one to use in arc welding malleable iron is 34._____

    A. mild steel   B. nickel base
    C. coated bronze   D. low hydrogen

35. MOST tool steels are characterized by a high _____ content.   35._____

    A. phosphorous   B. sulphur
    C. carbon   D. nickel

36. Of the following, the one that is the MOST likely cause of weld spatter is   36._____

    A. too low a welding current
    B. too small an electrode
    C. wrong polarity
    D. use of uncoated electrode

37. Porosity in a weld can be reduced by proper welding procedure.   37._____
    The one of the following procedures that will help to produce non-porous welds is to

    A. keep welding currents high
    B. puddle the weld
    C. use a series of stringer beads instead of weaving passes
    D. avoid the use of low hydrogen electrodes

38. The electrode MOST suited to high speed welding in the flat position is the   38._____

    A. E-6010   B. E-6014   C. E-6017   D. E-6020

39. Arc blow refers to the   39._____

    A. force with which the arc hits the base metal
    B. depth of penetration of the arc
    C. jumping of the arc away from the point at which the electrode is directed
    D. voltage that forces the arc across the gap

40. The one of the following that gives the CORRECT order of melting of the metals starting   40._____
    with the one that melts at the LOWEST temperature is

    A. tin, lead, copper, silver
    B. tin, lead, silver, copper
    C. lead, tin, silver, copper
    D. lead, tin, copper, silver

KEY (CORRECT ANSWERS)

1. D	11. D	21. C	31. A
2. D	12. B	22. C	32. D
3. B	13. C	23. D	33. A
4. C	14. A	24. A	34. C
5. C	15. D	25. C	35. C
6. A	16. B	26. A	36. C
7. B	17. D	27. D	37. B
8. C	18. C	28. A	38. D
9. B	19. B	29. A	39. C
10. A	20. A	30. C	40. B

MECHANICAL APTITUDE
TOOL RECOGNITION AND USE
EXAMINATION SECTION
TEST 1

DIRECTIONS: Each question or incomplete statement is followed by several suggested answers or completions. Select the one that BEST answers the question or completes the statement. *PRINT THE LETTER OF THE CORRECT ANSWER IN THE SPACE AT THE RIGHT.*

Questions 1-16.

DIRECTIONS: Questions 1 through 16 refer to the tools shown below. The numbers in the answers refer to the numbers below the tools. NOTE: These tools are NOT shown to scale.

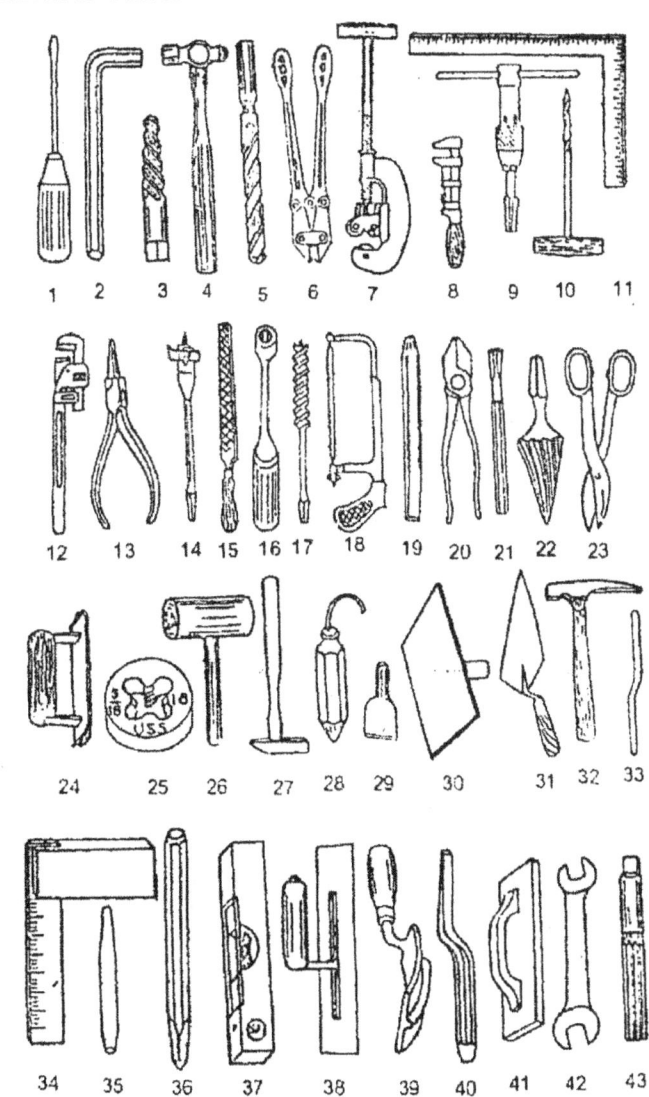

73

1. In order to cut a piece of 5/16" diameter steel scaffold hoisting cable, you should use tool number
   A. 6 B. 7 C. 19 D. 23

   1.____

2. Scaffold planks are secured to joisting irons by means of lag screws. To properly tighten these lag screws, you should use tool number
   A. 12 B. 13 C. 20 D. 42

   2.____

3. While installing a steel angle iron lintel, you find that the threads on the embedded holding bolts are damaged. You should repair the threads by using tool number
   A. 7 B. 9 C. 25 D. 43

   3.____

4. It is necessary to cut a hole in a concrete foundation wall in order to place a small bolt. To cut this small hole, you should use tool number
   A. 14 B. 19 C. 21 D. 40

   4.____

5. If tool number 17 bears the mark "7," this tool should be used to drill holes having a diameter of
   A. 7/64" B. 7/32" C. 7/16" D. 7/8"

   5.____

6. If the marking on the blade of tool number 18 reads "10-18," the "18" refers to the
   A. number of teeth per inch   B. weight
   C. thickness   D. length

   6.____

7. If two points are separated by a vertical distance of 12 feet, the tool that should be used to make certain that the points are in perfect vertical alignment is number
   A. 11 B. 28 C. 34 D. 37

   7.____

8. A 3/4" diameter hole must be made in a steel floor beam. The tool you should use is number
   A. 3 B. 5 C. 9 D. 22

   8.____

9. To cut the corner off a building brick, you should use tool number
   A. 4 B. 27 C. 29 D. 36

   9.____

10. A 2" x 2" x 3/16" steel angle should be cut using tool number
    A. 6 B. 7 C. 18 D. 19

    10.____

11. The term "snips" should be applied to tool number
    A. 6 B. 13 C. 20 D. 23

    11.____

12. To line-up the bolt holes in two structural steel beams, you should use tool number
    A. 1 B. 33 C. 35 D. 36

    12.____

13. A "hawk" is tool number 13.____
    A. 29 B. 30 C. 38 D. 41

14. After an 8" thick brick wall has been erected, it is discovered that a hole 14.____
    should have been left for a 4" sewer pipe.
    To cut that hole, you should use tool number
    A. 5 B. 19 C. 32 D. 36

15. A "float" is tool number 15.____
    A. 30 B. 31 C. 33 D. 41

16. A "Stillson" is tool number 16.____
    A. 2 B. 8 C. 12 D. 22

KEY (CORRECT ANSWERS)

1. A 11. D
2. D 12. C
3. C 13. B
4. C 14. D
5. C 15. D

6. A 16. C
7. B
8. B
9. C
10. C

TEST 2

DIRECTIONS: Each question or incomplete statement is followed by several suggested answers or completions. Select the one that BEST answers the question or completes the statement. *PRINT THE LETTER OF THE CORRECT ANSWER IN THE SPACE AT THE RIGHT.*

1. The stake shown in the sketch at the right is a _____ stake.
   A. hatchet
   B. conductor
   C. solid mandrel
   D. beak horn

   1._____

2. When a circle is too large to be drawn with a pair of dividers, the PROPER tool to use is a
   A. trammel
   B. protractor
   C. combination set
   D. flexible curve

   2._____

3. A rivet set is a tool used to
   A. shape the head of a rivet
   B. mark off the spacing of rivets
   C. remove a loose rivet
   D. check the shank length of a rivet

   3._____

4. The hammer shown in the sketch at the right is a _____ hammer.
   A. raising
   B. ball peen
   C. setting
   D. cross-over

   4._____

5. Of the following, the BEST tool to use to scribe a line parallel to the straight edge of a piece of sheet metal is a(n)
   A. outside caliper
   B. pair of dividers
   C. template
   D. scratch gage

   5._____

6. Of the following, the BEST device to use to check the condition of the insulation of a cable is the
   A. ohmmeter
   B. wheatstone bridge
   C. voltmeter
   D. megger

   6._____

7. Of the following fittings, the one used to connect two lengths of conduit in a straight line is a(n)
   A. elbow
   B. nipple
   C. tee
   D. coupling

   7._____

8. If a nut is to be tightened to an exact specified value, the wrench that should be used is a(n) _____ wrench.
   A. torque
   B. lock-jaw
   C. alligator
   D. spaner

   8._____

76

9. A stillson wrench is also called a _____ wrench.
   A. strap   B. pipe   C. monkey   D. crescent

9.____

10. A machine screw is indicated on a drawing as . The head is the American Standard type called
    A. flat
    B. oval
    C. fillister
    D. round

10.____

11. The tool that is shown at the right is properly referred to as a(n) _____ tap.
    A. bottoming
    B. acme
    C. taper
    D. plug

11.____

12. The tool indicated at the right is referred to as an Arc Punch. This tool should be used to
    A. cut holes in 1/16" steel
    B. cut large diameter holes in masonry
    C. run through a conduit prior to pulling a cable or wires
    D. make holes in rubber or leather gasket material

12.____

13. The plumbing fitting shown at the right is called a
    A. street elbow
    B. return bend
    C. running trap
    D. reversing "el"

13.____

14. For which one of the following uses would it be unsafe to use a carpenter's hammer?
    A. casing mail   B. hand punch
    C. hardened steel surface   D. plastic surface

14.____

15. Of the following, the MAIN advantage in using a Phillips head screw is that
    A. the threads of the Phillips head screw have a deeper bite than standard screw threads
    B. the screwdriver used on this type of screw is more likely to keep its edge than a standard screwdriver
    C. a single screwdriver fits all size screws of this type
    D. the screwdriver used on this type of screw is less likely to slip than a standard screwdriver

15.____

16. One of the reasons why a polyester rope is considered to be the BEST general purpose rope is that it
    A. does not stretch as much as ropes made of other materials
    B. is available in longer lengths than ropes made of other materials
    C. does not fray as much as ropes made of other materials
    D. contains more strands than ropes made of other materials

17. The PROPER saw to use to cut wood with the grain is a _____ saw.
    A. hack   B. crosscut   C. back   D. rip

18. Assume that the instruction manual for a machine indicates that a certain bolt must be tightened with a specified amount of force.
    Of the following tools, the one which should be used to tighten the bolt with the specified amount of force is a(n) _____ wrench.
    A. torque   B. adjustable   C. stillson   D combination

19. The power source of a pneumatic tool is
    A. manual   B. water pressure
    C. compressed air   D. electricity

20. The tool used to cut internal pipe threads is a
    A. broach   B. tap   C. die   D. rod

KEY (CORRECT ANSWERS)

1. A   11. A
2. A   12. D
3. A   13. B
4. C   14. C
5. D   15. D

6. D   16. A
7. D   17. D
8. A   18. A
9. B   19. C
10. B   20. B

ARITHMETICAL REASONING

EXAMINATION SECTION
TEST 1

DIRECTIONS: Each question or incomplete statement is followed by several suggested answers or completions. Select the one that BEST answers the question or completes the statement. *PRINT THE LETTER OF THE CORRECT ANSWER IN THE SPACE AT THE RIGHT.*

1. If it takes 2 men 9 days to do a job, how many men are needed to do the same job in 3 days?
   A. 4   B. 5   C. 6   D. 7

2. Suppose that a department operates 1,644 buildings. If one employee is needed for every 2 buildings, and one foreman is needed for every 18 employees, the number of foremen needed is CLOSEST to
   A. 45   B. 50   C. 55   D. 60

3. If 60 bars of soap cost the same as 2 gallons of wax, how many bars of soap can be bought for the price of 5 gallons of wax?
   A. 120   B. 150   C. 180   D. 300

4. An employee waxes 275 sq.ft. of floor on Monday, 352 sq.ft. on Tuesday, 179 sq.ft. on Wednesday, and 302 sq.ft. on Thursday.
   In order to average 280 sq.ft. of floor waxed a day, how many square feet of floor must he wax on Friday?
   A. 264   B. 278   C. 292   D. 358

5. A project covers 35 acres altogether. Lawns, playgrounds, and walks take up 28 acres and the rest is given over to buildings.
   What percentage of the total area is given over to buildings?
   A. 7%   B. 20%   C. 25%   D. 28%

6. When preparing for a mopping operation, fill the standard 16 quart bucket to the 3/4 full mark with warm water. Then add detergent at the rate of 2 oz. per gallon of water and disinfectant at the rate of 1 oz. to 3 gallons of water. According to these directions, the amount of detergent and disinfectant to add to 3/4 of a bucket of warm water is _____ oz. detergent and _____ oz. disinfectant.
   A. 4; 1/2   B. 5; 3/4   C. 6; 1   D. 8; 1 1/4

7. If corn brooms weigh 32 lbs. a dozen, the average weight of one corn broom is CLOSEST to _____ lbs. _____ oz.
   A. 2; 14   B. 2; 11   C. 2; 9   D. 2; 6

8. At the beginning of the year, a foreman has 7 dozen electric bulbs in stock. During the year, he receives a shipment of 14 dozen bulbs, and also replaces 5 burned out bulbs a month in each of 3 buildings in his area. How many electric bulbs does he have on hand at the end of the year? _____ dozen.

   A. 3   B. 6   C. 8   D. 12

9. A project has 4 buildings, each 14 floors high. Each floor has 10 apartments. If 35% of the apartments in the project have 3 rooms or less, how many apartments have 4 or more rooms?

   A. 196   B. 210   C. 364   D. 406

10. An employee takes 1 hour and 30 minutes a day to sweep 30 flights of stairs. How many flights of stairs does he sweep in a month if he spends a total of 30 hours doing this job and works at the same rate?

    A. 200   B. 300   C. 600   D. 900

11. During a month, Employee A washed 30 windows, Employee B washed 4 times as many windows as Employee A, and Employee C washed half as many windows as Employee B. The TOTAL number of windows washed by all three men together during this month is

    A. 180   B. 210   C. 240   D. 330

12. How much would it cost to completely fence in the playground area shown at the right with fencing costing $7.50 a foot?
    A. $615.00
    B. $820.00
    C. $885.00
    D. $960.00

13. A drill bit measures .625 inches. The fractional equivalent, in inches, is

    A. 9/16   B. 5/8   C. 11/16   D. 3/4

14. The number of cubic yards of sand required to fill a bin measuring 12 feet by 6 feet by 4 feet is MOST NEARLY

    A. 8   B. 11   C. 48   D. 96

15. Assume that you are assigned to put down floor tiles in a room measuring 8 feet by 10 feet. Individual tiles measure 9 inches by 9 inches. The total number of floor tiles required to cover the entire floor is MOST NEARLY

    A. 107   B. 121   C. 142   D. 160

16. Lumber is usually sold by the board foot, and a board foot is defined as a board one foot square and one inch thick.
    If the price of one board foot of lumber is 90 cents and you need 20 feet of lumber 6 inches wide and 1 inch thick, the cost of the 20 feet of lumber is

    A. $9.00   B. $12.00   C. $18.00   D. $24.00

    16._____

17. For a certain plumbing repair job, you need three lengths of pipe, 12 1/4 inches, 6 1/2 inches, and 8 5/8 inches.
    If you cut these three lengths from the same piece of pipe, which is 36 inches long, and each cut consumes 1/8 inch of pipe, the length of pipe REMAINING after you have cut out your three pieces should be _____ inches.

    A. 7 1/4   B. 7 7/8   C. 8 1/4   D. 8 7/8

    17._____

18. A maintenance bond for a roadway pavement is in an amount of 10% of the estimated cost.
    If the estimated cost is $8,000,000, the maintenance bond is

    A. $8,000   B. $80,000   C. $800,000   D. $8,000,000

    18._____

19. Specifications require that a core be taken every 700 square yards of paved roadway or fraction thereof. A 100 foot by 200 foot rectangular area would require _____ core(s).

    A. 1   B. 2   C. 3   D. 4

    19._____

20. An applicant must file a map at a scale of 1" = 40'. Six inches on the map represents _____ feet on the ground.

    A. 600   B. 240   C. 120   D. 60

    20._____

21. A 100' x 110' lot has an area of MOST NEARLY _____ acre.

    A. 1/8   B. 1/4   C. 3/8   D. 1/2

    21._____

22. 1 inch is MOST NEARLY equal to _____ feet.

    A. .02   B. .04   C. .06   D. .08

    22._____

23. The area of the triangle EFG shown at the right is MOST NEARLY _____ sq. ft.

    A. 36   B. 42   C. 48   D. 54

    23._____

24. Specifications state: As further security for the faithful performance of this contract, the Comptroller shall deduct, and retain until the final payment, 10% of the value of the work certified for payment in each partial payment voucher, until the amount so deducted and retained shall equal 5% of the contract price or in the case of a unit price contract, 5% of the estimated amount to be paid to the Contractor under the contract.
    For a $300,000 contract, the amount to be retained at the end of the contract is

    A. $5,000   B. $10,000   C. $15,000   D. $20,000

    24._____

25. Asphalt was laid for a length of 210 feet on the entire width of a street whose curb-to-curb distance is 30 feet. The number of square yards covered with asphalt is MOST NEARLY

    A. 210   B. 700   C. 2,100   D. 6,300

    25._____

KEY (CORRECT ANSWERS)

1.	C	11.	B
2.	A	12.	C
3.	B	13.	B
4.	C	14.	B
5.	B	15.	C
6.	C	16.	A
7.	B	17.	C
8.	B	18.	C
9.	C	19.	D
10.	C	20.	B

21. B
22. D
23. A
24. C
25. B

SOLUTIONS TO PROBLEMS

1. (2)(9) = 18 man-days. Then, 18 ÷ 3 = 6 men

2. The number of employees = 1644 ÷ 2 = 822. The number of foremen needed = 822 ÷ 18 ≈ 45

3. 1 gallon of wax costs the same as 60 ÷ 2 = 30 bars of soap. Thus, 5 gallons of wax costs the same as (5)(30) = 150 bars of soap.

4. To average 280 sq.ft. for five days means a total of (5)(280) = 1400 sq.ft. for all five days. The number of square feet to be waxed on Friday = 1400 - (275+352+179+302) = 292

5. The acreage for buildings is 35 - 28 = 7. Then, 7/35 = 20%

6. (16)(3/4) = 12 quarts = 3 gallons. The amount of detergent, in ounces, is (2)(3) = 6. The amount of disinfectant is 1 oz.

7. One corn broom weighs 32 ÷ 12 = 2 2/3 lbs. ≈ 2 lbs. 11 oz.

8. Number of bulbs at the beginning of the year = (7)(12) + (14)(12) = 252. Number of bulbs replaced over an entire year = (5)(3)(12) = 180. The number of unused bulbs = 252 - 180 = 72 = 6 dozen.

9. Total number of apartments = (4)(14)(10) = 560. The number of apartments with at least 4 rooms = (.65)(560) = 364.

10. 30 ÷ 1 1/2 = 20. Then, (20)(30) = 600 flights of stairs

11. The number of windows washed by A, B, C were 30, 120, and 60. Their total is 210.

12. The two missing dimensions are 26 - 14 = 12 ft. and 33 - 9 = 24 ft. Perimeter = 9 + 12 + 33 + 26 + 24 + 14 = 118 ft. Thus, total cost of fencing = (118)($7.50) = $885.00

13. $.625 = \dfrac{625}{1000} = \dfrac{5}{8}$

14. (12)(6)(4) = 288 cu.ft. Now, 1 cu.yd. = 27 cu.ft.; 288 cu.ft. is equivalent to 10 2/3 or about 11 cu.yds.

15. 144 sq.in. = 1 sq.ft. The room measures (8 ft.)x(10 ft.) = 80 sq.ft. = 11,520 sq.in. Each tile measures (9)(9) = 81 sq.in. The number of tiles needed = 11,520 ÷ 81 = 142.2 or about 142.

16. 20 ft. by 6 in. = (20 ft.)(1/2 ft.) = 10 sq.ft. Then, (10X.90) = $9.00

17. There will be 3 cuts in making 3 lengths of pipe, and these 3 cuts will use (3)(1/8) = 3/8 in. of pipe. The amount of pipe remaining after the 3 pieces are removed = 36 - 12 1/4 - 6 1/2 - 8 5/8 - 3/8 = 8 1/4 in.

18. The maintenance bond = (.10)($8,000,000) = $800,000

19. (100)(200) = 20,000 sq.ft. = 20,000 ÷ 9 ≈ 2222 sq.yds. Then, 2222 ÷ 700 ≈ 3.17. Since a core must be taken for each 700 sq.yds. plus any left over fraction, 4 cores will be needed.

20. Six inches means (6)(40) = 240 ft. of actual length.

21. (100 ft.)(110 ft.) = 11,000 sq.ft. ≈ 1222 sq.yds. Then, since 1 acre = 4840 sq.yds., 1222 sq.yds. is equivalent to about 1/4 acre.

22. 1 in. = 1/12 ft. ≈ .08 ft.

23. Area of $\triangle$ EFG = (1/2)(8)(6) + (1/2)(4)(6) = 36 sq.ft.

24. The amount to be retained = (.05)($300,000) = $15,000

25. (210)(30) = 6300 sq.ft. Since 1 sq.yd. = 9 sq.ft., 6300 sq.ft. equals 700 sq.yds.

TEST 2

DIRECTIONS: Each question or incomplete statement is followed by several suggested answers or completions. Select the one that BEST answers the question or completes the statement. *PRINT THE LETTER OF THE CORRECT ANSWER IN THE SPACE AT THE RIGHT.*

1. The TOTAL length of four pieces of 2" pipe, whose lengths are 7'3 1/2", 4'2 3/16", 5'7 5/16", and 8'5 7/8", respectively, is

    A. 24'6 3/4"
    B. 24'7 15/16"
    C. 25'5 13/16"
    D. 25'6 7/8"

    1.____

2. Under the same conditions, the group of pipes that gives the SAME flow as one 6" pipe is (neglecting friction) _____ pipes.

    A. 3 3"   B. 4 3"   C. 2 4"   D. 3 4"

    2.____

3. A water storage tank measures 5' long, 4' wide, and 6' deep and is filled to the 5 1/2' mark with water.
   If one cubic foot of water weighs 62 pounds, the number of pounds of water required to COMPLETELY fill the tank is

    A. 7,440   B. 6,200   C. 1,240   D. 620

    3.____

4. A hot water line made of copper has a straight horizontal run of 150 feet and, when installed, is at a temperature of 45°F. In use, its temperature rises to 190°F.
   If the coefficient of expansion for copper is 0.0000095" per foot per degree F, the total expansion, in inches, in the run of pipe is given by the product of 150 multiplied by 0.0000095 by

    A. 145
    B. 145 x 12
    C. 145 divided by 12
    D. 145 x 12 x 12

    4.____

5. To dig a trench 3'0" wide, 50'0" long, and 5'6" deep, the total number of cubic yards of earth to be removed is MOST NEARLY

    A. 30   B. 90   C. 140   D. 825

    5.____

6. If it costs $65 for 20 feet of subway rail, the cost of 150 feet of this rail will be

    A. $487.50   B. $512.00   C. $589.50   D. $650.00

    6.____

7. The number of cubic feet of concrete it takes to fill a form 10 feet long, 3 feet wide, and 6 inches deep is

    A. 12   B. 15   C. 20   D. 180

    7.____

8. The sum of 4 1/16, 5 1/4, 3 5/8, and 4 7/16 is

    A. 17 3/16   B. 17 1/4   C. 17 5/16   D. 17 3/8

    8.____

9. If you earn $10.20 per hour and time and one-half for working over 40 hours, your gross salary for a week in which you worked 42 hours would be

    A. $408.00   B. $428.40   C. $438.60   D. $770.80

    9.____

10. A drill bit, used to drill holes in track ties, has a diameter of 0.75 inches. When expressed as a fraction, the diameter of this drill bit is

    A. 1/4"   B. 3/8"   C. 1/2"   D. 3/4"

11. Three dozen shovels were purchased for use.
    If the shovels were used at the rate of nine a week, the number of weeks that the three dozen lasted was

    A. 3   B. 4   C. 9   D. 12

12. Assume that you earn $20,000 per year.
    If twenty percent of your pay is deducted for taxes, social security, and pension, your weekly take-home pay will be MOST NEARLY

    A. $280   B. $308   C. $328   D. $344

13. If a measurement scaled from a drawing is one inch, and the scale of the drawing is 1/8 inch to the foot, then the one inch measurement would represent an ACTUAL length of

    A. 8 feet   B. 2 feet
    C. 1/8 of a foot   D. 8 inches

14. Tiles 12" x 12" are used to lay a floor having the dimensions 10'0" x 12'0".
    The MINIMUM number of tiles needed to completely cover the floor is

    A. 60   B. 96   C. 120   D. 144

15. The volume of concrete in a strip of sidewalk 30 feet long by 4 feet wide by 3 inches thick is _____ cubic feet.

    A. 30   B. 120   C. 240   D. 360

16. To change a quantity of cubic feet into an equivalent quantity of cubic yards, _____ the quantity by _____.

    A. multiply; 9   B. divide; 9
    C. multiply; 27   D. divide; 27

17. If a pump can deliver 50 gallons of water per minute, then the time needed for this pump to empty an excavation containing 5,800 gallons of water is _____ hour(s) _____ minutes.

    A. 2; 12   B. 1; 56   C. 1; 44   D. 1; 32

18. The sum of 3 1/6", 4 1/4", 3 5/8", and 5 7/16" is

    A. 15 9/16"   B. 16 1/8"   C. 16 23/48"   D. 16 3/4"

19. If a measurement scaled from a drawing is 2 inches, and the scale of the drawing is 1/8 inch to the foot, then the two inch measurement would represent an ACTUAL length of

    A. 8 feet   B. 4 feet
    C. 1/4 of a foot   D. 16 feet

20. A room is 7'6" wide by 9'0" long with a ceiling height of 8'0". One gallon of flat paint will cover approximately 400 square feet of wall.
    The number of gallons of this paint required to paint the walls of this room, making no deductions for windows or doors, is MOST NEARLY

    A. 1/4   B. 1/2   C. 2/3   D. 1

21. The cost of a certain job is broken down as follows:

    Materials $3,750
    Rental of equipment 1,200
    Labor   3,150

    The percentage of the total cost of the job that can be charged to materials is MOST NEARLY

    A. 40%   B. 42%   C. 44%   D. 46%

22. By trial, it is found that by using two cubic feet of sand, a 5 cubic foot batch of concrete is produced. Using the same proportions, the amount of sand required to produce 2 cubic yards of concrete is MOST NEARLY _____ cubic feet.

    A. 20   B. 22   C. 24   D. 26

23. It takes 4 men 6 days to do a certain job.
    Working at the same speed, the number of days it will take 3 men to do this job is

    A. 7   B. 8   C. 9   D. 10

24. The cost of rawl plugs is $27.50 per gross. The cost of 2,448 rawl plugs is

    A. $467.50   B. $472.50   C. $477.50   D. $482.50

25. In a certain district, the area of a building may be no longer than 55% of the area of the lot on which it stands. On a rectangular lot 75 ft. by 125 ft., the maximum permissible area of building is, in square feet, MOST NEARLY

    A. 5,148   B. 5,152   C. 5,156   D. 5,160

KEY (CORRECT ANSWERS)

1. D
2. B
3. D
4. A
5. A

6. A
7. B
8. D
9. C
10. D

11. B
12. B
13. A
14. C
15. A

16. D
17. B
18. C
19. D
20. C

21. D
22. B
23. B
24. A
25. C

SOLUTIONS TO PROBLEMS

1. $3\frac{1}{6}" + 4\frac{1}{4}" + 3\frac{5}{8}" + 5\frac{7}{16}" = 3\frac{8}{48}" + 4\frac{12}{48}" + 3\frac{30}{48}" + 5\frac{21}{48}" = 15\frac{71}{48}" = 16\frac{23}{48}"$

2. The flow of a 6" pipe is measured by the cross-sectional area. Since diameter = 6", radius = 3", and so area = 9π sq.in. A single 3" pipe would have a cross-sectional area of $(3/2)\pi$ sq.in. = 2.25π sq.in. Now, 9 ÷ / 2.25 = 4. Thus, four 3" pipes is equivalent, in flow, to one 6" pipe.

3. (5x4x6) - (5x4x5 1/2) = 10. Then, (10)(62) = 620 pounds.

4. The total expansion = (150')(.0000095"/1 ft.)(190°-45°). So, the last factor is 145.

5. (3')(50')(5 1/2') = 825 cu.ft. Since 1 cu.yd. = 27 cu.ft., 825 cu.ft. cu.yds.

6. 150 ÷ 20 = 7.5. Then, (7.5)($65) = $487.50

7. (10')(3')(1/2') = 15 cu.ft.

8. $4\frac{1}{16} + 5\frac{4}{16} + 3\frac{10}{16} + 4\frac{7}{16} = 16\frac{22}{16} = 17\frac{3}{8}$

9. Gross salary = ($10.20)(40) + ($15.30)(2) = $438.60

10. $75" = \frac{75}{100}" = \frac{3}{4}"$

11. 3 dozen = 36 shovels. Then, 36 ÷ 9 = 4 weeks

12. Since 20% is deducted, the take-home pay = ($20,000)(.80) = $16,000 for the year, which is $16,000 ÷ 52 ≈ $308 per week.

13. A scale drawing where 1/8" means an actual size of 1 ft. implies that a scale drawing of 1" means an actual size of (1')(8) = 8'

14. (10')(12') = 120 sq.ft. Since each tile is 1 sq.ft., a total of 120 tiles will be used.

15. (30')(4')(1/4') = 30 cu.ft.

16. To convert a given number of cubic feet into an equivalent number of cubic yards, divide by 27.

17. 5800 ÷ 50 = 116 min. = 1 hour 56 minutes

18. $3\frac{1}{6}" + 4\frac{1}{4}" + 3\frac{5}{8}" + 5\frac{7}{16}" = 3\frac{8}{48}" + 4\frac{12}{48}" + 3\frac{30}{48}" + 5\frac{21}{48}" = 15\frac{71}{48}" = 16\frac{23}{48}"$

19. 2 ÷ 1/8 = 16, so a 2" drawing represents an actual length of 16 feet.

20. The area of the 4 walls = 2(7 1/2')(8') + 2(9')(8') = 264 sq.ft. Then, 264 ÷ 400 = .66 or about 2/3 gallon of paint.

21. $3750 + $1200 + $3150 = $8100. Then, $3750/$8100 ≈ 46%

22. 2 cu.yds. ÷ 5 cu.ft. = 54 ÷ 5 = 10.8. Now, (10.8)(2 cu.ft.) ≈ 22 cu.ft. Note: 2 cu.yds. = 54 cu.ft.

23. (4)(6) = 24 man-days. Then, 24 ÷ 3 = 8 days

24. 2448 ÷ 144 = 17. Then, (17)($27.50) = $467.50

25. (75')(125') = 9375 sq.ft. The maximum area of the building = (.55)(9375 sq.ft.) ≈ 5156 sq.ft.

TEST 3

DIRECTIONS: Each question or incomplete statement is followed by several suggested answers or completions. Select the one that BEST answers the question or completes the statement. *PRINT THE LETTER OF THE CORRECT ANSWER IN THE SPACE AT THE RIGHT.*

1. A steak weighed 2 pounds, 4 ounces. How much did it cost at $4.60 per pound?

    A. $7.80   B. $8.75   C. $9.90   D. $10.35

2. twenty pints of water just fill a pail. the capacity of the pail, in gallons, is

    A. 2   B. 2 1/4   C. 2 1/2   D. 2 3/4

3. The sum of 5/12 and 1/4 is

    A. 7/12   B. 2/3   C. 3/4   D. 5/6

4. The volume of earth, in cubic yards, excavated from a trench 4'0" wide by 5'6" deep by 18'6" long is MOST NEARLY

    A. 14.7   B. 15.1   C. 15.5   D. 15.9

5. 5/8 written as a decimal is

    A. 62.5   B. 6.25   C. .625   D. .0625

6. The number of cubic feet in a cubic yard is

    A. 9   B. 12   C. 27   D. 36

7. If it costs $16.20 to lay one square yard of asphalt, to lay a patch 15' by 15', it will cost MOST NEARLY

    A. $405.00   B. $3,645.00   C. $134.50   D. $243.00

8. You are assigned thirty (30) asphalt workers to be divided into two crews so that one crew will have 2/3 as many men as the other.
The number of men you would put into the SMALLER crew is

    A. 10   B. 12   C. 14   D. 20

9. It takes 12 asphalt workers, working 6 hours a day, 5 days to complete a certain job. The number of days it will take 10 men, working 8 hours a day, to do the same job, assuming all work at the same rate, is

    A. 2 1/2   B. 3   C. 4 1/2   D. 6

10. A street is laid to a 3% grade. This means that in 150 ft., the street grade will rise

    A. 4 1/2 inches   B. 45 inches
    C. 4 1/2 feet   D. 45 feet

11. The sum of the following dimensions, 3 4/8, 4 1/8, 5 1/8, and 6 1/4, is

    A. 19   B. 19 1/8   C. 19 1/4   D. 19 1/2

12. A worker is paid $9.30 per hour.
    If he works 8 hours each day on Monday, Tuesday, and Wednesday, 3 1/2 hours on Thursday, and 3 hours on Friday, the TOTAL amount due him is

    A. $283.65   B. $289.15   C. $276.20   D. $285.35

13. The price of metal lath is $395.00 per 100 square yards. The cost of 527 square yards of this lath is MOST NEARLY

    A. $2,076.50   B. $2,079.10   C. $2,081.70   D. $2,084.30

14. The total cost of applying 221 square yards of plaster board is $3,430.
    The cost per square yard is MOST NEARLY

    A. $14.00   B. $14.50   C. $15.00   D. $15.50

15. In a three-coat plaster job, the scratch coat is 1/8 in. thick in front of the lath, the brown coat is 3/16 in. thick, and the finish coat is 1/8 in. thick.
    The TOTAL thickness of this plaster job, measured from the face of the lath, is

    A. 7/16"   B. 1/2"   C. 9/16"   D. 5/8"

16. If an asphalt worker earns $38,070 per year, his wages per month are MOST NEARLY

    A. $380.70   B. $735.00   C. $3,170.00   D. $3,807.00

17. The sum of 4 1/2 inches, 3 1/4 inches, and 7 1/2 inches is 1 foot _____ inches.

    A. 3   B. 3 1/4   C. 3 1/2   D. 4

18. The area of a rectangular asphalt patch, 9 ft. 3 in. by 6 ft. 9 in., is _____ square feet.

    A. 54   B. 54 1/4   C. 54 1/2   D. 62 7/16

19. The number of cubic feet in a cubic yard is

    A. 3   B. 9   C. 16   D. 27

20. A 450 ft. long street with a grade of 2% will have one end of the street higher than the other end by _____ feet.

    A. 2   B. 44   C. 9   D. 20

21. If the drive wheel of a roller is 6 ft. in diameter and the tiller wheel is 4 ft. in diameter, whenever the drive wheel makes a complete revolution on a straight pass, the tiller wheel makes _____ revolution(s).

    A. 1   B. 1 1/4   C. 1 1/2   D. 2

22. A point on the centerline of a street is marked: Station 42 + 51. Another point on the centerline 30 feet from the first is marked Station 42+81.
    A third should be marked Station

    A. 12+51   B. 42+21   C. 45+51   D. 72+51

23. In twenty minutes, a truck moving with a speed of 30 miles an hour will cover a distance of _____ miles. 23._____

   A. 3 B. 5 C. 10 D. 30

24. The number of pounds in a ton is 24._____

   A. 500 B. 1,000 C. 2,000 D. 5,000

25. During his summer vacation, a boy earned $45.00 per day and saved 60% of his earnings. 25._____
   If he worked 45 days, how much did he save during his vacation?

   A. $15.00 B. $18.00 C. $1,215.00 D. $22.50

KEY (CORRECT ANSWERS)

1.	D	11.	A
2.	C	12.	A
3.	B	13.	C
4.	B	14.	D
5.	C	15.	A
6.	C	16.	C
7.	A	17.	B
8.	B	18.	D
9.	C	19.	D
10.	C	20.	C

21.	C
22.	B
23.	C
24.	C
25.	C

SOLUTIONS TO PROBLEMS

1. ($4.60)(2 1/4 lbs.) = $10.35

2. 1 gallon = 8 pints, so 20 pints = 20/8 = 2 1/2 gallons

3. $\dfrac{5}{12}+\dfrac{1}{4}=\dfrac{5}{12}+\dfrac{3}{12}=\dfrac{8}{12}=\dfrac{2}{3}$

4. (4')(5 1/2')(18 1/2') = 407 cu.ft. Since 1 cu.yd. = 27 cu.ft., 407 cu.ft. ≈ 15.1 cu.yds.

5. 5/8 = 5 ÷ 8.000 = .625

6. There are (3)(3)(3) = 27 cu.ft. in a cu.yd.

7. (15')(15') = 225 sq.ft. = 25 sq.yds. Then, ($16.20)(25) = $405.00

8. Let 2x = size of smaller crew and 3x = size of larger crew. Then, 2x + 3x = 30. Solving, x = 6. Thus, the smaller crew consists of 12 workers.

9. (12)(6)(5) = 360 worker-days. Then, 360 ÷ [(10)(8)] = 4 1/2 days

10. (.03)(150') = 4 1/2 ft.

11. $3\dfrac{4}{8}+4\dfrac{1}{8}+5\dfrac{1}{8}+6\dfrac{2}{8}=18\dfrac{8}{8}=19$

12. ($9.30)(8+8+8+3 1/2+3) = ($9.30)(30 1/2) = $283.65

13. The cost of 527 sq.yds. = (5.27)($395.00) = $2081.65 ≈ $2081.70

14. $3430 ÷ 221 ≈ $15.50

15. $\dfrac{1}{8}"+\dfrac{3}{16}"+\dfrac{1}{8}"=\dfrac{2}{16}"+\dfrac{3}{16}"+\dfrac{2}{16}"=\dfrac{7}{16}"$

16. $38,070 ÷ 12 = $3172.50 ≈ $3170.00 per month

17. 4 1/2" + 3 1/4" + 7 1/2" = 15 1/4" = 1 ft. 3 1/4 in.

18. 9 ft. 3 in. = 9 1/4 ft., 6 ft. 9 in. = 6 3/4 ft. Area = (9 1/4)(6 3/4) = 62 7/16 sq.ft.

19. A cubic yard = (3)(3)(3) = 27 cubic feet

20. (450')(.02) = 9 ft.

21. 6/4 = 1 1/2 revolutions

22. Station 42 + 51
    30 ft away would be 51 + 30 = 81 OR 51 - 30 = 21
    Station 42 + 81 or 42 + 21 (ANSWER: B)

23. 30 miles in 60 minutes means 10 miles in 20 minutes.

24. There are 2000 pounds in a ton.

25. ($45.00)(.60) = $27.00 savings per day. For 45 days, his savings is (45)($27.00) = $1215.00

BASIC FUNDAMENTALS OF MECHANICAL MEASUREMENT

1. SCALED INSTRUMENTS AND ACCESSORIES

    The hand-measuring devices used in machined-parts inspection include both precision and nonprecision instruments. Precision instruments mean measuring devices that have the accuracy and sensitivity to measure dimensions to thousandths and tenths of thousandths of an inch and hundredths and thousandths of a millimeter. Nonprecision instruments mean devices in which the accuracy of measurement largely depends on the ability to line up and read the graduations of a scale.

2. SCALE VS. RULE

    A scale is a measuring device which is graduated for the purpose of increasing or decreasing the size of an object on a drawing. It is also used as a descriptive term such as "the ruler has a scale of..." or "that vernier scale..."

    A rule is a measuring device which is graduated in full scale, whatever that particular scale may be. The illustrations shown below are good examples of the basic differences between the scale and the rule.

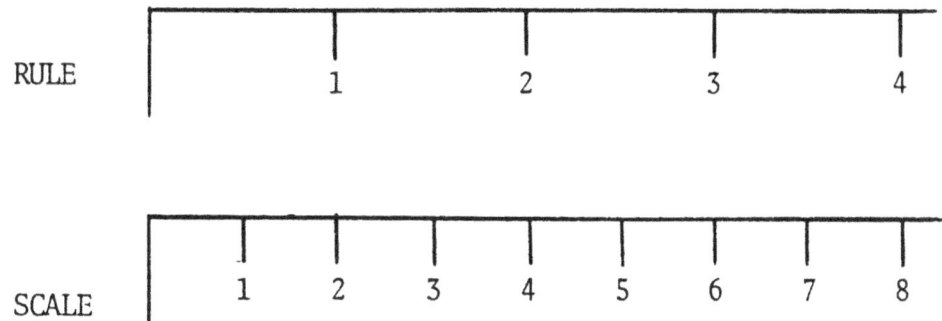

3. THE STEEL RULE

    One of the simplest and most widely used hand measuring devices is the line-graduated steel rule - sometimes erroneously called a scale. Basically, the steel rule is a narrow strip of steel with one or more scales graduated in fractional or decimal inches, or centimeters. It is read by direct comparison of the graduations with an edge or surface. As will be seen later, there are many types and sizes of steel rules. Lengths vary from a fraction of an inch to several feet. Some have a fixed or sliding hook on one end to facilitate alignment of the starting point of the rule with an edge. The short rules usually include a removable clamping shaft or holder to facilitate handling. Some steel rules have fractional inch scales on one side and decimal or metric scales on the other. Likewise, some have conversion charts engraved on the reverse side. The most popular rule - possibly because it's easily carried in a pocket - is the standard six-inch machinist's steel rule.

Some typical examples of steel rules are shown:

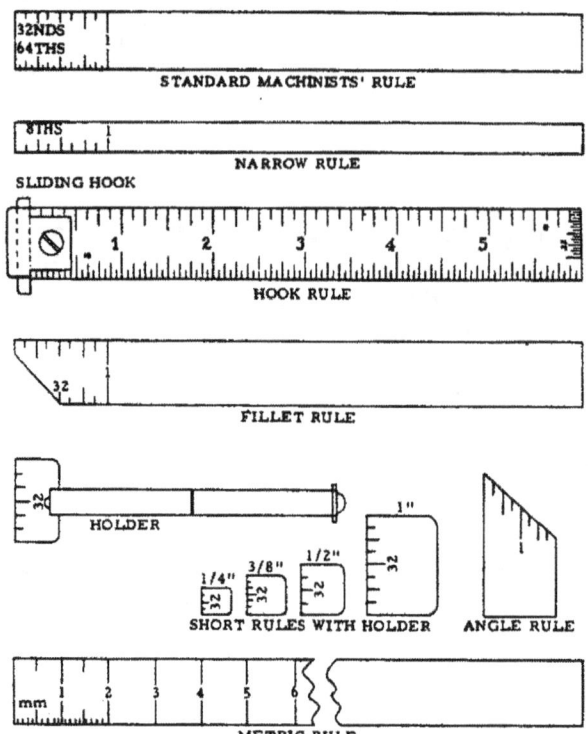

While considering the different steel rules, it should be remembered that fractional inch scales found on steel rules are usually graduated in 8ths, 16ths, 32nds, and 64ths of an inch. Decimal inch scales are available in 10ths and either 50ths or 100ths of an inch. The metric scales are divided into centimeters, millimeters and half millimeters.

4. SELECTING A STEEL RULE

In choosing a steel rule for accomplishing a particular measurement, first select a rule with scales that agree with the part or object to be measured. That is, use fractional inch scales in measuring fractional inch parts, decimal inch scales for decimal parts, and metric scales for metric parts.

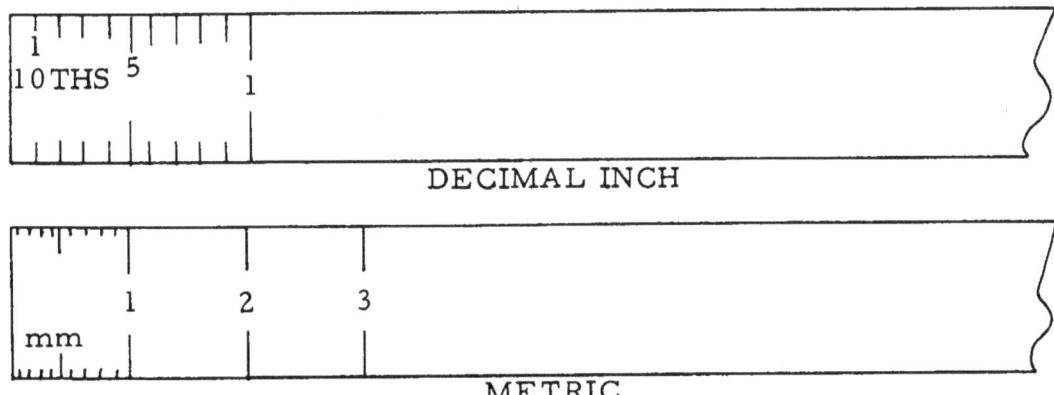

DECIMAL INCH

METRIC

Of the three rules illustrated above, as an example, determine which rule would be used to measure a dimension of 44/64 inches.

It should be obvious that the rule containing the fractional inch scales is the correct choice since the dimension given is in fractional inches.

It should also be realized that in selecting a rule, no steel rule - or any other line-graduated measuring device for that matter - is capable of controlling the accuracy of measurement to a degree finer than that of the finest graduation on its scale. This is called "discrimination."

If, for example, the finest graduation on the rule is 1/32 inch, the dimension to be measured must be in terms of units not smaller than 32nds of an inch. A dimension in 64ths would fall between graduations and would have to be made or an interpolation made to get the actual dimension. For reliable readings, scale discrimination must be such that guessing or interpolation is held to a minimum.

Which of the following scales provides the finer discrimination?

DECIMAL INCHES

You should realize that the 50ths (.02 inch) scale would provide the finer discrimination.

The next consideration is to select the appropriate type or size of steel rule. If the dimension lies in a recess or cramped area where space does not allow the use of regular size rules, a short rule must be used. If the measurement involves a fillet, a fillet rule is required. A narrow rule may be required in measuring the depth of a narrow slot. Steel rules or excessive length also can be a factor in that they become unwieldly in measuring small objects and short distances, making it difficult to obtain a reliable measurement.

In other words, select the rule that will best do the job. The primary considerations in selecting a steel rule are the physical characteristics and the size or dimensions of the object to be measured. Convenience and adaptability are secondary.

5. MEASURING WITH A STEEL RULE

All linear measurements, and that includes measuring with a steel rule, are basically point-to-point measurements involving a "reference point" and a "measured point." The "points" in turn may be true points, a pair of lines or edges, two sides, or two planes.

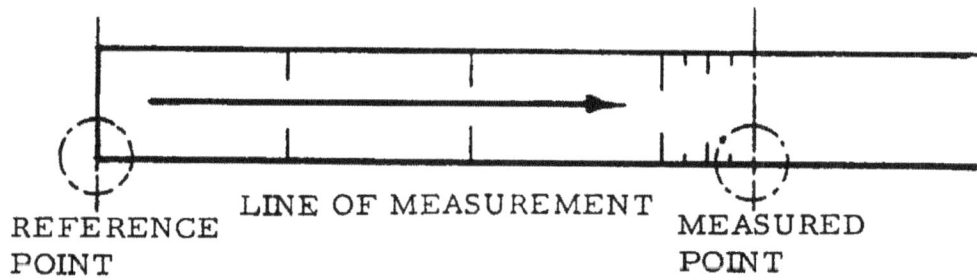

REFERENCE POINT   LINE OF MEASUREMENT   MEASURED POINT

In measuring with a steel rule, the rule is generally held or supported so that scale graduations rest on the line of measurement, with the starting point of the rule aligned with the reference point. The measured point is then read directly from the scale.

Should the measured point not coincide with a rule graduation, the rule is turned to a successively finer scale until the measured point does coincide with a graduation, or until the required discrimination or the finest scale is reached.

In measuring with a steel rule, it is the measured point that is read to the nearest graduation.

6. SOURCES OF ERROR

Now that we have an idea of how steel rules are used, look at some possible sources of error in using a steel rule and how they can be avoided. Shown below are some examples of what might be encountered in aligning a steel rule with a reference point.

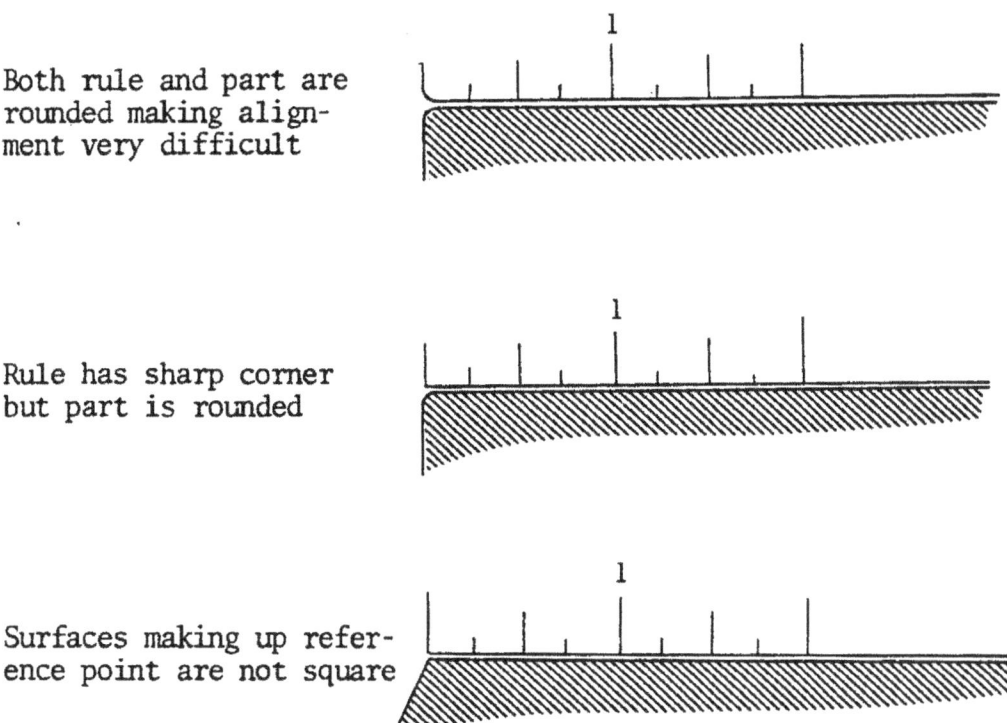

Both rule and part are rounded making alignment very difficult

Rule has sharp corner but part is rounded

Surfaces making up reference point are not square

As probably noted, using the end of a rule to establish the starting point is to invite error. Not only may the corners of the rule be worn or rounded - a fact easily confirmed by examination under a magnifying glass - the edge or surface of the part coinciding with the reference point may not be sharp or square. A much more reliable method is to butt the part and rule against a butt plate, knee or similar flat surface. Another is to use a hook rule or hook attachment to establish a firm reference point, or use a scale graduation and ignore the end of the rule altogether.

Therefore, to get any degree of accuracy in performing measurement, the steel rule must be properly aligned with the reference point and the measurements should always be read to the center of graduations.

A significant factor to remember when reading a rule or scale is the degree a unit of length is subdivided. This is called discrimination. It is also the finest division that can be read reliably.

Another form of observational error that must be known is "parallax error"...the apparent shifting of a measurement when viewed from different directions. Parallax occurs when the graduations of a rule are not positioned directly on the line of measurement.

To avoid parallax, the head must be positioned so that line of sight is perpendicular to the line of measurement.

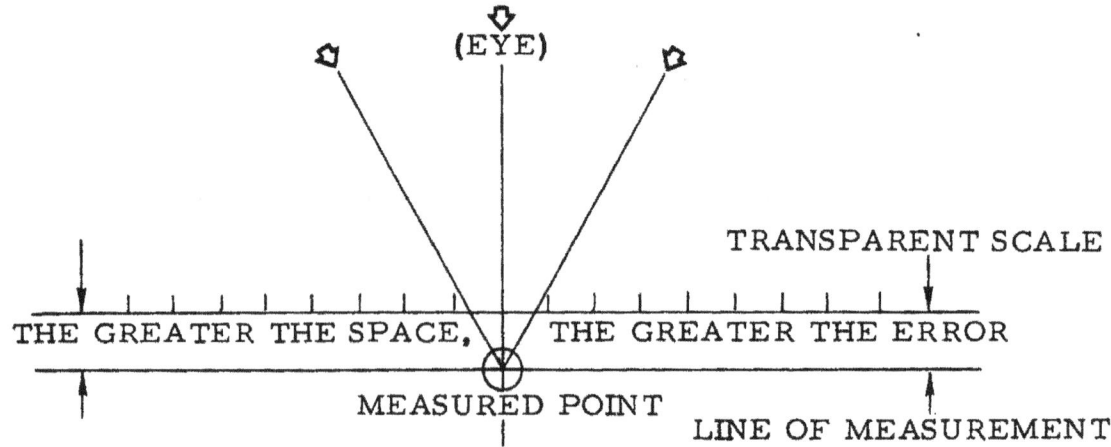

Avoiding manipulative or manual error is also important. This is the error that generally results from using too little or too much force and bending or cocking the rule. It is the error that results from improper handling of the part and rule. The name of the game is to let the rule do the work.

THE RULE SHOULD BE POSITIONED ON THE LINE OF MEASUREMENT AND HELD LIGHTLY BUT FIRMLY.

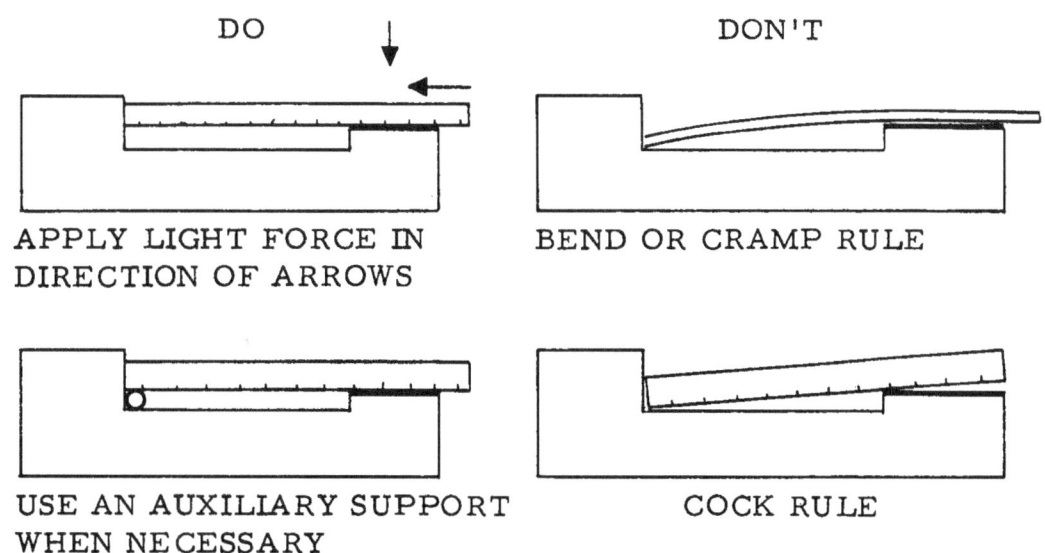

Visual bias is another source of error and is caused by unconscious influencing a measurement. An example is when measuring the diameter of a hole, the blueprint calls for 2 1/4 inches. The rule is positioned over the hole and moved back and forth slightly, using the reference point as the pivot until the longest dimension, the measured point, can be read at the opposite side of the hole.

It is obviously easier to read 2 1/4 inches than 2 15/64 or 2 17/64, particularly when 2 1/4 inches is the dimension we want. So unless some conscious effort is made we tend to read the easier dimension. Add to this the fact that part and rule are subject to slip when moving the eye from the reference point to the measured point, particularly when both the part and rule are held by hand, and we have still another source of possible error.

It is well to remember that repetition is the test of an accurate measurement. If a part is measured several times in the same location and different readings are made, then the measurements are not being taken accurately.

Lack of repetition is a reliable indicator that something is wrong. Either the procedures are at fault or the measuring device itself is defective. A frequent source of error is a bent, loose, or worn rule hook.

In summary, there are several sources of error when using a rule or scale. The most common were reviewed for student awareness. They are:

Improper Alignment   Parallax
Discrimination   Manipulative or Manual
            Visual Bias

7. ACCESSORIES AND USES

There are a number of accessories other than the hook attachment that are used with rules. Some of these are listed with their use in applications:

Key seat clamps - for aligning a rule with the axis of a cylinder.

Parallel clamps - for clamping two or more rules together.

Right angle clamps - for clamping two or more rules together.

Square heads - for measuring and scribing lines normal to a straight edge.

Center heads - for measuring and scribing lines through the center of a circular surface.

Protractor heads - for measuring angles.

Combination square - consists of a steel rule or blade with a sliding square head and scriber.

Combination set - the same as the combination square but has included a center head and a protractor head.

The combination set is probably the most useful of the steel rule variations. It can be used to check squareness and plumb as well as measure height and depth. It can be used to lay out 45- and 90-degree angles. By adding a right angle clamp and another steel rule, it can often be used to measure an otherwise inaccessible point. Substituting the center head in place of the square head, it can be used to find the center of a shaft, etc., or to speed measurement of diameters. Substituting the protractor head provides a convenient means for checking angles.

In using rule accessories and attachments, keep in mind that none of them change the basic principles of the steel rule. They merely add convenience or extend the rule's range of application to jobs which otherwise could not be performed with rules. They make rule measurement easier which in turn generally increases the reliability of measurements.

8. DEPTH GAUGE

This popular variation of the steel rule is the simple depth gauge consisting of a T-head or stock, a screw clamp, and a sliding rod or narrow flat rule. The sliding rods may be plain or graduated. Some versions of the depth gauge use hooked rules for measuring the depth of through holes. Some have heads which pivot with respect to their rules.

To use the depth gauge, the gauge head is held against the workpiece so that is spans the shoulders of the recess or hole to be measured. The sliding rule or rod is pushed into the hole until it bottoms, and the screw clamp tightened. The gauge is then withdrawn and the rule's scale read. When plain rods are used, the length of the rod protruding from the head is measured with a separate rule.

9. THE STEEL MEASURING TAPE

The steel measuring tape is an extension of the steel rule consisting of a narrow and fairly flexible strip of tempered steel, marked off in either inches or centimeters, and housed in a protective case. The tape is extended by pulling on the end of the tape and retracted using a small crank on the side of the case. The pocket sizes generally include a spring-driven retraction mechanism which retracts the tape when a small button is pushed.

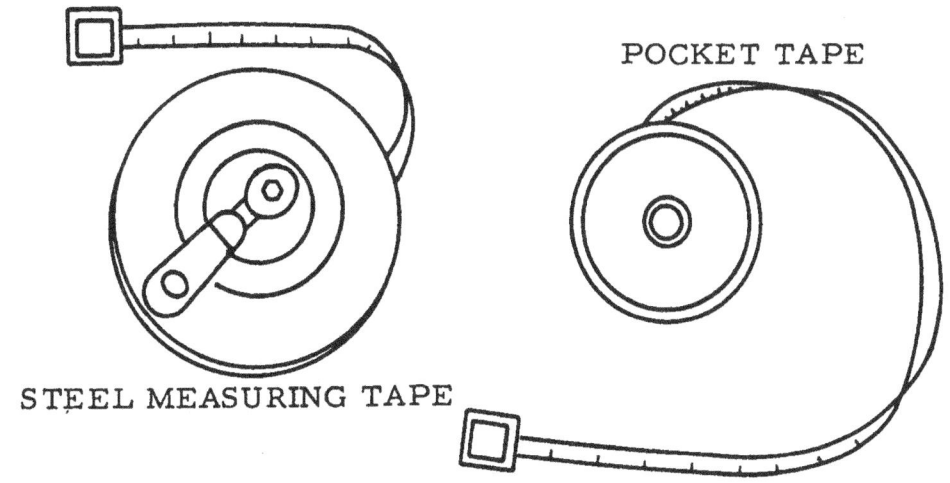

STEEL MEASURING TAPE   POCKET TAPE

Steel measuring tapes are available in 25, 50, 75, and 100 foot lengths. The pocket tapes come in 6 and 8 foot lengths, although other lengths are not uncommon. Graduations are usually in 8ths of an inch for the standard tapes and in 16ths of an inch for the pocket tapes.

The same basic principles of measurement which apply to steel rules also apply to steel measuring tapes. Like the steel rule, the start of the tape is carefully aligned with the reference point. The tape is stretched along the line of measurement and the measured point is read directly from the tape. In using steel measuring tapes, however, particular attention must be paid to supporting the tape and applying the proper tension. The tape must be held substantially flat and not be allowed to sag. Applied tension should be moderate (10 pounds).

It should also be remembered that steel measuring tapes are sensitive to variations in ambient temperatures. This means that when measuring with steel tapes, consideration must be given to contraction and expansion of the tape.

10. SIMPLE CALIPERS

In using steel rules the position of the measured point or edge in relation to scale graduations is judged by sight. Frequently, however, two contact points are necessary to measure a dimension more accurately or to reach surfaces or features otherwise inaccessible. This is where calipers come into the picture.

Calipers are instruments that physically duplicate the separation between two points. The simpler forms, of which we are concerned with here, consist of two legs or points which can be adjusted to duplicate any dimension within their range. They require the use of a separate scale to read the measurement. Below are some examples.

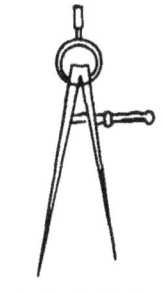
DIVIDER

OUTSIDE CALIPER

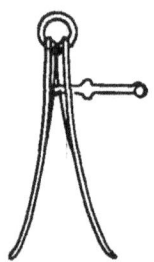
INSIDE CALIPER

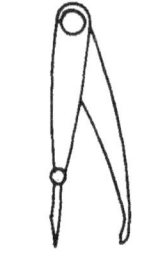
HERMAPHRODITE CALIPER

The divider is used to scribe arcs, radii and circles, and to lay out distances set from a rule. It also can be used to transfer distances for measuring with a rule. In transferring a measurement from a part to the scale on a rule, the customary procedure is to locate one point on the reference point, then turn the adjusting nut so that the other point falls exactly on the measured point. When properly set, there should be no pressure tending to spring the points either in or out.

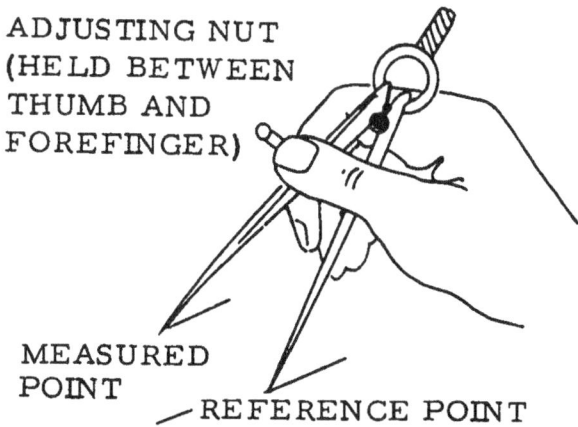

The divider is then placed on a rule with one point in one of the graduations and the scale is read at the other point as shown below.

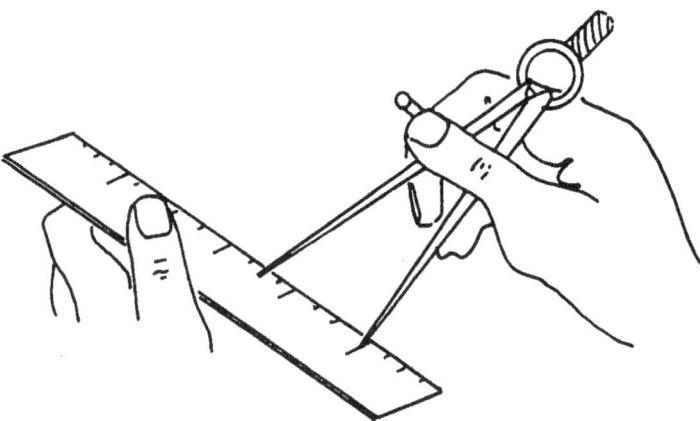

Inside and outside calipers perform the same general function as the divider in transferring measurements except one is used to measure inside surfaces and the other measures outside surfaces.

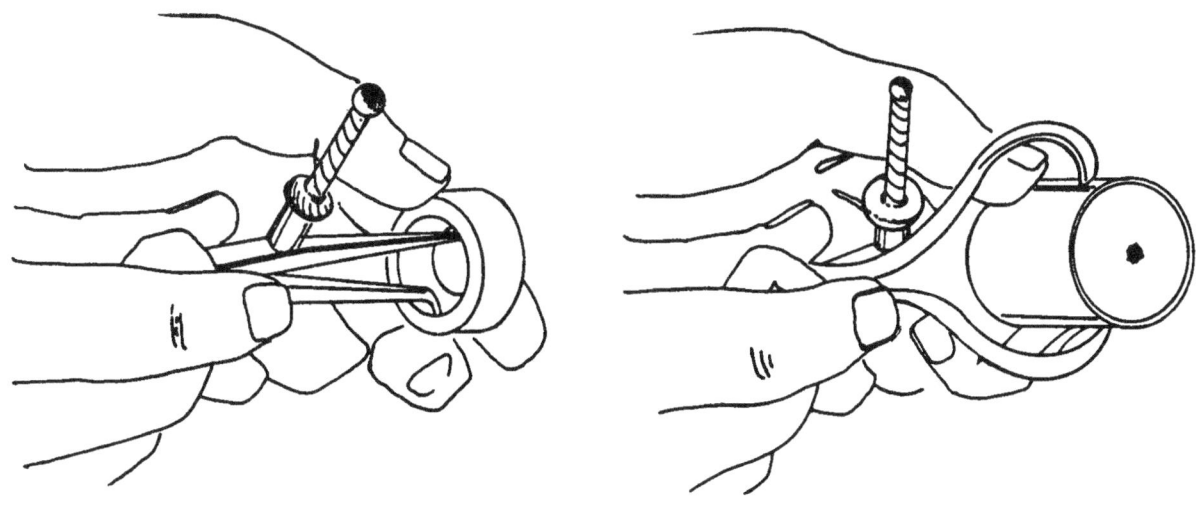

The caliper is first set to the opening or feature of the part. The separation is then transferred to a rule and read. In reading the inside caliper, the rule and one leg of the caliper are generally butted against a flat surface to provide a stable reference point (below right).

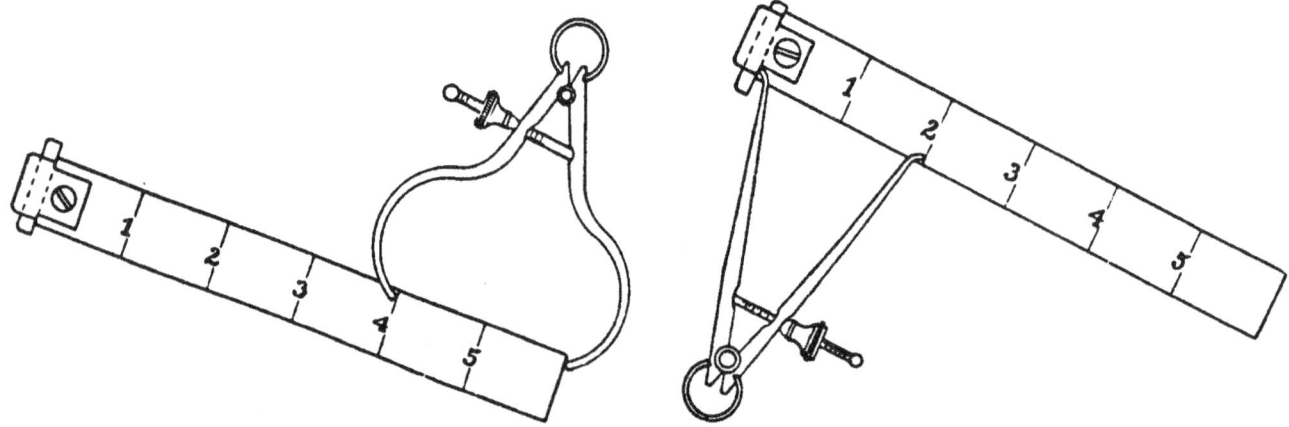

In reading the outside caliper, one leg is positioned in contact with the end of the rule (above left).

Two important factors in taking measurements with inside and outside calipers are caliper alignment and the gauging pressure or force used. In taking measurements, one leg or point should be set as the reference point and the caliper then rocked and adjusted until correct measurement is obtained.

The correct measurement is obtained by the "feel" of the force exerted on the part as the caliper moves over center. Since only a slight force is necessary to spring the caliper legs, the lighter the "feel" is kept the more reliable the measurement.

11. SLIDE CALIPERS

The slide caliper is actually another variation of the steel rule with one fixed jaw and one sliding jaw to permit direct reading of measurements. It comes in a number of sizes with fractional inch, decimal inch, or metric scales. It comes equipped with a slide lock for locking the jaws in any desired position. It includes a "nib" on the tip of each jaw to permit the taking of inside measurements.

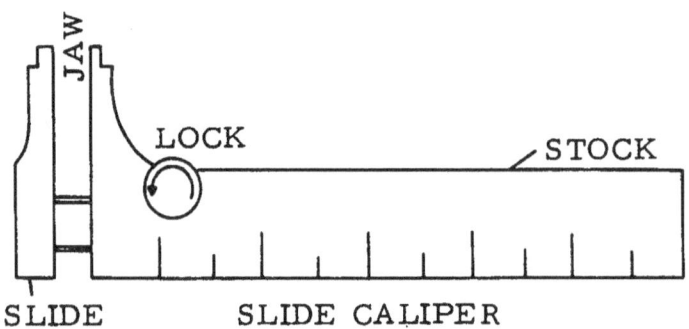

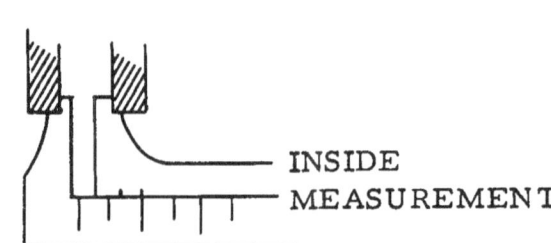

When the jaws are brought in contact with surfaces being measured, the distance between them may be read from the scale.

An advantage in using a slide caliper over the steel rule is that the slide caliper provides positive contact between instrument and the reference and measured points.

12. BEAM TRAMMELS

The beam trammel is simply a divider with extended range. It consists of a rod or beam to which trams may be clamped. The trams in turn carry chucks for inserting divider points, or caliper points. Its use is confined chiefly to measurements beyond the range of dividers and calipers.

Below you will notice one of the trams is equipped with an adjusting screw to provide fine adjustments.

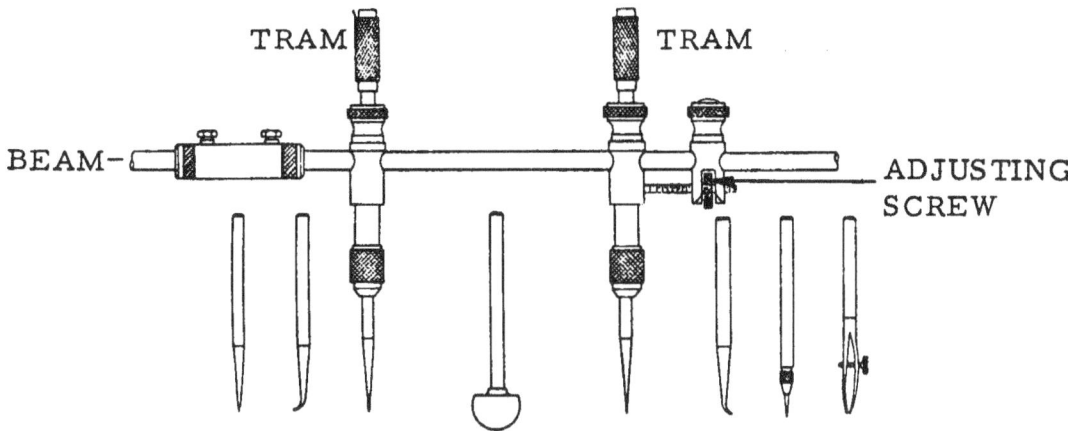

BEAM TRAMMEL AND ATTACHMENTS

A summary of what has been presented in this chapter is as follows:

1. A "scale" is a graduated surface for decreasing or increasing a unit of length.

2. The "rule" is a direct measuring device graduated in actual units in length. It may carry fractional inch, decimal inch, or metric scales.

3. The scales used should agree with the dimensioning of the part or object to be measured. That is, use fractional inch scales for franctional inch parts, decimal inch scales for decimal inch parts, and metric scales for metric parts.

4. "Reference point" is the term used to identify the start of a measurement.

5. "Measured point" identifies the end of a measurement.

6. The "line of measurement" is a straight line drawn between and and intersecting the reference point and measured point.

7. "Discrimination" refers to the degree a scale subdivides a unit of length. It is also the finest division that can be read reliably.

8. Rules are read to the center of graduations.

9. The measured point is read to the nearest graduation.

10. To use the end of a rule to align rule with reference point is to invite error.

11. "Parallax error" is the apparent shifting of a measurement when viewed from different directions.

12. "Manipulative or manual error" is the error that results from using too little or too much force and not positioning the rule properly.

13. "Visual bias" is the unconscious influencing of a measurement.

14. The same basic principles of measurement which apply to steel rules apply to all the scaled instruments and their accessories.

15. Instruments are selected on the basis of which one will best do the job.

16. Accessories and attachments add errors. Use should be confined to measurements in which the added convenience, or their application, increases the reliability of a measurement more than they decrease it.

17. Every transfer of measurement adds steps and added steps add errors...a factor that should be considered in using transfer instruments such as the caliper.

18. Transfer instruments depend on the "feel" of the user for accuracy.

19. In using steel measuring tapes, one should also consider the effects of changes in ambient temperature on measurements.

20. It is good practice to repeat measurements until satisfied as to their accuracy...write down measurements rather than trust them to memory...use mechanical support as opposed to hand support whenever possible... ensure both part and the measuring device are clean before taking measurement.

13. SELF ACTIVITIES

    1. Review and ensure personal knowledge of the various rules and gauges.

    2. Obtain a steel scale, measuring tape and accessories from the home workshop, or school metal shop, and practice measuring various items. Awareness should be made of the types of errors described in the resource guide. Attempt to duplicate parallax, discrimination, measured point, and manipulative errors.

    3. Using a 10 foot rule, measure the height of students in your class. Make a comparison of these measurements with the metric conversions.

    4. Using a 2 foot rule measure pre-cut stock. The length of stock should be cut to various lengths and include fractions which correspond to graduations of the rule.

    5. Using a 6' wood rule or metal tape, measure a classroom. Then use a 50 or 100 foot measuring tape and compare the results.

    6. With a steel rule measure various lengths of metal stock in the metal shop. Measure in various fraction accuracy, such as 1/8", 1/16", 1/32", and 1/64".

    7. Visit the metal shop and ask the teacher to show you the various types of steel rules, accessories, and calipers. Perhaps the teacher will demonstrate the uses for you.

14. VERNIER INSTRUMENTS

    Vernier hand measuring devices are very essential to the entry level industrial manufacturing employee. Therefore, an in-depth review is made to familiarize the student with the basic requirements.

15. THE VERNIER CALIPER

The vernier caliper is essentially a slide caliper that incorporates a vernier scale and a fine adjustment.

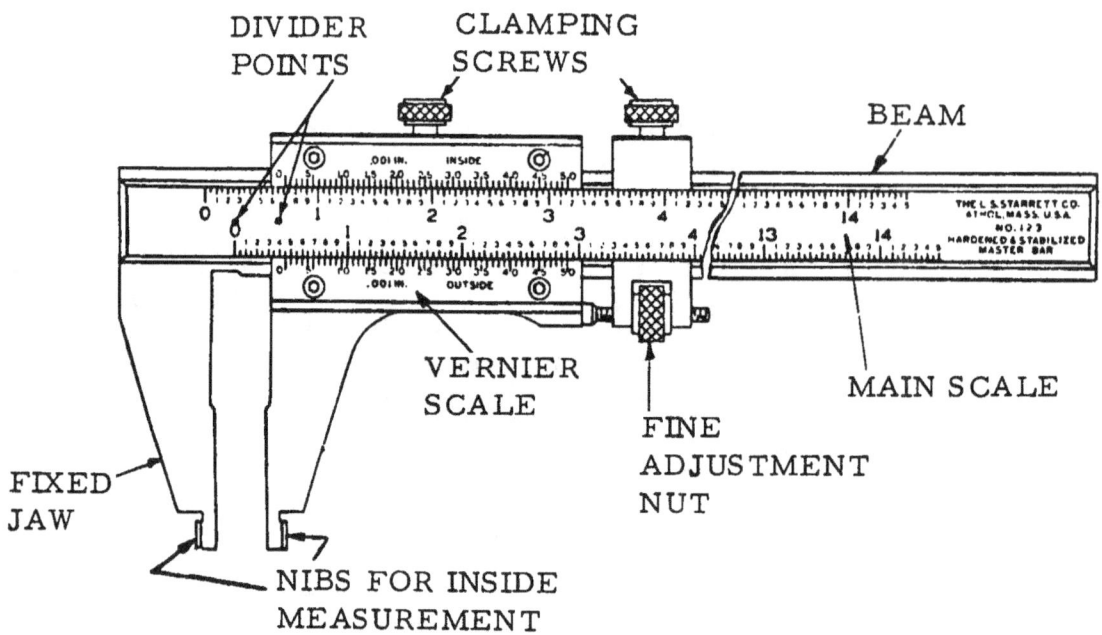

The typical instrument consists of an L-shaped frame or beam, the end of which forms the fixed jaw, and a sliding jaw assembly made up of two sections joined by a screw and adjustment nut. The vernier scale attaches to the sliding jaw and moves parallel to a main scale engraved on the caliper beam. Design is such that readings are made from one scale to the other with minimum parallax error. Two center points are usually provided on the side of the instrument for setting dividers to close dimensions. The "nibs" for inside measurement are ground to a radius to permit single-point contact with small holes and bores. A variation of the vernier caliper uses knife-edged jaws for gauging surfaces.

The vernier and main scales on one side of the instrument generally read outside measurements while the scales on the opposite side read inside measurements. Sometimes both the inside and outside scales are found on the same side of the instrument, one above the other.

16. READING VERNIER SCALES

First consider the standard 25-division vernier. The main scale itself is graduated in full inches. Each inch is divided into ten parts and each of the tenths is again subdivided into quarters.

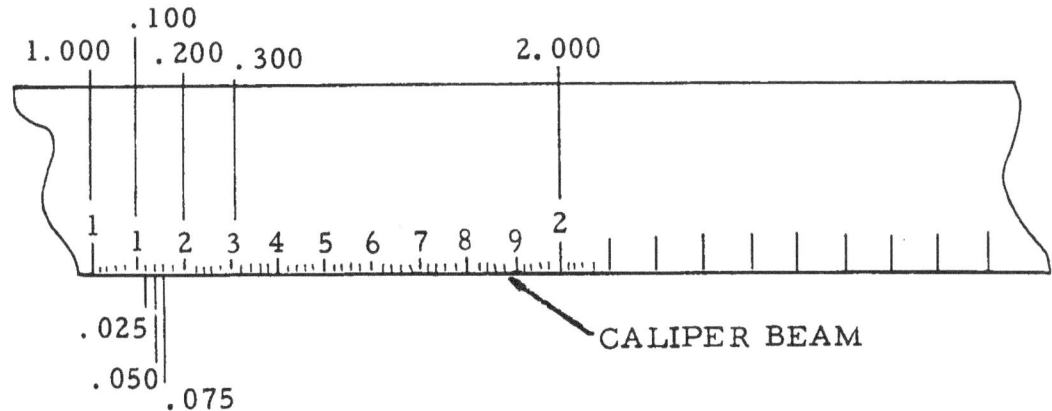

(The scale is read by adding the inches, tenths and quarters together.)

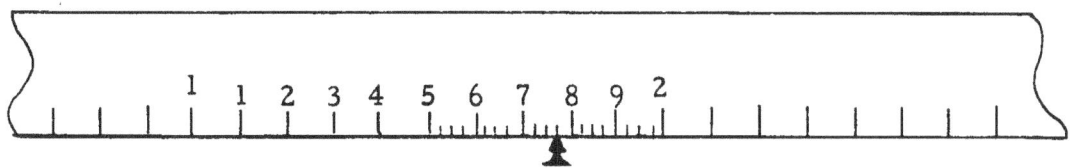

The reading of the above scale is therefore 1.775.

The vernier scale contains 25 divisions in the same length that the main scale has 24. Each vernier division is 1/25th smaller than its main scale counterpart. Since each main scale division equals 1/40th of an inch (.025 inch), this means each vernier division equals 1/25th of 1/40th of an inch or 1/1000th of an inch (.001 inch).

There are also metric vernier calipers.

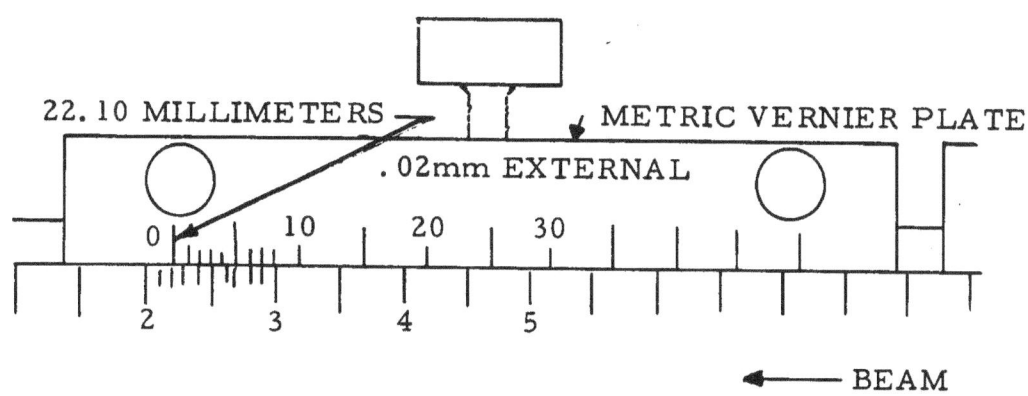

Using the vernier "0" line as the index, the above metric scale reads 20 + 2 beam graduations, or 22 millimeters, plus the vernier reading of the line which coincides with beam line. In the example, that line is "5". Thus 22 millimeters (the beam scale reading) + 5 X .02 (the vernier scale reading) equals 22.10 millimeters...the sum of the beam and vernier scales.

An example of reading a metric scale is:

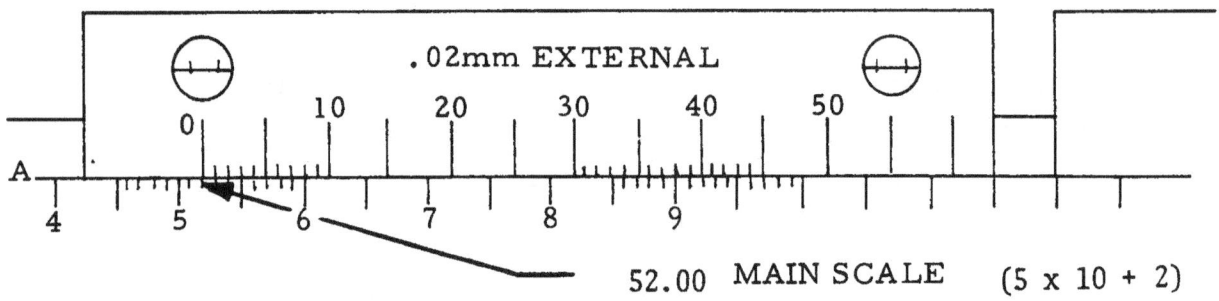

52.00 MAIN SCALE   (5 x 10 + 2)

17. MEASURING WITH VERNIER CALIPERS

In taking outside or exterior measurements, the caliper jaws are set slightly larger than the distance to be measured and the adjustment nut carrier locked to the beam by tightening the appropriate clamping screw. The sliding jaw clamping screw is in turn snugged up but not so tight as to lock the jaw.

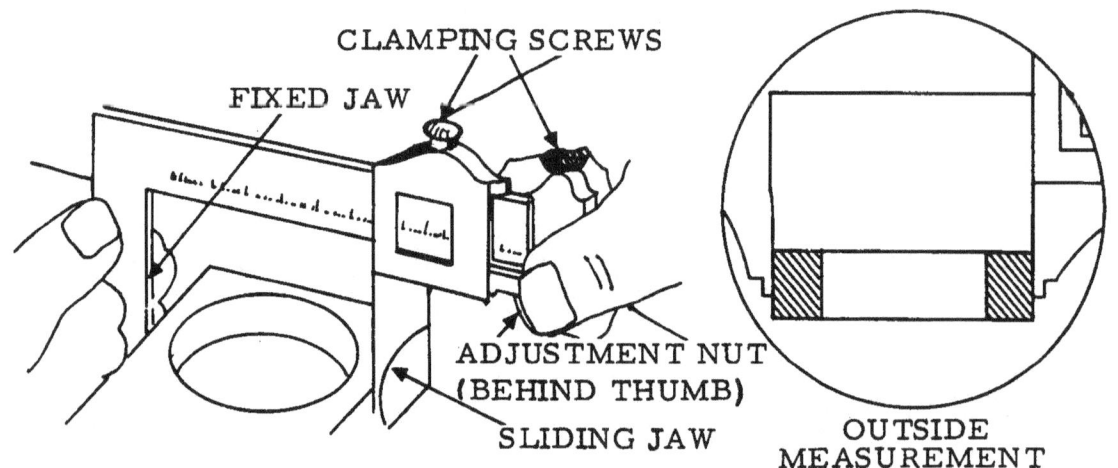

The caliper is then gripped near or opposite the jaws - one hand at the fixed jaw and the other generally supporting the sliding jaw - and the caliper carefully positioned on the part or feature to be measured. With the fixed jaw held against the reference point and the axis of the instrument parallel and in plane with the line of measurement, the sliding jaw is moved using the fine adjustment nut until it just contacts the measured point. The sliding jaw is locked by tightening the appropriate clamping screw and the "feel" between the caliper and part rechecked. The student should remember that "feel" refers to the gauging pressure or force used in setting the instrument to measure a part dimension or feature.

Inside or interior measurements are performed in essentially the same manner except at start of measurement, the jaws are set slightly smaller than distance to be measured, and the measurement is read from the scales marked "INSIDE" or "INTERIOR."

In measuring a diameter, the procedure is to hold the fixed jaw against the reference point and swing the sliding jaw back and forth past center while turning the fine adjustment nut. Correct setting is obtained when the sliding jaw just contacts the measured point as it passes center.

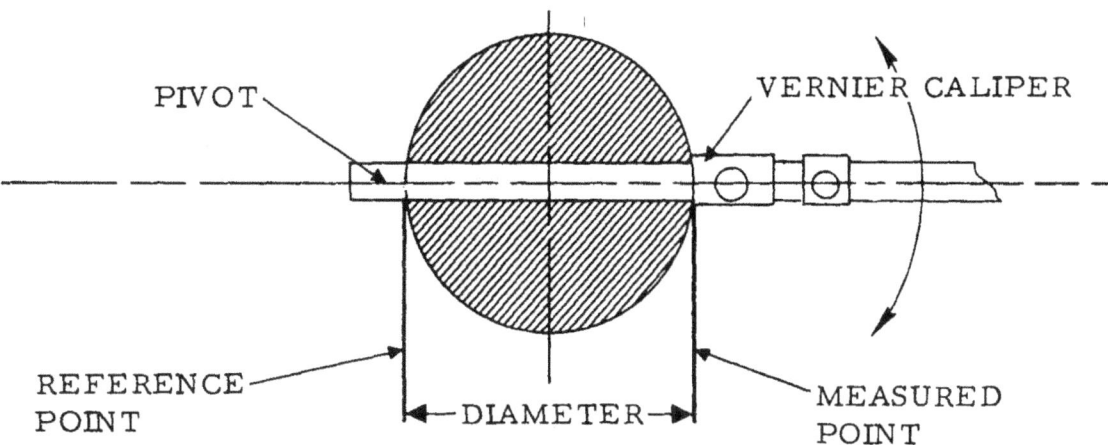

In measuring the vernier calipers, whether it is an outside measurement, an inside measurement, or the measurement of a diameter, it is the fixed jaw that is always used as the reference point.

18. SOURCES OF ERROR

A basic law of measurement states that maximum accuracy is obtainable only when the axis of the instrument lies on the same line as the line of measurement. Because caliper jaws are offset from the axis of the instrument, alignment therefore becomes a very important consideration when measuring with vernier calipers.

In taking measurements, always make sure the caliper beam and the plane of the jaws are truly perpendicular to the surfaces being measured. Other important factors are:

1. Never allow the instrument to tip, twist or become canted. In other words, greatest accuracy is obtained when the axis of the instrument is held parallel and in plane with line of measurement.

2. Centralizing - rocking the instrument slightly on the reference point and the sliding jaw adjusted until the measured point falls on the true diameter. The procedure is to hold the fixed jaw against the reference point, move the sliding jaw in a small circle, and at the same time turn the adjustment nut until contact is felt. The sliding jaw is then backed off slightly and the process repeated using smaller and smaller circles until the caliper jaws rest squarely on the reference and measured points.

3. Another source of error is the use of excessive gauging pressure. Over-tightening in fact can not only result in inaccurate and unreliable measurements, it could burnish the part...it could even damage the instrument. Correct gauging pressure is obtained when contact between part and caliper jaws can just be felt.

4. Lack of magnification can also lead to discrimination error.

5. In obtaining accurate and reliable measurements, it is required that both the part and measuring device are clean. Surfaces should be wiped free of any dirt, grit, or oil. Along the same line, you should make certain there are no burrs or other obstructions which could affect measurement.

6. As in measuring with steel rules, it is a good practice to write down a measurement rather than trust it to memory. It is good practice to repeat a measurement until satisfied as to accuracy.

19. CARE OF VERNIER CALIPERS

A primary consideration in the care of vernier calipers is the condition of the jaws. For example, they may become bent or sprung. They are also vulnerable to wear. Some of the common wear patterns are:

Wear from measuring outside diameters.
Wear from general use.

Wear from measuring inside diameters.
Sliding jaw-fame wear and warpage.

The calipers could be easily checked for these wear patterns by closing the calipers tightly and hold them up to the light and sighting through the crack. If light can be seen, it means some degree of wear exists. When wear does exist and it exceeds .0002 inch, the instrument should be returned to a gauge maker or the calibration laboratory for reconditioning.

Zero setting - is checked by closing the caliper and observing if the vernier reads zero. If not, it can be adjusted by loosening the vernier plate screws and respositioning the scale.

Precautionary Note: The accuracy and reliability of the vernier caliper depends on how much care it receives. Some very basic hints on maintenance are:

Handle the instrument gently
Keep free of dirt, and grit.
Keep in appropriate box when not in use.
Never use the vernier caliper as a wrench
hammer or pry bar.

20. VERNIER DEPTH GAUGES

The vernier depth gauge is essentially a rule depth gauge incorporating a vernier scale and fine adjustment.

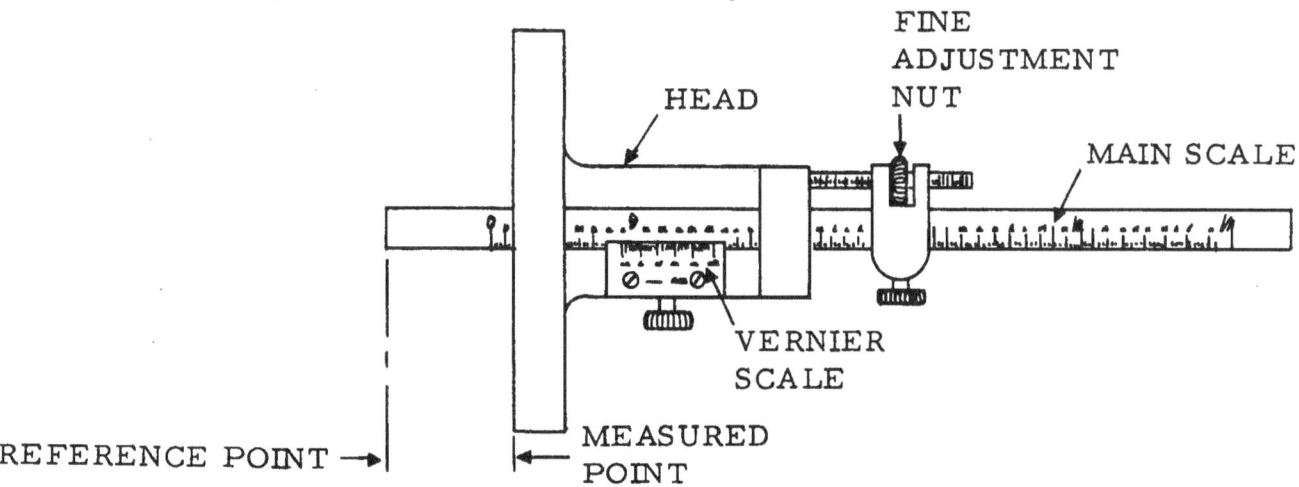

To use the instrument, the head or base is generally rested on or against the reference point and the graduated beam adjusted to contact the measured point. Reading of the scales is identical to the vernier caliper.

Like the vernier caliper, the vernier depth gauge is subject to a number of manipulative errors. In fact, it is probably easier to make manipulative errors with a vernier depth gauge than any other measuring device. Some of the errors associated with the use of vernier depth gauges are:

>Part features not square or true.
>Base lifted from reference point.
>Base tilted.
>Manipulative errors.

Therefore, a firm pressure must be maintained in holding the base against the reference point, while at the same time using a very light touch to set the graduated beam against the measured point.

21. UNIVERSAL BEVEL PROTRACTORS

The universal bevel protractor, also called a bevel protractor or vernier protractor, is a precision angle-measuring instrument designed for layout and checking of angles. It consists of a base and a blade which can be revolved in relation to each other and set in any desired position. An acute angle attachment permits a longer line of contact in measuring small angles. Below is a typical bevel protractor.

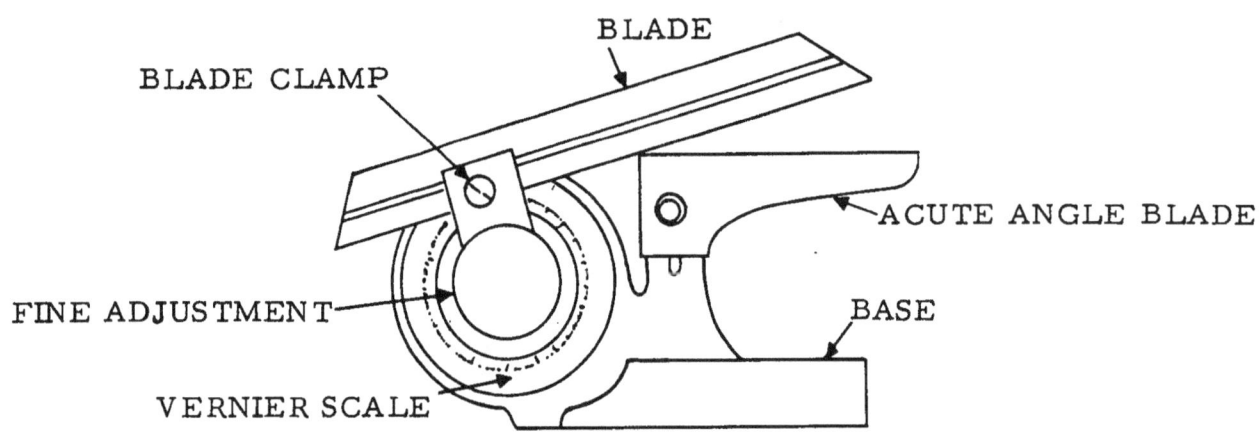

22. SELF ACTIVITIES

1. Visit the metal shop and ask the teacher to demonstrate the various vernier measuring instruments. Perhaps you will be able to practice taking some actual measurements.

2. Review the differences in reading the regular scales and the metric scales if they are available.

3. For the student or entry-level employee, effort should be made to learn the care and handling of the vernier measuring instruments.

4. The student should remember that there is only one way to become proficient in using delicate and precise measuring instruments, this is with practice. Considering this, the student should expend all available time in getting the "feel" of the instruments.

23. MICROMETER INSTRUMENTS

Micrometer instruments achieve even greater precision than the vernier instruments by using a finely threaded screw to amplify readings. There are many types of micrometers. The most commonly used are:

    Outside micrometer calipers
    Inside micrometer calipers
    Micrometer depth gauges

The most general reference to the term micrometer is the outside micrometer caliper. The basic components of the outside micrometer caliper include a frame, anvil, spindle, barrel, and thimble. Many have a ratchet stop to help establish the proper "feel" or torque when making measurements. Many have a clamp ring to "lock" measurement.

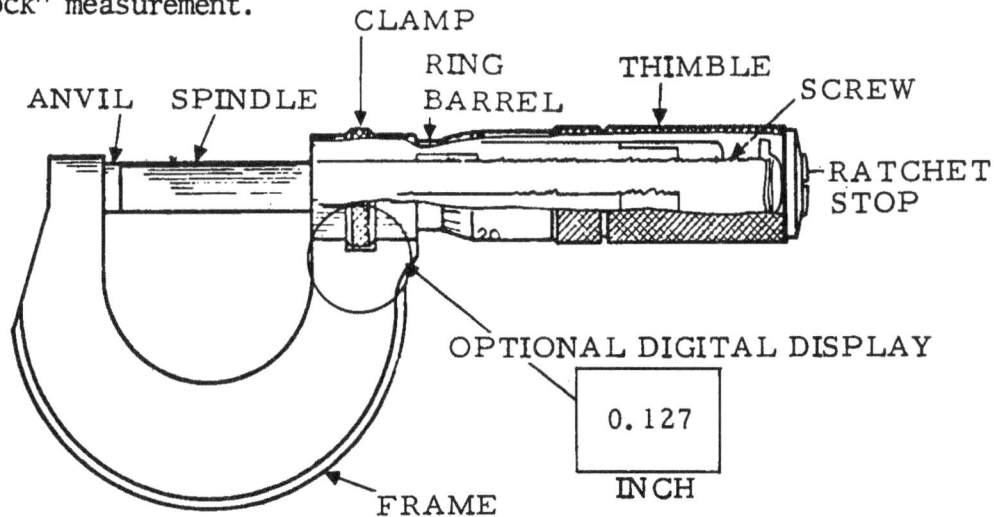

Micrometer screw, which is actually a part of the spindle, threads through a stationary nut located within the barrel. The thimble attaches to the spindle and acts as a dust cover. A linear scale is provided on the barrel to measure the axial movement of the spindle. A circumferential scale on the thimble indicates the amount of partial rotation of the thimble. Some micrometers include a vernier scale on the barrel for measuring in still finer increments of thimble rotation. Some include a digital display for faster and easier reading. The part of the micrometer that moves back and forth with thimble rotation is the spindle. The anvil represents the fixed reference point of a micrometer measurement.

In addition to different types of micrometers, there are different sizes. The designated size of a micrometer being its largest opening - not its range. For example, the 1-inch micrometer has a measurement range of 0 to 1 inch; the 25-millimeter metric micrometer measures from 0 to 25 millimeters. Larger "inch" sizes are designated 2 inch, 3 inch, 4 inch, 5 inch, while metric sizes run 25, 50, 75, and 100 millimeters. Regardless of micrometer size, however, the range of measurement is usually limited to 1 inch for inch micrometers and 25 millimeters for metric micrometers. This means that a 6-inch micrometer can be used for measuring dimensions of 5 to 6 inches only.

24. READING THE "INCH" MICROMETER

Reading a micrometer is simply a matter of counting the revolutions of the thimble and adding to this any fraction of a revolution shown on the thimble scale. The pitch of the "inch" micrometer screw is usually 40 threads per inch. This means that each complete turn of the thimble moves the spindle 1/40 or .025 inch. The barrel scale is in turn graduated so that each division represents one revolution of the thimble or .025 inch.

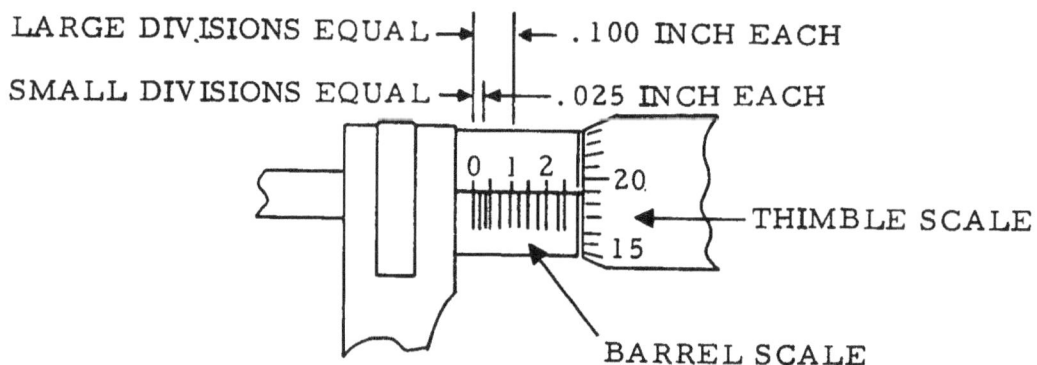

From 0 to 1 on the barrel scale are four divisions, so that "1" on the scale represents 4 x .025 or .100 inch; "2" is equivalent to .200 inch; and "3" to .300 inch.

If "3" on the barrel scale is equivalent to .300 inch, "5" on the scale represents 5 x .025 or .125 inch. The barrel scale shown below reads .200 + .025 x 3 (the number of divisions showing to the right of .200) or .275 inch + a part of a division.

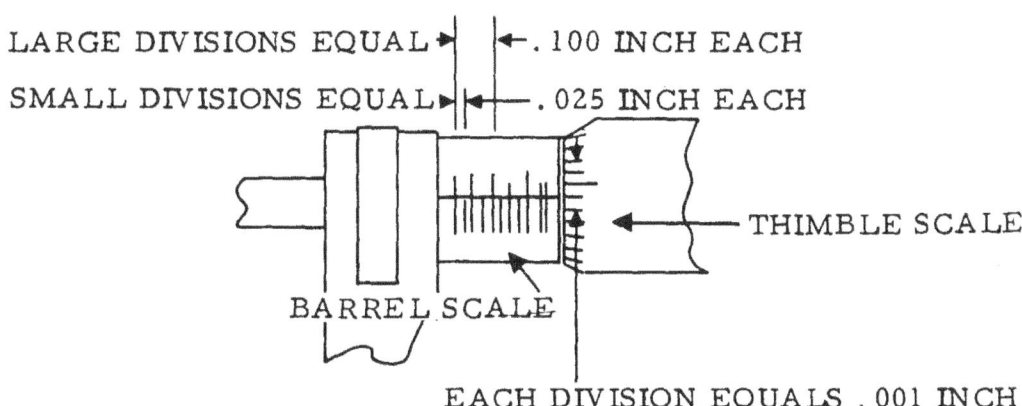

The thimble scale has 25 divisions, each division representing 1/25 x .025 or .001 inch. Using the horizontal line on the barrel scale as the index, note that the part of a revolution indicated on the thimble scale above is 19, meaning 19 x .001 or .019 inch. Adding this value to the whole divisions showing on the barrel, we have the measured distance.

```
      .275 (reading from barrel scale)
  +   .019 (reading from thimble scale)
      .294 (measured distance)
```

25. THE VERNIER MICROMETER

These are micrometers that include a vernier scale on the micrometer barrel for carrying a measurement to four places (.0000).

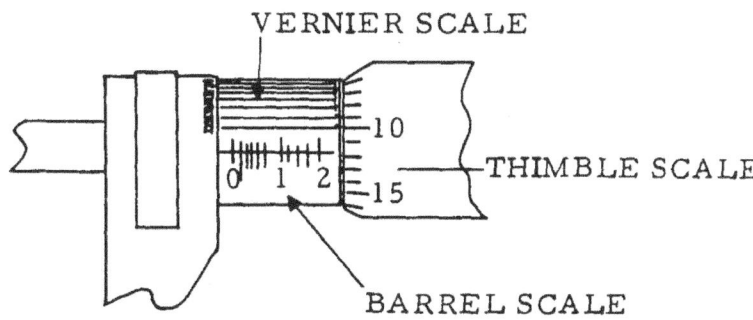

The vernier scale consists of 11 equally spaced lines. The first ten are numbered zero through nine, with the eleventh line identified as another zero. The vernier is read by matching a vernier graduation to a thimble graduation, noting the vernier number and adding this number as the fourth digit. Shown below are two examples.

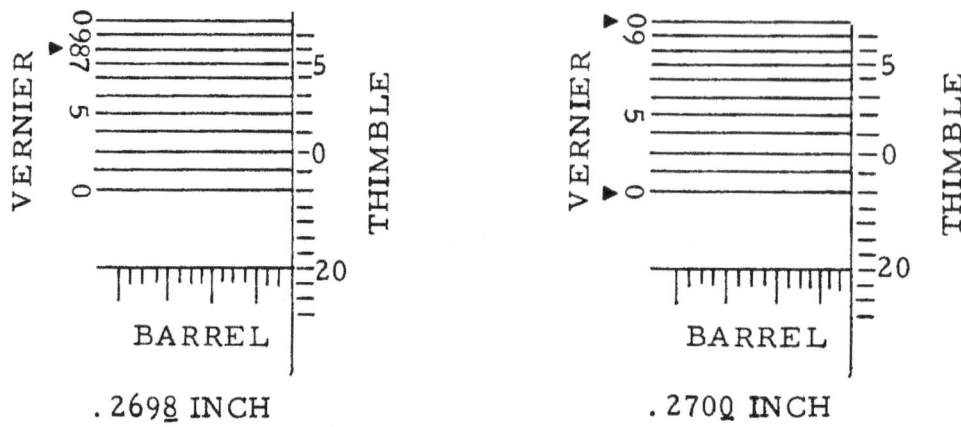

.269<u>8</u> INCH   .270<u>0</u> INCH

Notice that when micrometer reads in whole thousandths, both zeros on the vernier scale match up with thimble lines.

26. SOURCES OF ERROR

The following are possibly the most common sources of error in reading micrometer scales:

Barrel scales are frequently misread an additional .025 inch.

The thimble is read in the wrong direction.

27. READING THE "METRIC" MICROMETER

With metric micrometers, several variations of the barrel scale are used. Below are two typical examples.

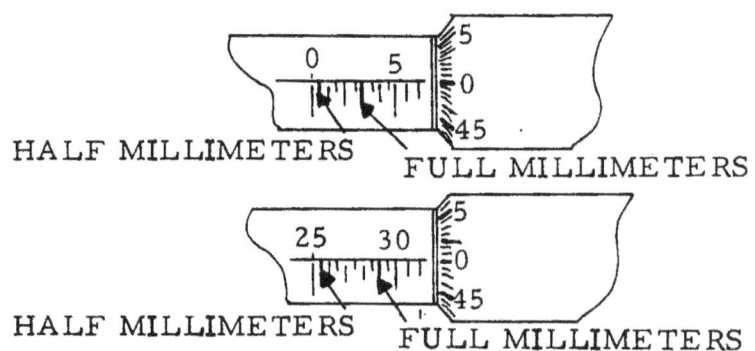

Each complete turn of the thimble moves the spindle 1/2 millimeter (.5mm). Two turns equal 1 millimeter (1mm). The thimble scale in turn has 50 divisions dividing the 1/2 millimeter graduations of the barrel scale into hundredths of a millimeter (.01 mm). To read the metric micrometer, first count the "full" or whole millimeter graduations. Add the next 1/2 millimeter graduation if visible, plus the thimble reading.

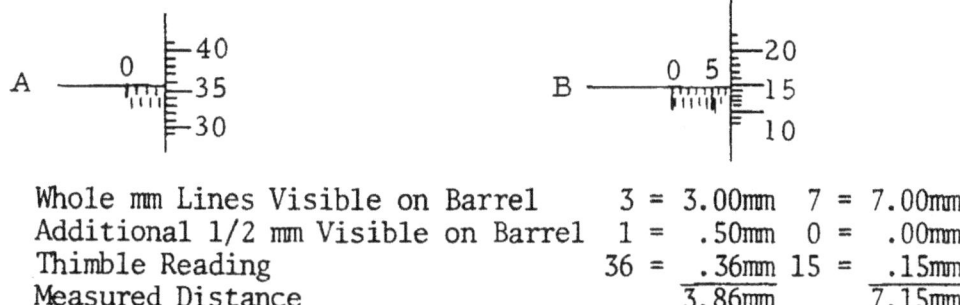

Whole mm Lines Visible on Barrel	3 = 3.00mm	7 = 7.00mm
Additional 1/2 mm Visible on Barrel	1 = .50mm	0 = .00mm
Thimble Reading	36 = .36mm	15 = .15mm
Measured Distance	3.86mm	7.15mm

28. USING THE MICROMETER

The basic principles of measurement with micrometers are essentially the same as for the instruments already discussed. Specifically, measurement with a micrometer involves a reference point, measured point, and a line of measurement.

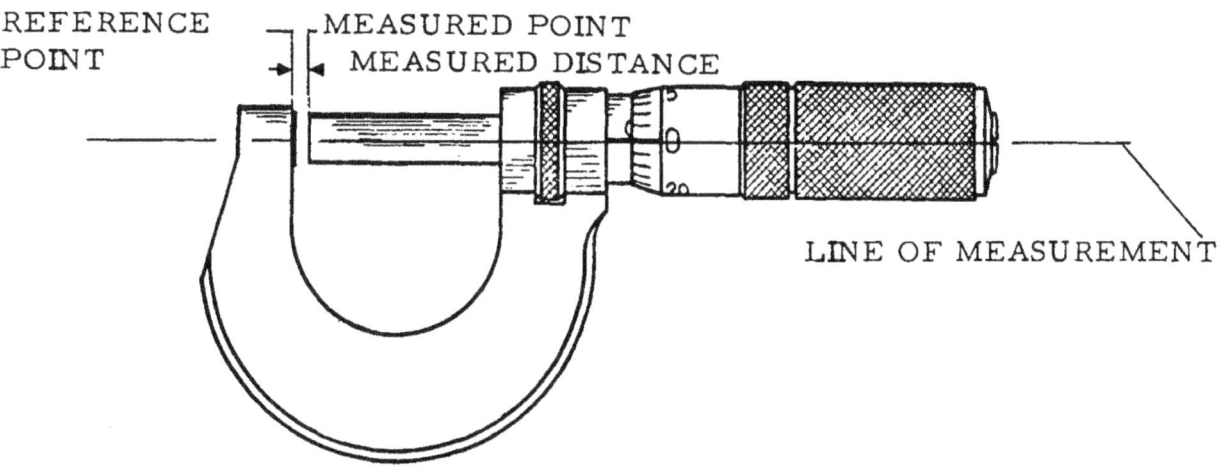

The most common application of micrometers is the measurement of length dimensions between two parallel end surfaces on the outside of an object or feature. The micrometer is set to duplicate the separation between reference point and measured point, with the axis of the instrument on the line of measurement.

The part or object is held in the left hand while the right hand holds the micrometer so that the thimble can be turned between the thumb and combined index and third fingers. The fourth and fifth fingers are used to clamp the frame against the palm of the hand. A drawback of this method is that in most instances the fingers are too short to reach the ratchet stop.

A more reliable method is to use a bench stand or equivalent device to support the micrometer thus leaving the hands free to concentrate on measurement. The ratchet stop is also accessible.

On larger and bulkier work, different methods of holding the micrometer are used. One hand is generally used to hold and align the micrometer while the other hand is free to turn the thimble either directly or using the ratchet stop.

The micrometer is first set to an opening slightly larger than the distance to be measured. This is easily and quickly done by rolling the thimble along your hand or arm. Never change the setting by grasping the micrometer by the thimble and twirling the frame. To do so only accelerates threadwear. It could also damage the micrometer should the spindle be jammed into the anvil.

In gauging flat surfaces, the micrometer is placed on the work and the anvil positioned squarely against the reference plane. (A feeling of stability usually occurs when the axis of the micrometer is perpendicular to the reference plane.)

The spindle is then closed on the measured plane by slowly turning the ratchet stop until it releases one click. The measurement is read. The purpose of the ratchet stop is to control the torque applied to the spindle thereby ensuring a more uniform measuring force.

Very small diameters are gauged in much the same manner as flat surfaces. For larger cylindrical parts, however, a different method must be used in aligning the micrometer with the line of measurement.

In measuring large diameters it is necessary to "feel" the setting to be sure the spindle is on the diameter. This is accomplished by rocking the micrometer back and forth over center while closing the micrometer by small steps. When contact is felt, the micrometer is then rocked sideways slightly to find the position of last contact. The rocking back and forth and sideways is repeated until the perpendicular position is found and the spindle just contacts the measured point as it passes over center. The measurement is then read from the micrometer barrel and thimble scales.

In other words, cylindrical surfaces are measured by rocking the micrometer over center and turning the thimble in very small increments until the spindle just contacts the diameter. Flat surfaces are measured by placing the micrometer anvil squarely against the part and using the ratchet stop to set measuring pressure.

Another point to keep in mind is that even though many micrometers read to .0001 inch, their structural design is not sufficiently rigid for reliable measurement to .0001 inch. Generally speaking, don't expect to measure with any accuracy to closer than .0002 inch.

29. CARE OF MICROMETERS

   1. Dirt not only causes rapid wear but buildup on measuring surfaces can create errors of as much as several thousandths of an inch. This means that before a micrometer is used it should be wiped free of oil, dirt, dust, and grit. A popular method of cleaning the measuring surfaces of the 1-inch micrometer caliper is to close the micrometer lightly but firmly on a piece of soft paper, then withdraw the paper. The spindle is then opened a few turns and any remaining fuzz or dust is blown away.

   2. A micrometer may also become gummy and the thimble fail to turn freely. This requires disassembly and washing of the micrometer components in a suitable cleaning solvent, then relubricating with a light oil and assembling the parts. Just soaking the assembled micrometer will only transfer the dirt to another part of the micrometer and perhaps make it even more difficult to clean. It also washes away needed lubrication. Furthermore, the apparent sticking may not be due to gum and grit at all but to a damaged thread or a sprung frame or bent spindle. In checking the micrometer, the spindle should turn freely with no play at any point in its travel. Any adjustment or repair should be done according to the manufacturer's instructions.

   3. Perspiration as well as cutting oils are highly corrosive to the finely finished surfaces of a micrometer. At the end of the work day, the micrometer should be wiped clean and lightly oiled before it is returned to its case. Oiling of micrometer surfaces is highly essential for protection against rust and corrosion.

   4. Never leave a 1-inch micrometer with the spindle in contact with the anvil or leave any micrometer tightened on its standard. (The finely finished contact surfaces corrode quite rapidly when left "wrung" together, probably because of electrolytic action.)

5. Never use force or cramp the micrometer to make it fit because it can be sprung or bent.

6. Never overtighten a micrometer or use it as a snap gauge.

7. Some typical cautions are listed below for additional student clarity:

DO	DO NOT
Keep micrometer clean	Twirl micrometer frame
Take care in aligning micrometer with part	Force or cramp micrometer
Use uniform gauging pressure	Overtighten micrometer
Avoid tendency to make micrometer fit	Use micrometer as a snap gauge

Some other major points for the micrometer user to remember are:

1. A check of zero setting will often alert the user to errors in micrometer readings. The check involves closing the micrometer using the same gauging pressure that would be used in making measurements, then observing if micrometer reads zero. Any difference, depending on the direction of error, should be added or substracted from measurements or the micrometer reset according to the manufacturer's instructions.

2. The contact surfaces of a micrometer should be checked periodically for parallelism and flatness. This is readily accomplished using a precision ball to "explore" the contact surfaces. The ball is simply moved from location to location around the contact surfaces and measurements taken of ball diameter. Any deviation in parallelism appears as a change in reading.

3. The contact surfaces of a micrometer could also be checked with an optical flat. The optical flat has the advantage of readily and accurately detecting combinations of wear such as waviness and humps as well as lack of parallelism appears as a change in reading.

4. Micrometers should be checked periodically to verify their accuracy. Calibration usually consists of measuring a selected group of precision gauge blocks and noting any variations from true dimensions.

5. "Standards" are also purchased and/or furnished with micrometers for checking calibration. For 1- and 2-inch micrometers, the standard is usually a disc. For larger micrometers, they are rods. In measuring gauge blocks and standards, the gauging pressure used should be the same as that used in measuring.

30. VARIATIONS OF THE OUTSIDE MICROMETER CALIPER

Some of the more common variations of the outside micrometer are listed for student and user information. They are:

Disc micrometers - for measuring closely spaced sections.

Blade micrometers - for measuring to the bottom of narrow grooves.

Thread micrometers - for measuring pitch diameters.

Round anvil micrometer - for measuring tubing wall thickness.

Micrometer with interchangeable anvils - to cover a wide range of sizes.

Bench micrometer - for reliably measuring small parts. (The stable position of this micrometer permits a more precise locating of a workpiece and the heavy base adds to the rigidity of the instrument.) Bench micrometers also have a larger diameter spindle and thimble, thus permitting a finer pitch thread for greater sensitivity and direct reading in tenths of thousandths of an inch.

Variations of the outside micrometer caliper are generally according to their anvil configuration. This configuration generally serves as the means of identification excepting the bench micrometer.

31. INSIDE MICROMETER CALIPERS

The inside micrometer caliper is essentially an outside micrometer caliper with fixed and movable jaws substituted in place of the frame and anvils. Available in three sizes, the smallest dimension that can be measured is .200 inch. The largest is 2 inches.

Designed specifically for inside measurement, the "nibs" or jaw gauging surfaces are ground to a small radius to ensure single point contact. Besides using jaws for gauging surfaces, the inside micrometer is common with the vernier caliper in that both have the instrument axis offset from the line of measurement. Therefore, the same rules regarding rocking and centralizing apply to both instruments.

The inside micrometer has two different scale arrangements. One has the linear scale located on the spindle, while the other has the scale on the barrel. In reading the barrel scale, however, only the covered graduations are read left to right in the conventional manner.

32. INSIDE MICROMETERS

The inside micrometer generally comes as a set consisting of a micrometer head, handle, spacing collar, and a number of extension rods. The rods are made in different lengths, usually in 1-inch steps, and are assembled to the head by means of a threaded connection or chuck. The smaller heads have a screw travel of 1/2 inch, and the rods are attached either directly or by using the 1/2-inch spacing collar. The handle can be attached to the head to permit measuring at greater depths. A typical inside micrometer set includes the following items:

```
Handle                3 to 4 inch rod
Micrometer head       4 to 5 inch rod
Spacing collar        5 to 6 inch rod
2 to 3 inch rod       6 to 7 inch rod
```

The smallest bore which can be measured is generally 2 inches while the largest diameter depends on the extension rod used, the practical limit being about 32 inches. The gauging surfaces or contacts are spherical to permit measuring holes, bores, etc., at their true diameter.

In measuring an inside diameter, the spindle or extension rod is generally held against the reference point and the instrument centralized until contact points rest squarely on the reference and measured points, with axis of the instrument on line of measurement.

Sources of error - in addition to the usual measurement precautions, there are two other possible sources of error when using an inside micrometer. They are:

1. Make sure extension rods are properly seated and locked in their sockets before performing measurement.

2. Do not handle the extension rods unnecessarily. Warming from handling too long can substantially increase their length and thus produce errors.

33. SELF ACTIVITIES

1. The same activities pertain to the micrometer instruments as with other instruments except that perhaps more care must be taken when using them.

2. Visit the metal shop in your school and ask the teacher to demonstrate the micrometer instruments.

3. Perhaps you may enroll in a basic mechanical measurements class and get first hand knowledge of the instrument through actual use.

4. For the entry-level manufacturing industry employee, the basic tools such as the steel rule, vernier caliper, and one-inch micrometer should be purchased as personal tools. Once purchased, read all directions carefully and then practice using the tools on objects in the home or shop.

5. Once the basic tools are fully understood, then the use of the less common micrometers could be learned.

34. LIMIT GAUGES

Limit gauges (gages) provide a fast economical way to check for tolerance limits and makes possible quantity production. Mass production would be seriously hampered if it was necessary to measure all parts with adjustable tools.

Basically limit gauges are made to measure a single dimension. Some of the most common of these are presented for student/entry-level employees familiarity:

35. PLUG GAUGES

These are called go/no-go gauges for the fast inspection of holes, inside diameters, and slots. They are available in single ended models and are ordinarily used in pairs held by hexagonal handles. Types of plug gauges are:

> Single ended go
> Single ended go for deep bores
> No-go
> Go/no-go double ended combination
> Progressive go/no-go

Descriptive terms for securing gauging members to the handle are:

1. Taperlock - taper shanks fitted into tapered receptable that are limited to smaller diameters through 1.510 inches.

2. Reversible - held by color coded locking nuts, green for go and red for no-go. (May be withdrawn from handle when worn and reversed to present a fresh gaging surface.) It is restricted to 0.760 inches or less.

3. Trilock - three prongs on the handle are forced into corresponding groves of the gaging members by means of a screw passing through the center of the plug and threading into the handle. It is for diameter measurements of 1.510 inches to 8.010 inches.

4. Annular - a wheel type, single ended unit with removable screw-in handles to facilitate the gaging process.

36. RING GAUGES

These gauges have a bore of known dimensional accuracy with which cylindrical male test pieces may be compared. Also used for outside diameters, thickness, and lengths.

Go-Gauge - represents the maximum tolerance.

No-Go Gauge - represents the minimum tolerance. For identification the no-go is supplied with an annular groove or ring in the knurled periphery. For rings less than or equal to 1.510 inches the gauges are made of solid cylindrical stock. For larger sizes, the gauges are flanged.

37. MASTER SETTING DISKS

Widely employed for setting and checking micrometers, adjustable snap gauges and all types of comparators whenever a cylindrical test piece is to be compared.

These disks are cylindrical in shape to resemble the part to be checked.

Have insulating grips to help avoid handling the measuring surface.

38. SNAP GAUGES

The group of fixed or slightly adjustable calipers used for the size control of external dimensions. They are also used for thickness and lengths.

>Go/No-go
>Double ended combinations on a common frame
>Progressive types

39. TAPER GAUGES - TAPERED PARALLELS

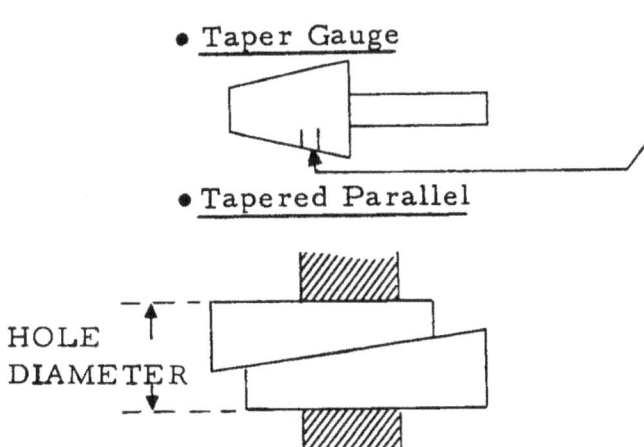

- Taper Gauge

Have two marks on the taper. (If taper enters hole to a point where it stops between marks, the taper is acceptable.)

- Tapered Parallel

Using two tapered surfaces facing each other and placed in a hole. The external edges are gauged to give the hole diameter.

40. OTHER GAUGE TYPES

Feeler Gauges - blades of various thicknesses.

Radius Gauges - a series of thin steel leaves used as templates.

Fillet Gauges - a series of thin steel leaves used as templates.

Flush Pin Gauges - single purpose gauges designed for the control of a particular dimension on a particular dimension with a particular component.

There are some cautions to be taken when using limit gauges. They are:

>Do not force gauges.
>For close tolerances, keep part and gauge moving or they may freeze up.
>Lubricate when tolerances are close.

Conditions that are difficult to detect with limit gauges are: (when size differences are small):

>Ovality
>Taper
>Bell-mouth
>Hour-glass
>Barrel

41. ADJUSTABLE LIMIT GAUGES

A fixed gauge cannot be used for any check other than the dimension and tolerance for which it is made. In contrast, adjustable gauges have threaded contacts which can be adjusted to various limits of tolerance and wear.

1. Indicating gauges - which are also adjustable, include a direct reading device such as the dial indicator, to show the amount of variation from the specified dimension.

2. Dial Indicators - basic to measurement by comparison with the following features:

    a. Simplest indication is a lever which allows very small movements to be greatly enlarged.

    b. Range from low amplification test indicators in setup and in-process inspection, to highly precise electronic instruments.

    c. The amplification is the expansion of the gear train multiplied by the increase contributed by the pointer.

    d. All measurement requires movement.

    e. Direct measurement is static.

    f. Comparison measurement is dynamic.

    The dial indicator consists of a graduated dial with an indicating hand; a contact point attached to a spindle, and an enclosed gear or lever amplifying movement. A short linear movement of the spindle is amplified by the internal mechanism and shows on the dial by a broad sweep of the indicating hand. An internal spring returns the spindle to its original position when pressure is removed. The spring provides the optimum measuring pressure without reliance of manual "feel."

The use of the dial indicator as a dynamic limit gauge is complicated and not generally used by entry-level workers until experience is gained in the more basic limit gauges.

42. SELF ACTIVITIES

1. Visit a manufacturing plant where large lots of hardware are received. Perhaps you may ask the tour director to illustrate the various limit gauges.

2. Ask the teacher if the metal shop uses limit gauges other than the feeler type gauges.

3. The entry-level employee in a manufacturing plant will become familiar with the many limit gauges through experience.

43. HISTORY AND BACKGROUND OF THREADS WHICH ARE IMPORTANT TO GAUGES

Screw threads and their standardization have proven to be one of the world's most difficult and costly problems. The British Screw System was devised in 1841 and was based on the inch measurement while the American industry was just starting. The American system was also based on the inch and was not developed until 1864. The development was brought about by the lack of standardization in the railroad development.

France and other countries used screw thread systems based on the metric system of measurement. World War I brought about a need for standards in screw thread systems, but it was not until World War II re-emphasized the problem that eventually the British, Canadians, and Americans agreed on the Unified Thread Standards.

A screw thread is a ridge of uniform section in the form of a helix generated on the external or internal surface of a cylinder or cone. Its purpose is to hold two components together.

44. ELEMENTS OF SCREW THREAD MEASUREMENT

1. Major Diameter - Largest diameter of a straight thread. (For a tapered thread, the largest diameter at any given plane normal to the axis.)

2. Minor Diameter - The smallest diameter of a single thread. (On a taper thread, the smallest diameter at any given plane normal to the axis.)

3. Pitch Diameter - Diameter of an imaginary cylinder, the surface of which would pass through the threads at points so as to make the width of the thread and the space between threads equal.

4. Angle of Thread - The angle included between the sides of the thread measured in the axial plane.

5. Lead (or Pitch of Thread) - The distance a screw thread advances axially in one complete turn.

>Single Thread - lead and pitch equal.
>Double Thread - lead is double the pitch.
>Triple Thread - lead is triple the pitch.

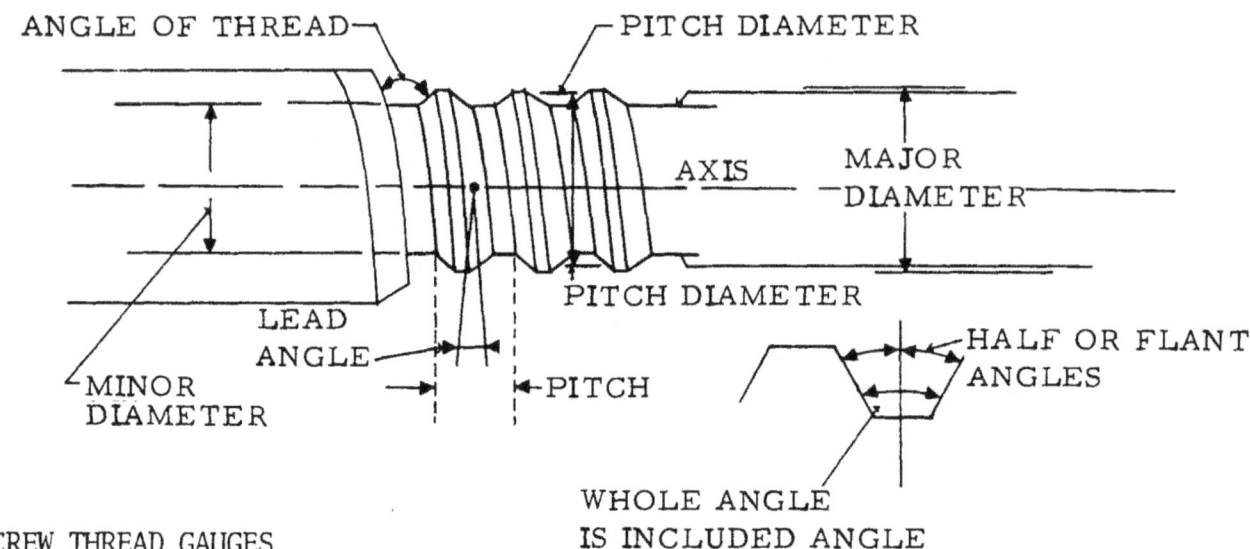

45. SCREW THREAD GAUGES

Thread gauges are usually classified into two groups:

Group I Working Gauges and Inspection Gauges (Used to check a product to maintain a tolerance as it is being machined and after completion.)

Group II Setting of Master Gauges (Used as standards against which the reference gauges are checked.)

Tha gauge tolerance accuracy is classed as follows:

Class W - Closest to which thread gauges are manufactured.
Class X - Average tolerance (largest percentage).
Class Y - Least accurate.

46. TEST AND INSPECTION FACTORS

The following are some of the test and inspection factors that are commonly considered in thread gauge checks:

1. Thread ring and plug gauges are commonly used for go/no-go inspections.

2. "Drunken" helix can be accurately checked optically.

3. Angle deviation of a gauge can also be checked optically by accurate alignment of a test point with a thread and microscope examination.

4. Thread comparators give direct indication of variation between production threads and a master setting gauge.

5. Optical comparators are used to check external threads. (With a master template, the inspector is able to observe the outside diameter, pitch diameter, form, thread angle, and lead error simultaneously.)

6. Minor diameters require special chisel-shaped anvils designed to engage only the minor diameter and not make contact along the flanks of the thread tooth.

7. The lead error in a thread can also be checked with a toolmaker's microscope.

47. SCREW THREAD ELEMENTS OF DEVIATION (DO NOT HAVE TOLERANCES)

   1. Out-of-roundness - limits thread engagement and allows for only line contact with the mating thread. Two types are:

   <u>Multi-lobe</u>
   3 Point
   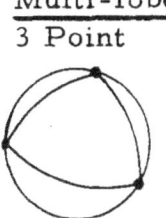

   <u>Oval</u>
   Point
   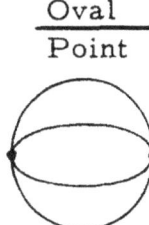

   a. Lead deviation
   b. Flank angle deviation

   2. Drunkenness - when the helix variation of a thread is a wavy deviation from the true helical advancement (advance of thread is irregular). An exaggerated sketch of this feature is:

   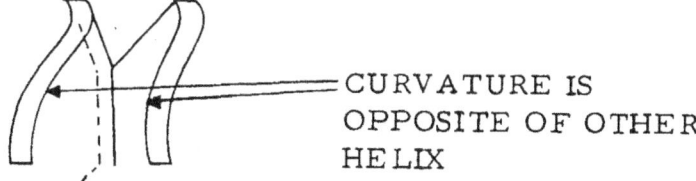
   CURVATURE IS OPPOSITE OF OTHER HELIX

   NOTE: Number of threads per inch could vary.

3. Surface Defects - nicks or bruises on threads.

4. Taper - causes uneven torquing pressures.

48. TORQUE AND TORQUE MEASUREMENT

Associated with screw thread applications is the method of inserting screws and the corresponding control of the insertion. One of the major controls is torque.

Torque - The tendency of an application of force to produce rotation. (Measured in inch-grams, inch-ounces, inch-pounds, foot-pounds or corresponding metric units.) Basic techniques of torque measurement are:

1. Static measurements of force at a fixed distance from the pivot point.

2. Dynamic or static measurements of a torsion produced in the shaft of a "prime mover" delivery torque to a load.

3. Dynamic or static measurements of the force and distance required to hold the housing of a torque generator or its load.

4. Measurement of the chain or belt tension required to rotate a pulley or load.

A gauging tool, torque wrench, is used to measure the resistance to turning. Features are:

1. Direct reading with mechanical or sensory options.

2. Very critical and must be closely controlled.

3. Equation is $T = F \times D$; where -

   T = Torque
   F = Applied Force
   D = Distance of lever arm

   NOTE: Lever length must be perpendicular to direction of applied force.

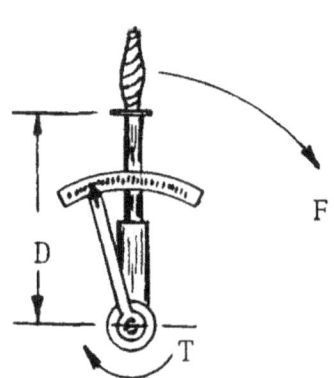

49. SELF ACTIVITIES

1. Learn the basic features of screw-thread application in order to be prepared for future involvement.

2. Visit the metal shop and ask the teacher to demonstrate screw-thread applications and point out the major parts of the screw.

3. Ask the metal shop teacher to demonstrate the torque wrench and how it applies to screw-threads and associated criticality of insertion into various material.

50. PLANAR SURFACES

Planar surfaces are very important in the applications of inspection and quality control in the manufacturing industry. Accurate mechanical measurement would be practically impossible without the bases of these measurements. The two bases are surface plates and gauge blocks.

51. SURFACE PLATES

When discussing planar surfaces, flatness becomes a major consideration. Flatness, although considered basic, is a stranger to nature. The discovery of flatness, in reality, was a major breakthrough for the industrial revolution. It refers to the measure of deviation from a reference plane.

Surface plates are very relevant for two reasons:

1. They serve as a horizontal reference plane of sufficient strength and rigidity on which measurement operations may be supported.

2. Every linear measurement starts at a reference point and ends at a measured point.

52. APPLICATIONS OF THE SURFACE PLATE

1. The surface plate has many uses, some of them are:

    Grinding Table   Planing Table   Lathe Way

2. They are used to check the following:

    Fixed gauging (go/no-go)   Roundness
    Scribing   Squareness
    Comparative gauging   Parallelism
    Hold location   Angles

3. Tolerances of the surface plate per unit length can be up to .050 or 50 thousandths of an inch or more.

4. The materials, cleaning, care and use of surface plates:

    a. Materials

        Black Granite (most superior flatness)

            Closer tolerances and lower cost
            Non-corrosive and non-rusting
            Not subject to contact interference
            Non-magnetic
            Hard, stable, and long wearing
            Easy to clean
            Has thermal stability

        Cast Iron and Steel

            Used mostly for separate reference surfaces
            Expensive
            Rusts and induce rust
            Must be oiled (oil collects dust causing error)
            Must be kept covered

    b. Cost - depends on:

        Accuracy required
        Material used

    c. Degradation of Workmanship

        The plane surface can be developed to a high order of accuracy because there is no standard.

        A product is not as precise as the machines. The machines are not as precise as the gauges, the gauges are not as precise as...

    d. Applications

        Use surface plates when setting up to check first article and/or when measurements/perpendicularity is in the 10 thousandths.

        When comparing two articles.

        When measuring one feature to another with no reference available on the part.

        Apply degradation of workmanship principles to personal work and importance of care when working.

53. GAUGE BLOCKS

Gauge blocks are end standards that combine arithmetically to form combinations and are considered to be the keystone to measurement. Some of the important features of gauge blocks are:

1. They are the basic tool of precision measurement.

2. They allow greater precision than other instruments.

3. They must be considered when:

    Precision increases
    Length increases
    Importance of reliability increases
    Skill of the measure decreases

4. They are the most important metrological tool that will be encountered.

5. They are the most rugged and most delicate devices used.

6. They have a built-in (designed and produced) cushion of accuracy.

54. ENVIRONMENTAL AND THERMAL CONSIDERATIONS OF GAUGE BLOCKS

1. Must have environmentally controlled atmosphere for maximum accuracy.

2. Very stable, change little with age and care.

3. Very susceptible to corrosion due to moisture (should not breathe on or touch surfaces).

4. Must be cleaned and lubricated.

5. Will shrink if too much solvent is used (evaporation of solvent cools blocks).

55. RULES FOR GAUGE BLOCK CARE

1. Never attempt to wring or otherwise use gauge blocks that have been in contact with chips, dust, or dirt-laden cutting fluids.

2. Before using, clean blocks with a high-grade solvent or commercial gauge block cleaner. Wipe dry with a lint-free tissue.

3. Do not allow blocks to remain wrung together for long periods. Separate daily.

4. When not in use, place blocks in a safe place where they will not be damaged, preferrably in their case.

5. Before putting blocks away, clean the blocks and cover with a non-corrosive oil, or grease, or commercial preservative.

6. Be on constant guard for burrs. If anything has been placed on a block or if it does not wring readily, use a conditioning stone immediately.

7. Thoroughly clean gauge block case periodically.

56. PHYSICAL AND METROLOGICAL CONSIDERATIONS

Considerations that must be given to gauge blocks are two-fold, physical and metrological. They are:

<u>Physical</u>

Surface finish
Physical properties
Identification
Material:
    Alloy steel (most common)
    Carbide
    Stainless steel
    Chrome plate
Heat sensitive

<u>Metrological</u>

Measured plane
Reversible reference surfaces
Reference plane
(All reference surfaces are parallel to line of measurement)

57. GAUGE BLOCK GRADES

Grade AA - Laboratory grade
Grade A   - Inspection grade
Grade B   - Working grade
Grade AAA - The grand master for top level industrial calibration

58. TYPICAL SETS

The typical gauge block sets manufactured can be: rectangular, square, or cylindrical.

The sets are in groups of 121, 86, 56, 38, and 35. (With a set of 81 blocks, over 100,000 combinations are possible.)

The smallest size is 0.010 inches and the largest is 20.000 inches.

59. PRESENT INCH SETS (81 PIECE SET)

Inches	Series	Blocks	Sizes
0.039439 0.039755 0.000039	First	9	0.1001 through 0.1009 inches (increments of .0001)
0.039794 0.058661 0.000394	Second	49	0.101 through 0.001 inches (increments of .001)
0.0197 0.9646 0.0197	Third	19	0.050 through 0.950 inches (increments of .050 inches)
0.9842 0.9370 0.9843	Fourth	4	1.000 through 4.000 inches (increments of 1.0000 inches)

60. IMPORTANT FEATURES OF GAUGE BLOCKS

   Wringing -   Bringing two flat and smooth surfaces intimately together causing adherence (due to molecular attraction).

   -    Very important in the use of gauge blocks.

   -    Space between blocks can be reduced to a fraction of a mike (0.0001 inch) but 2 mikes are most common (90% of the time).

   -    Wringing interval is space between blocks, and is caused by:

         Poor surface finish (irregularities)
         Air films
         Oil films
         Grease films

   Combining -   Stacking various sized blocks to form a length dimension.

   Example: Choose blocks to elimate figures from right to left (combination for the value of 1.605 is 1.605 - .105 - .500 - 1.000) = 0.

   Example: For a value of 2.4817, the following combinations are made:

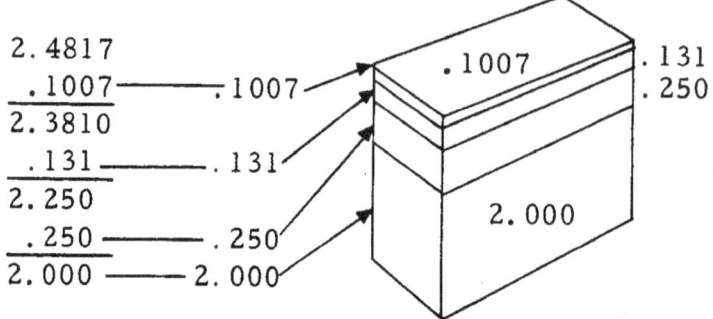

61. WHEN TO USE GAUGE BLOCKS (SLIDE-PRINCIPLE USES FOR GAUGE BLOCKS)

   Calibration of other instruments and lesser standards.
   Setting of comparators and indicator-type instruments.
   Attribute gauging.
   Machine set-up and precision assembly.
   Layout.

62. HOW TO USE GAUGE BLOCKS FOR MEASUREMENT

   Measurement by comparison.
   Compare an unknown with a known quantity (standard).
   Depends on:

   1. Accuracy of standard.
   2. Discrimination of standard.
   3. Reading of instrument.

63. WEAR BLOCKS AND ACCESSORIES

   Special carbide or steel blocks reserved for use as reference.

   Used to minimize wear of blocks.

   Surfaces at the ends of gauge block stacks.

   Recommended when blocks are used for direct comparison.

   Not needed when block holders are used.

   Extends useful life of gauge block sets.

64. SELF ACTIVITIES

   1. The student in high school is limited to availability of surface plates and gauge blocks. Therefore, study must be made by reviewing textbooks on the subjects and/or films that may be available that explain the usage.

2. Ask the metal shop teacher to arrange a plant visitation where surface plates and gauge blocks are used. Perhaps a demonstration of the usage of these planar surfaces will be possible.

3. The entry-level employee, although in most situations will not be required to use surface plates and gauge blocks, could observe more experienced employees when these basic tools are being used.

BASIC FUNDAMENTALS OF MEASURING TOOLS AND TECHNIQUES

CONTENTS

	Page
I. RULES AND TAPES	1
II. SIMPLE CALIPERS	5
III. VERNIER CALIPER	10
IV. MICROMETER	14
V. SQUARES	20
VI. MISCELLANEOUS GAGES	24

BASIC FUNDAMENTALS OF MEASURING TOOLS AND TECHNIQUES

In performing many jobs during your career, you will be required to take accurate measurements of materials and objects. It is common practice in the shop to fabricate material for installation in a shop or in the field. For example, suppose you need a box of certain size to fit a space in a compartment. You would have to take measurements of the space and send them to a shop where the box would be built. This example suggests that the measurements you took and those taken in the process of building the box must be accurate. However, the accuracy of the measurements will depend on the measuring tools used and one's ability to use them correctly.

Measuring tools are also used for inspecting a finished product or partly finished product. Inspection operations include testing or checking a piece of work by comparing dimensions of the workpiece to the required dimensions given on a drawing or sketch. Again, the measurements taken must be accurate and accuracy depends on one's ability to use measuring tools correctly.

After studying this chapter, you should be able to select the appropriate measuring tool to use in doing a job and be able to operate properly a variety of measuring instruments.

I. RULES AND TAPES

There are many different types of measuring tools in use in the shop. Where exact measurements are required, a micrometer caliper (mike) is used. Such a caliper, when properly used, gives measurements to within .001 of an inch accuracy. On the other hand, where accuracy is not extremely critical, the common rule or tape will suffice for most measurements.

Figure 1 shows some of the types of rules and tapes commonly used. Of all measuring tools, the simplest and most common is the steel rule. This rule is usually 6 or 12 inches in length, although other lengths are available. Steel rules may be flexible or nonflexible, but the thinner the rule, the easier it is to measure accurately because the division marks are closer to the work.

Generally a rule has four sets of graduations, one on each edge of each side. The longest lines represent the inch marks. On one edge, each inch is divided into 8 equal spaces; so each space represents 1/8 in. The other edge of this side is divided into sixteenths. The 1/4-in. and 1/2-in. marks are commonly made longer than the smaller division marks to facilitate counting, but the graduations are not, as a rule, numbered individually, as they are sufficiently far apart to be counted without difficulty. The opposite side is similarly divided into 32 and 64 spaces per inch, and it is common practice to number every fourth division for easier reading.

There are many variations of the common rule. Sometimes the graduations are on one side only, sometimes a set of graduations is added across one end for measuring in narrow spaces, and sometimes only the first inch is divided into 64ths, with the remaining inches divided into 32nds and 16ths.

A metal or wood folding rule may be used for measuring purposes. These folding rules are usually 2 to 6 feet long. The folding rules cannot be relied on for extremely accurate measurements because a certain amount of play develops at the joints after they have been used for a while.

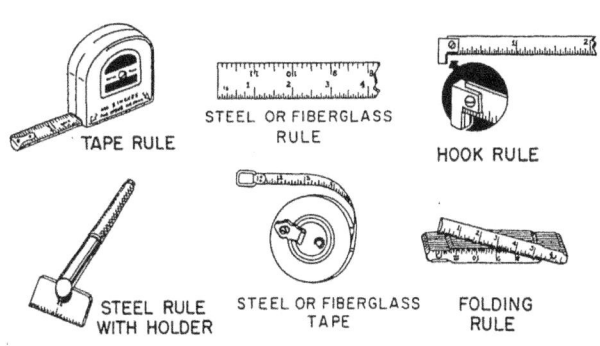

Figure 1.—Some common types of rules.

MEASURING TOOLS AND TECHNIQUES

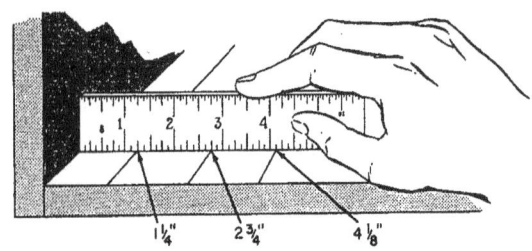

Figure 2.—Measuring with and reading a common rule.

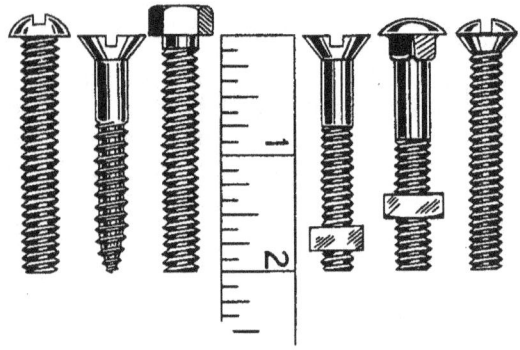

Figure 3.—Measuring the length of a bolt or screw.

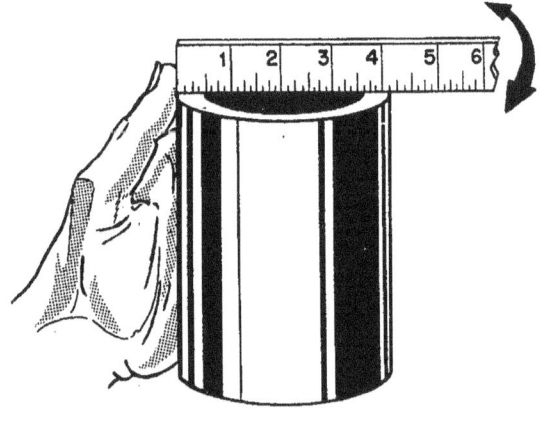

Figure 4.—Measuring the outside diameter of a pipe.

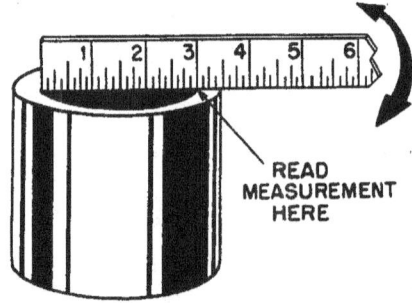

Figure 5.—Measuring the inside diameter of a pipe.

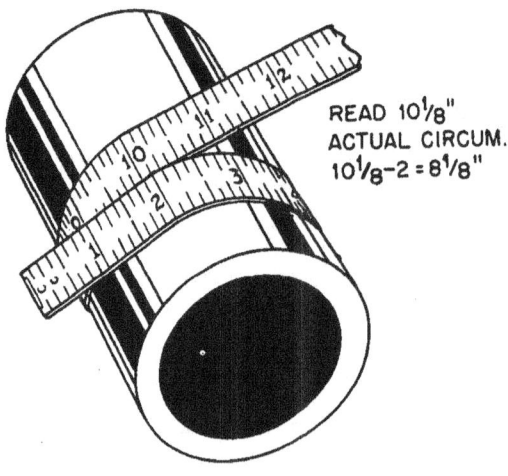

Figure 6.—Measuring the circumference of a pipe with a tape.

Steel tapes are made from 6 to about 300 ft. in length. The shorter lengths are frequently made with a curved cross section so that they are flexible enough to roll up, but remain rigid when extended. Long, flat tapes require support over their full length when measuring, or the natural sag will cause an error in reading.

The flexible-rigid tapes are usually contained in metal cases into which they wind themselves when a button is pressed, or into which they can be easily pushed. A hook is provided at one end to hook over the object being measured so one man can handle it without assistance. On some models, the outside of the case can be used as one end of the tape when measuring inside dimensions.

MEASURING PROCEDURES

To take a measurement with a common rule, hold the rule with its edge on the surface of the object being measured. This will eliminate parallax and other errors which might result

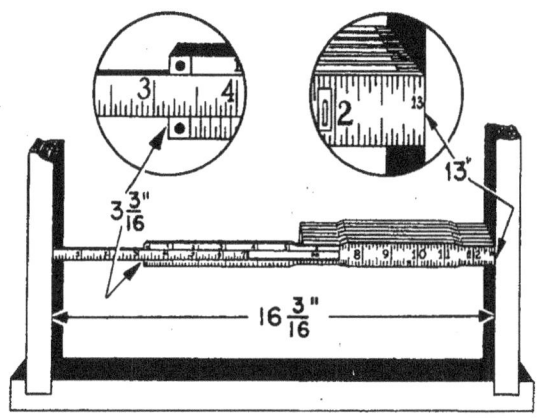

Figure 7.—Using a folding rule to measure an inside dimension.

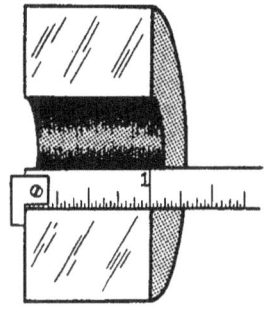

Figure 9.—Measuring the thickness of stock through a hole.

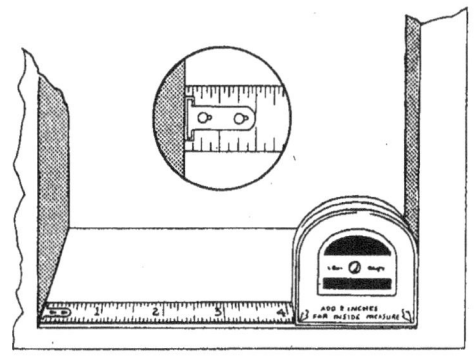

Figure 8.—Measuring an inside dimension with a tape rule.

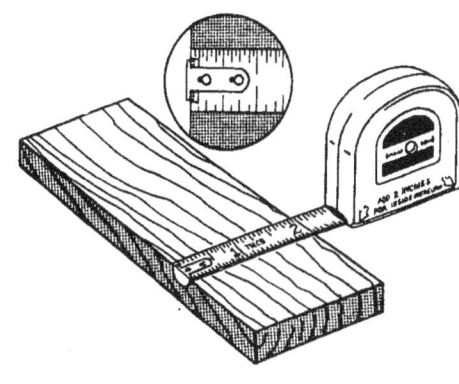

Figure 10.—Measuring an outside dimension using a tape rule.

due to the thickness of the rule. Read the measurement at the graduation which coincides with the distance to be measured, and state it as being so many inches and fractions of an inch. (Fig. 2.) Always reduce fractions to their lowest terms, for example, 6/8 inch would be called 3/4 inch. A hook or eye at the end of a tape or rule is normally part of the first measured inch.

Bolts or Screws

The length of bolts or screws is best measured by holding them up against a rigid rule or tape. Hold both the bolt or screw to be measured and the rule up to your eye level so that your line of sight will not be in error in reading the measurement. As shown in figure 3, the bolts or screws with countersink type heads are measured from the top of the head to the opposite end, while those with other type heads are measured from the bottom of the head.

Outside Pipe Diameters

To measure the outside diameter of a pipe, it is best to use some kind of rigid rule. A folding wooden rule or a steel rule is satisfactory for this purpose. As shown in figure 4, line up the end of the rule with one side of the pipe, using your thumb as a stop. Then with the one end held in place with your thumb, swing the rule through an arc and take the maximum reading at the other side of the pipe. For most practical purposes, the measurement obtained

MEASURING TOOLS AND TECHNIQUES

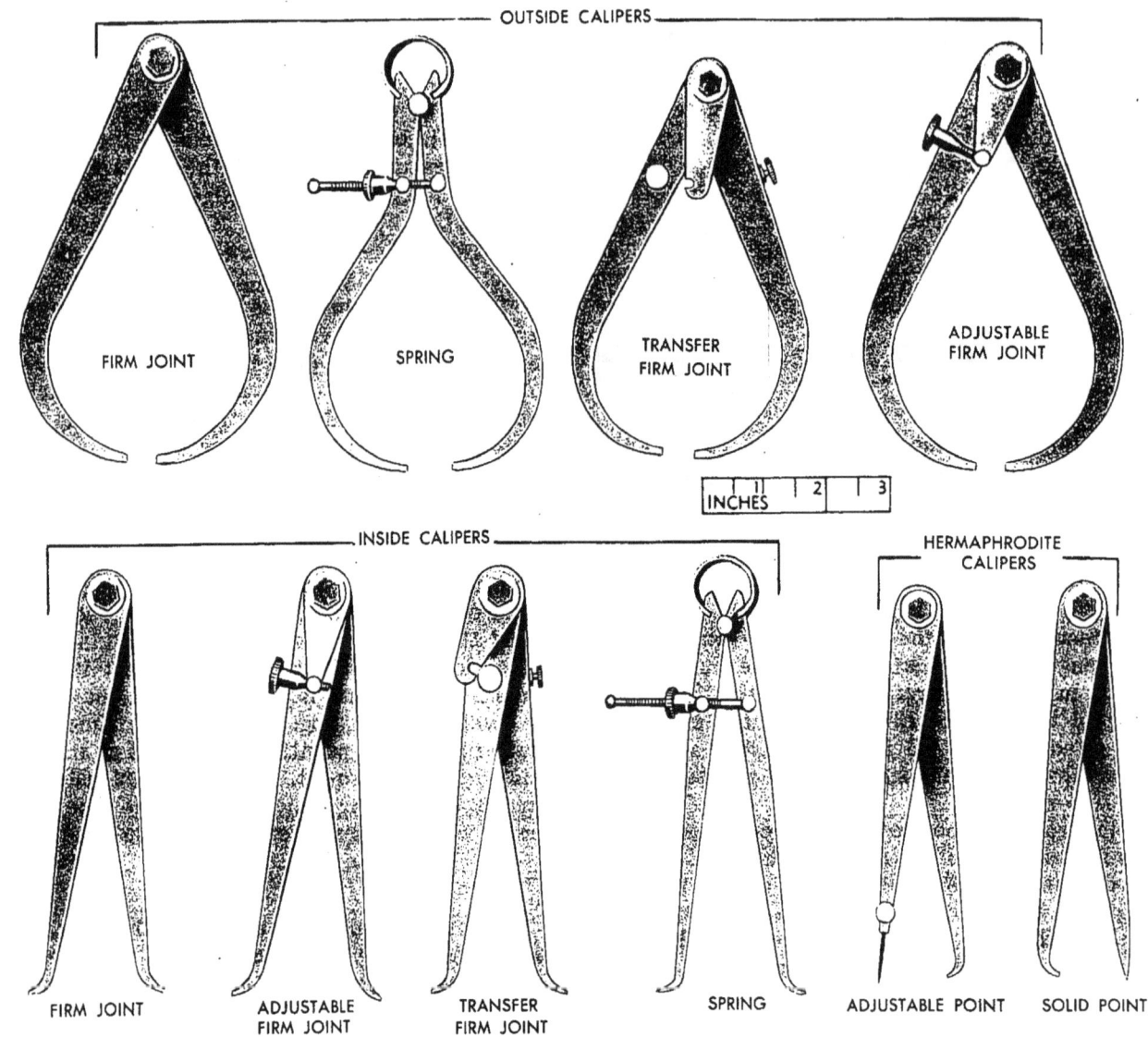

Figure 11.—Simple calipers—noncalibrated.

by using this method is satisfactory. It is necessary that you know how to take this measurement as the outside diameter of pipe is sometimes the only dimension given on pipe specifications.

Inside Pipe Diameters

To measure the inside diameter of a pipe with a rule, as shown in figure 5, hold the rule so that one corner of the rule just rests on the inside of one side of the pipe. Then, with one end thus held in place, swing the rule through an arc and read the diameter across the maximum inside distance. This method is satisfactory for an approximate inside measurement.

Pipe Circumferences

To measure the circumference of a pipe, a flexible type rule that will conform to the cylindrical shape of the pipe must be used. A tape rule or a steel tape is adaptable for this job. When measuring pipe, make sure the tape has been wrapped squarely around the axis of the pipe (i.e., measurement should be taken in a plane perpendicular to the axis) to ensure that the reading will not be more than the actual circumference of the pipe. This is extremely important when measuring large diameter pipe.

Hold the rule or tape as shown in figure 6. Take the reading, using the 2-inch graduation, for example, as the reference point. In this case the correct reading is found by subtracting 2 inches from the actual reading. In this way the first 2 inches of the tape, serving as a handle, will enable you to hold the tape securely.

Inside Dimensions

To take an inside measurement, such as the inside of a box, a folding rule that incorporates a 6- or 7-inch sliding extension is one of the best measuring tools for this job. To take the inside measurement, first unfold the folding rule to the approximate dimension. Then extend the end of the rule and read the length that it extends, adding the length of the extension to the length on the main body of the rule. (Fig. 7.) In this illustration the length of the main body of the rule is 13 inches and the extension is pulled out 3 3/16 inches. In this case the total inside dimension being measured is 16 3/16 inches.

In figure 8 notice in the circled insert that the hook at the end of the particular rule shown is attached to the rule so that it is free to move slightly. When an outside dimension is taken by hooking the end of the rule over an edge, the hook will locate the end of the rule even with the surface from which the measurement is being taken. By being free to move, the hook will retract away from the end of the rule when an inside dimension is taken. To measure an inside dimension using a tape rule, extend the rule between the surfaces as shown, take a reading at the point on the scale where the rule enters the case, and add 2 inches. The 2 inches are the width of the case. The total is the inside dimension being taken.

To measure the thickness of stock through a hole with a hook rule, insert the rule through the hole, hold the hook against one face of the stock, and read the thickness at the other face. (Fig. 9.)

Outside Dimensions

To measure an outside dimension using a tape rule, hook the rule over the edge of the stock. Pull the tape out until it projects far enough from the case to permit measuring the required distance. The hook at the end of the rule is designed so that it will locate the end of the rule at the surface from which the measurement is being taken. (Fig. 10.) When taking a measurement of length, the tape is held parallel to the lengthwise edge. For measuring widths, the tape should be at right angles to the lengthwise edge. Read the dimension of the rule exactly at the edge of the piece being measured.

It may not always be possible to hook the end of the tape over the edge of stock being measured. In this case it may be necessary to butt the end of the tape against another surface or to hold the rule at a starting point from which a measurement is to be taken.

Distance Measurements

Steel or fiberglass tapes are generally used for making long measurements. Secure the hook end of the tape. Hold the tape reel in the hand and allow it to unwind while walking in the direction in which the measurement is to be taken. Stretch the tape with sufficient tension to overcome sagging. At the same time make sure the tape is parallel to an edge or the surface being measured. Read the graduation on the tape by noting which line on the tape coincides with the measurement being taken.

CARE

Rules and tapes should be handled carefully and kept lightly oiled to prevent rust. Never allow the edges of measuring devices to become nicked by striking them with hard objects. They should preferably be kept in a wooden box when not in use.

To avoid kinking tapes, pull them straight out from their cases—do not bend them backward. With the windup type, always turn the crank clockwise—turning it backward will kink or break the tape. With the spring-wind type, guide the tape by hand. If it is allowed to snap back, it may be kinked, twisted, or otherwise damaged. Do not use the hook as a stop. Slow down as you reach the end.

II. SIMPLE CALIPERS

Simple calipers are used in conjunction with a scale to measure diameters. The calipers most commonly used are shown in figure 11.

MEASURING TOOLS AND TECHNIQUES

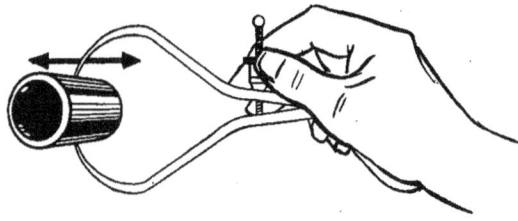

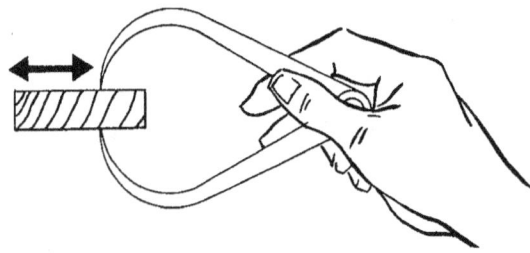

Figure 12.—Using an outside caliper.

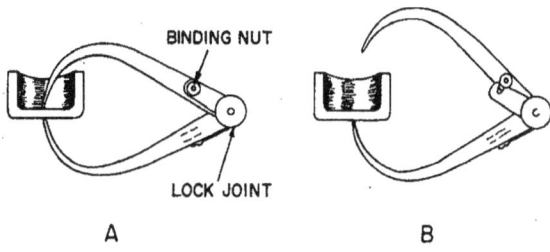

Figure 13.—Measuring the thickness of the bottom of a cup.

Outside calipers for measuring outside diameters are bow-legged; those used for inside diameters have straight legs with the feet turned outward. Calipers are adjusted by pulling or pushing the legs to open or close them. Fine adjustment is made by tapping one leg lightly on a hard surface to close them, or by turning them upside down and tapping on the joint end to open them.

Spring-joint calipers have the legs joined by a strong spring hinge and linked together by a screw and adjusting nut. For measuring chamfered cavities (grooves), or for use over flanges, transfer calipers are available. They are equipped with a small auxiliary leaf attached to one of the legs by a screw. (Fig. 11.) The measurement is made as with ordinary calipers; then the leaf is locked to the leg.

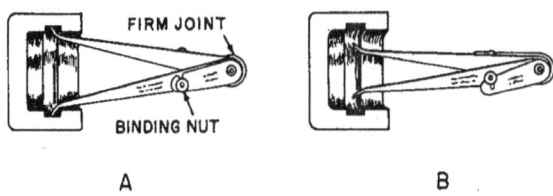

Figure 14.—Measuring a hard to reach inside dimension with an inside caliper.

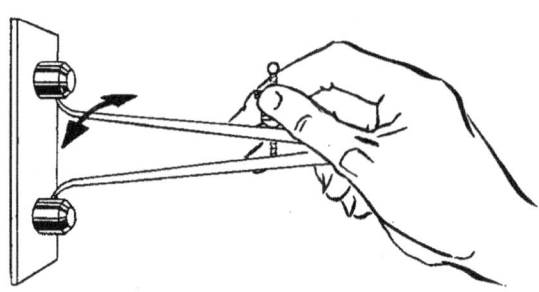

Figure 15.—Measuring the distance between two surfaces with an inside caliper.

The legs may then be opened or closed as needed to clear the obstruction, then brought back and locked to the leaf again, thus restoring them to the original setting.

A different type of caliper is the hermaphrodite, sometimes called odd-leg caliper. This caliper has one straight leg ending in a sharp point, sometimes removable, and one bow leg. The hermaphrodite caliper is used chiefly for locating the center of a shaft, or for locating a shoulder.

USING CALIPERS

A caliper is usually used in one of two ways. Either the caliper is set to the dimension of the work and the dimension transferred to a scale, or the caliper is set on a scale and the work machined until it checks with the dimension set up on the caliper. To adjust a caliper to a scale dimension, one leg of the caliper should be held firmly against one end of the scale and the other leg adjusted to the desired dimension. To adjust a caliper to the work, open the legs wider than the work and then bring them down to the work.

CAUTION: Never place a caliper on work that is revolving in a machine.

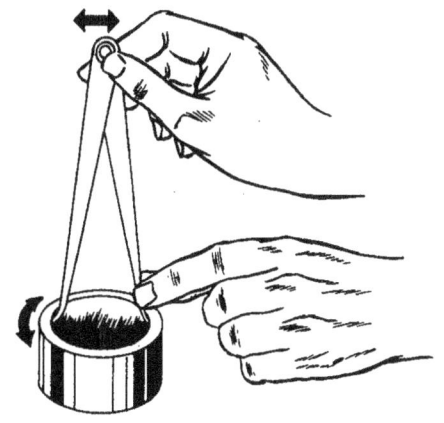

Figure 16.—Measuring an inside diameter with an inside caliper.

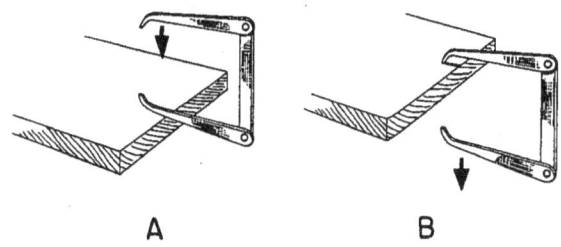

Figure 18.—Decreasing and increasing the setting of a firm joint caliper.

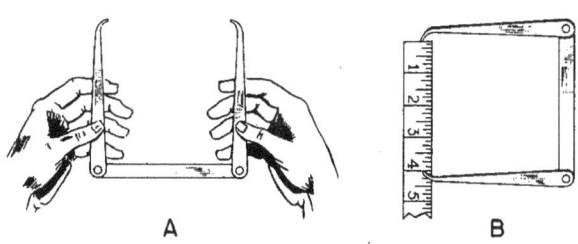

Figure 17.—Setting a combination firm joint caliper.

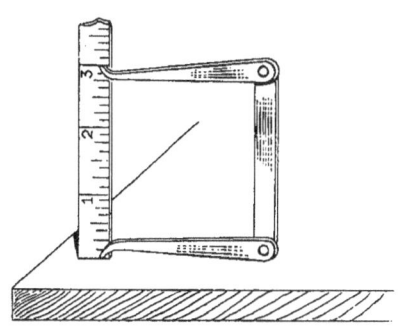

Figure 19.—Setting a combination firm joint caliper for inside measurements.

Measuring The Diameter of Round or
The Thickness of Flat Stock

To measure the diameter of round stock, or the thickness of flat stock, adjust the outside caliper so that you feel a slight drag as you pass it over the stock. (See fig. 12.) After the proper "feel" has been attained, measure the setting of the caliper with a rule. In reading the measurement, sight over the leg of the caliper after making sure the caliper is set squarely with the face of the rule.

Measuring Hard to Reach
Dimensions

To measure an almost inaccessible outside dimension, such as the thickness of the bottom of a cup, use an outside transfer firm-joint caliper as shown in figure 13. When the proper "feel" is obtained, tighten the lock joint. Then loosen the binding nut and open the caliper enough to remove it from the cup. Close the caliper again and tighten the binding nut to seat in the slot at the end of the auxiliary arm. The caliper is now at the original setting, representing the thickness of the bottom of the cup. The caliper setting can now be measured with a rule.

To measure a hard to reach inside dimension, such as the internal groove shown in figure 14, a lock-joint inside caliper should be used. The procedure followed for measuring a hard to reach outside dimension is used.

Measuring The Distance
Between Two Surfaces

To measure the distance between two surfaces with an inside caliper, first set the caliper to the approximate distance being measured. Hold the caliper with one leg in contact with one of the surfaces being measured. (See fig. 15.) Then as you increase the setting of the caliper, move the other leg from left to right. Feel for

MEASURING TOOLS AND TECHNIQUES

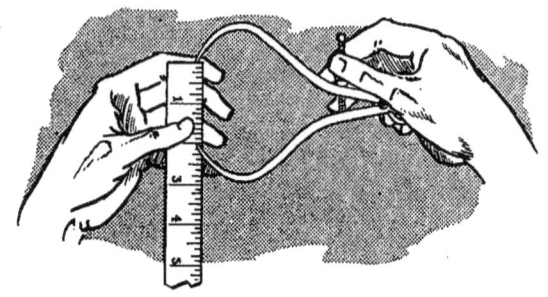

Figure 20.—Setting an outside spring caliper.

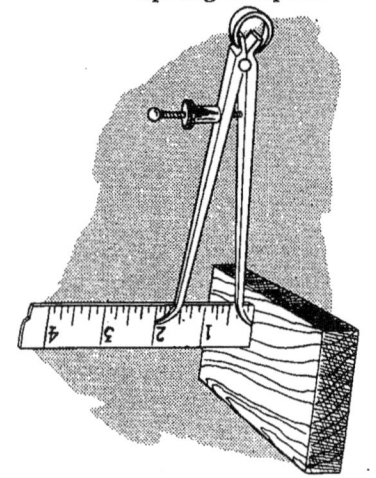

Figure 21.—Setting an inside spring caliper.

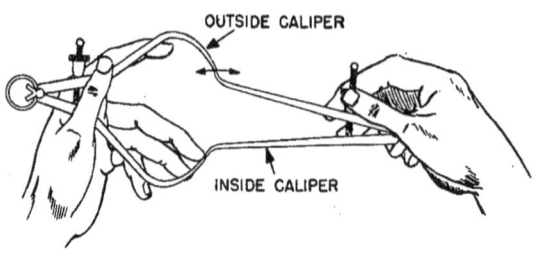

Figure 22.—Transferring a measurement from an outside to an inside caliper.

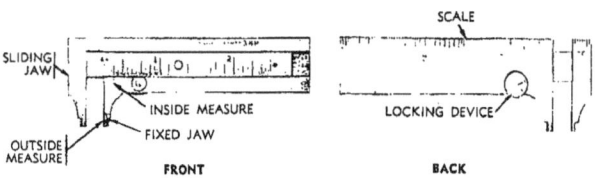

Figure 23.—Caliper square (slide caliper).

the slight drag indicating the proper setting of the caliper. Then remove the caliper and measure the setting with a rule.

Measuring Hole Diameters

To measure the diameter of a hole with an inside caliper, hold the caliper with one leg in contact with one side of the hole (fig. 16) and, as you increase the setting, move the other leg from left to right, and in and out of the hole. When you have found the point of largest diameter, remove the caliper and measure the caliper setting with a rule.

Setting A Combination
Firm Joint Caliper

To set a combination firm joint caliper with a rule, when the legs are in position for outside measurements, grasp the caliper with both hands, as shown in figure 17A, and adjust both legs to the approximate setting. By adjusting both legs, the shape of the tool will be approximately symmetrical. Thus it will maintain its balance and be easier to handle.

Check this approximate setting as shown in figure 17B. Sight squarely across the leg at the graduations on the rule to get the exact setting required.

If it is necessary to decrease or increase the setting, tap one leg of the caliper, as shown in figure 18. The arrow indicates the change in setting that will take place.

When the caliper is set for inside measurements, the same directions for adjusting the setting apply. Figure 19 shows how the end of the rule and one leg of the caliper are rested on the bench top so that they are exactly even with each other when the reading is taken.

Setting Outside And Inside
Spring Calipers

To set a particular reading on an outside spring caliper, first open the caliper to the approximate setting. Then, as shown in figure 20, place one leg over the end of the rule, steadying it with index finger. Make the final setting by sighting over the other leg of the

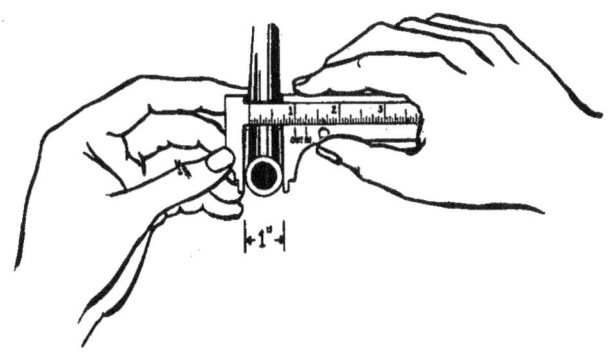

Figure 24.—Measuring an outside dimension with a pocket slide caliper.

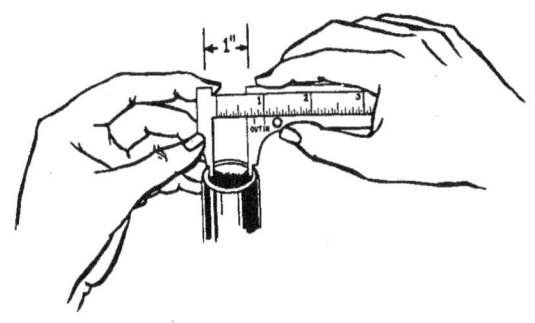

Figure 25.—Measuring an inside dimension with a slide caliper.

caliper, squarely with the face of the rule at the reading, and turning the knurled adjusting nut until the desired setting is obtained.

To set an inside spring caliper to a particular reading, place both caliper and rule on a flat surface as shown in figure 21. The rule must be held squarely or normal (90° in both directions) to the surface to ensure accuracy. Adjust the knurled adjusting nut, reading the setting on the rule with line of sight normal to the face of the rule at the reading.

Transferring Measurements From One Caliper To Another

To transfer a measurement from one spring caliper to another, hold the calipers as shown in figure 22. Note that one of the man's fingers is extended to steady the point of contact of the two lower caliper legs. In this figure the inside caliper is being adjusted to the size of the outside caliper. As careful measurements with calipers depend on one's sense of touch, which is spoken of as "feel," calipers are best held lightly. When you notice a slight drag, the caliper is at the proper setting.

CARE

Keep calipers clean and lightly oiled, but do not overoil the joint of firm joint calipers or you may have difficulty in keeping them tight. Do not throw them around or use them for screwdrivers or pry bars. Even a slight force may spring the legs of a caliper so that other measurements made with it are never accurate. Remember they are measuring instruments and must be used only for the purpose for which they are intended.

SLIDE CALIPER

The main disadvantage of using ordinary calipers is that they do not give a direct reading of a caliper setting. As explained earlier, you must measure a caliper setting with a rule. To overcome this disadvantage, use slide calipers (fig. 23). This instrument is occasionally called a caliper rule.

Slide calipers can be used for measuring outside, inside, and other dimensions. One side of the caliper is used as a measuring rule, while the scale on the opposite side is used in measuring outside and inside dimensions. Graduations on both scales are in inches and fractions thereof. A locking screw is incorporated to hold the slide caliper jaws in position during use. Stamped on the frame are two words, "IN" and "OUT." These are used in reading the scale while making inside and outside measurements, respectively.

To measure the outside diameter of round stock, or the thickness of flat stock, move the jaws of the caliper into firm contact with the surface of the stock. Read the measurement at the reference line stamped OUT. (See fig. 24.)

When measuring the inside diameter of a hole, or the distance between two surfaces, insert only the rounded tips of the caliper jaws into the hole or between the two surfaces. (See fig. 25.) Read the measurement on the reference line stamped IN.

Note that two reference lines are needed if the caliper is to measure both outside and inside dimensions, and that they are separated

MEASURING TOOLS AND TECHNIQUES

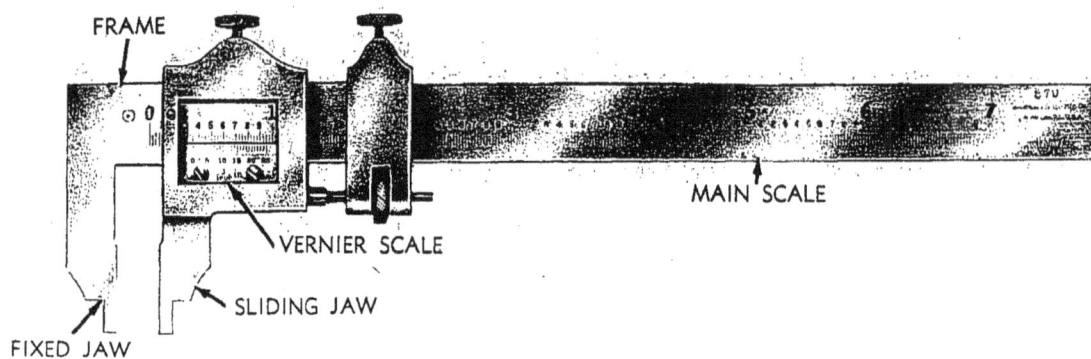

Figure 26.—Vernier caliper.

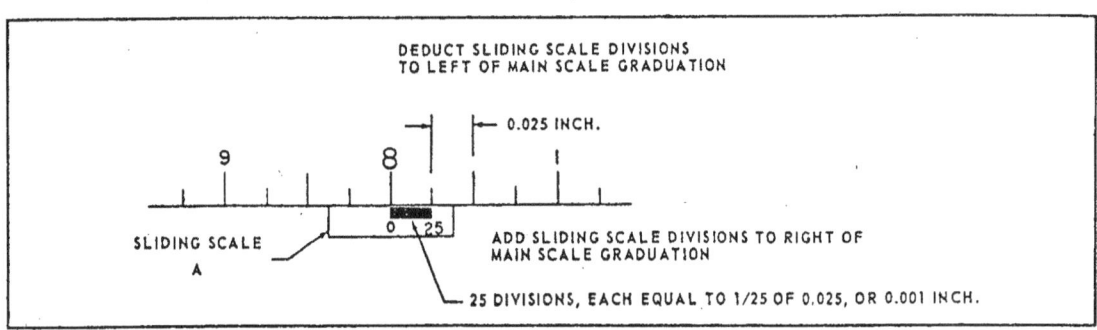

Figure 27.—Vernier scale principle.

by an amount equal to the outside dimension of the rounded tips when the caliper is closed.

Pocket models of slide calipers are commonly made in 3-in. and 5-in. sizes and are graduated to read in 32nds and 64ths. Pocket slide calipers are valuable when extreme precision is not required. They are frequently used for duplicating work when the expense of fixed gages is not warranted.

III. VERNIER CALIPER

A vernier caliper (fig. 26) consists of an L-shaped member with a scale engraved on the long shank. A sliding member is free to move on the bar and carries a jaw which matches the arm of the L. The vernier scale is engraved on a small plate that is attached to the sliding member.

Perhaps the most distinct advantage of the vernier caliper, over other types of caliper, is the ability to provide very accurate measurements over a large range. It can be used for both internal and external surfaces. Pocket models usually measure from zero to 3 in., but sizes are available all the way to 4 ft. In using the vernier caliper, you must be able to measure with a slide caliper and be able to read a vernier scale.

PRINCIPLES OF THE VERNIER SCALE

It would be possible to etch graduations 1/1000 inch (0.001) in. apart on a steel rule or sliding caliper as shown in figure 27. This enlarged illustration shows two graduated scales. The top scale has divisions which are 0.025 inches apart. The small sliding lower scale has 25 0.001 inch graduations which can divide any of the main scale divisions of 0.025 inch into 25 parts. When the first graduation marked "O" on this small scale aligns with a graduation on the main scale, the last, or 25th will also align with a graduation on the main scale as shown. Consequently, the small 0.00

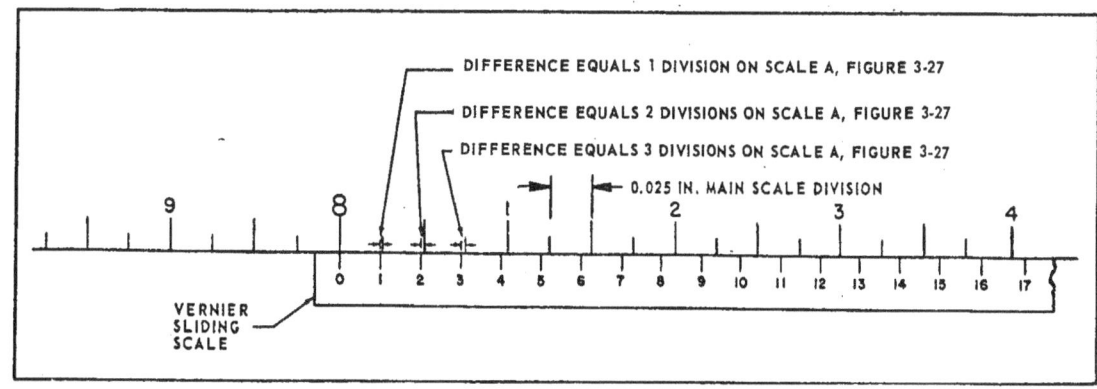

Figure 28.—Expanded view of the vernier scale.

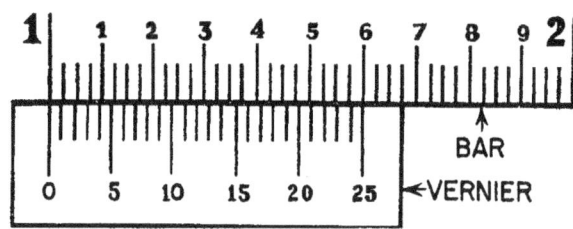

Figure 29.—English-measure vernier scale.

graduations are not significant in this position. But when the zero graduation does not align with a graduation on the main scale, it can be readily determined how many thousandths the zero missed the 0.025 inch graduation by counting the misaligned graduation at either end of the small scale. When the zero or index line on the sliding scale does not quite reach the graduation, the amount of misalignment must be subtracted, but when it passes the 0.025 graduation from which the reading is made, it must be added. This illustrates the simple arrangement to increase the accuracy of a common scale. Unfortunately, the 0.001 inch graduations are not too legible and so the system is not practical. A vernier arrangement overcomes this problem.

VERNIER SCALE ARRANGEMENT

The main difference between the vernier scale and the arrangement shown in fig. -27 is the spacing of the 25 divisions. Instead of 25 graduations crowded within the space of one main scale division, the vernier graduations are arranged at intervals exactly 0.001 inch less than the main scale graduations, as shown in fig. 28. This arrangement results in an accumulation of misalignments starting with the first vernier graduation past the zero so that each may be marked as shown with a number representing the space in thousandths to the next upper scale graduation. For example, if the zero index line would be moved past the 8 inch graduation until the vernier graduation number 5 aligned with the next main scale graduation, the exact reading would be 8 inches plus 0.005 or 8.005 inches.

READING A VERNIER CALIPER

Figure 29 shows a bar 1 inch long divided by graduations into 40 parts so that each graduation indicates one-fortieth of an inch (0.025 inch). Every fourth graduation is numbered; each number indicates tenths of an inch (4 x 0.025 inch). The vernier, which slides along the bar, is graduated into 25 divisions which together, are as long as 24 divisions on the bar. Each division of the vernier is 0.001 inch smaller than each division on the bar. Verniers that are calibrated as just explained are known as English-measure verniers. The metric-measure vernier is read the same, except that the units of measurement are in millimeters.

In figure 30, insert A illustrates the English measure vernier caliper. Insert B shows an enlarged view of the vernier section. As you can see in this figure, when the zero on the vernier coincides with the 1-inch mark, no other lines coincide until the 25th mark on the vernier.

MEASURING TOOLS AND TECHNIQUES

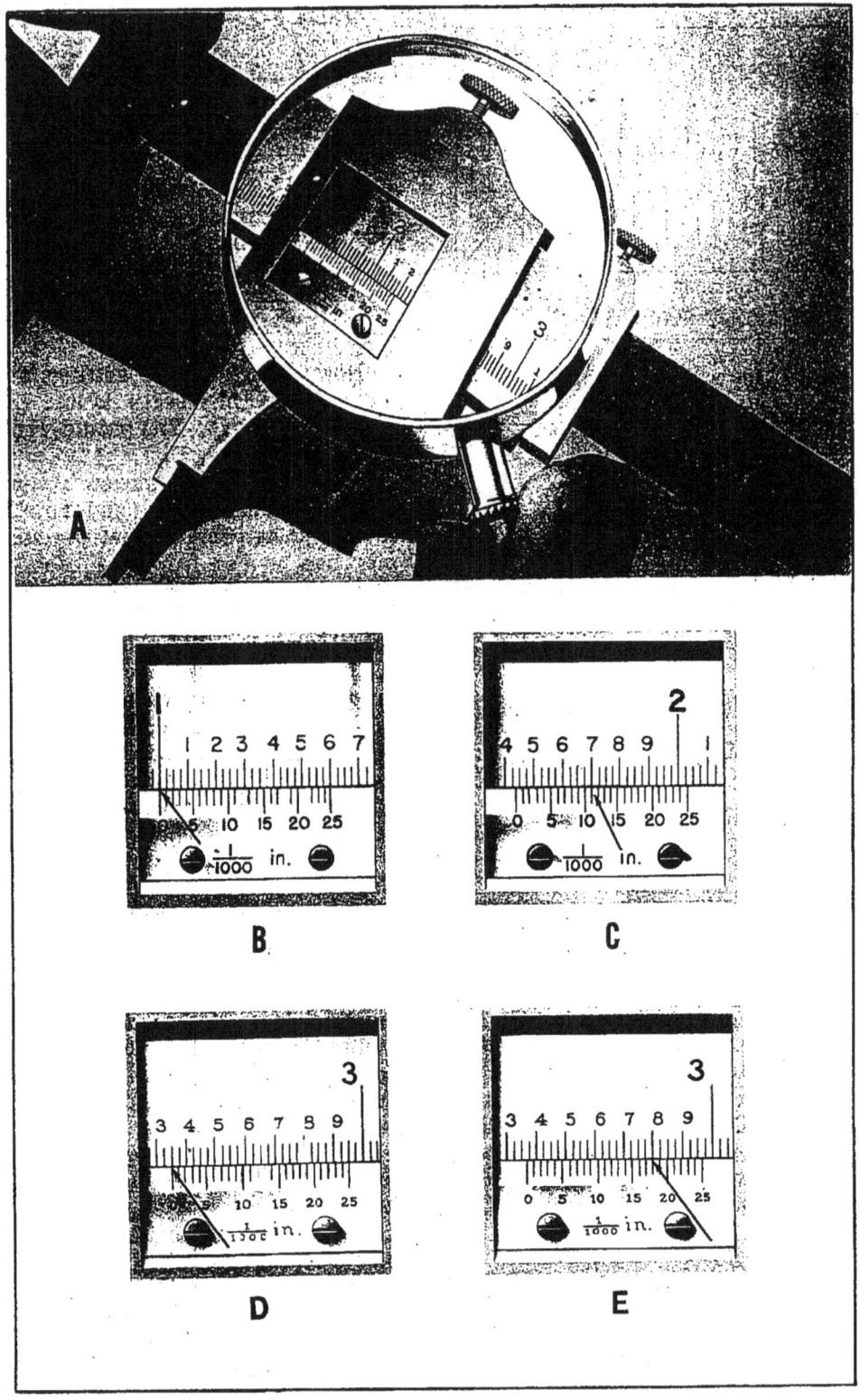

Figure -30.—Vernier caliper.

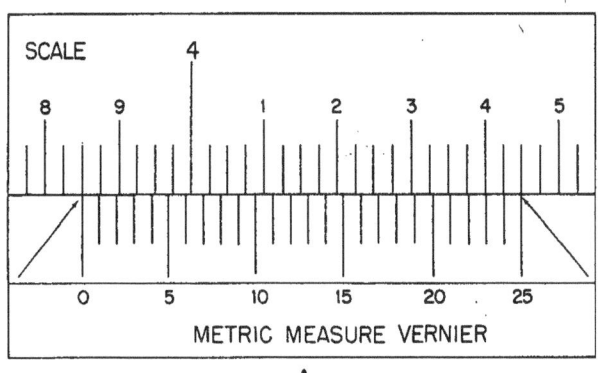

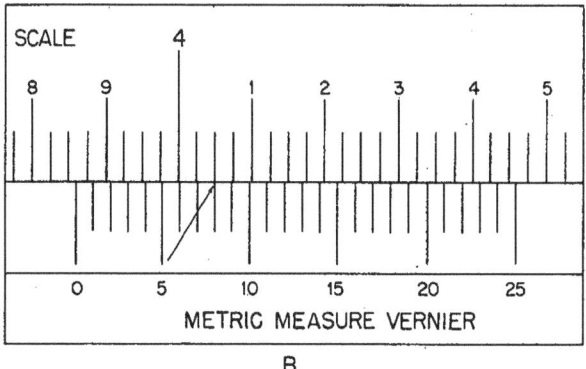

Figure 31.—Metric-measure vernier scales.

To read the caliper in insert C, write down in a column the number of inches (1.000 in.), of tenths of an inch (0.400 in.), and of thousandths of an inch that the zero mark on the vernier is from the zero mark on the rule. Because the zero mark on the vernier is a little past a 0.025 in. mark, write down the 0.025 in. and then note the highest number on the vernier where a line on the vernier coincides with one on the rule. In this case it is at the 0.011 in. line on the vernier, so you also write the 0.011 in. in the column which will then look like this:

```
1.000 in.
 .400 in.
 .025 in.
 .011 in.
1.436 in.
```

The reading on the caliper shown in insert C is 1.436 in. and was obtained by adding four separate "readings." After a little practice you will be able to make these calculations mentally.

Table 1.—Measuring Point Allowances
44.216

Size of Caliper	English Measure	Metric Measure
6" or 150 mm .	Add 0.250"...	Add 6.35 mm.
12" or 300 mm .	.300"...	7.62 mm.
24" or 600 mm .	.300"...	7.62 mm.
36" or 600 mm .	.500"...	12.70 mm.

Now try to read the settings of the two verniers shown in inserts D and E. Follow the above procedure. You should read 2.350 in. on D and 2.368 in. on E.

To read a metric-measure vernier, note the number of millimeters, and the 0.25 millimeter if the setting permits, that the zero on the vernier has moved from the zero on the scale. Then add the number of hundredths of a millimeter indicated by the line on the vernier that coincides with a line on the scale.

For example, figure 31A shows the zero graduation on the vernier coinciding with a 0.5-mm graduation on the scale resulting in a 38.50 mm reading. The reading in figure 31B indicates that 0.08 mm should be added to the scale reading and results in 38.00 mm + 0.50 mm + 0.08 mm = 38.58 mm.

If a vernier caliper is calibrated in either English measure or in metric measure, usually one side will be calibrated to take outside measurements and the other to take inside measurements directly. The vernier plate for inside measurements is set to compensate for the thickness of the measuring points of the tools. But if a vernier caliper is calibrated for both English and metric measure, one of the scales will appear on one side and one on the other. Then it will be necessary, when taking inside measurements over the measuring points, to add certain amounts to allow for their thickness. For example, table 1 shows the amounts to be added for various sizes of vernier calipers.

Outside Surface Measurements

To measure the distance between outside surfaces or the outside diameter of round stock with a vernier caliper, steady the stock with one hand and hold the caliper in the other as shown in figure 32. In the figure, the clamping

MEASURING TOOLS AND TECHNIQUES

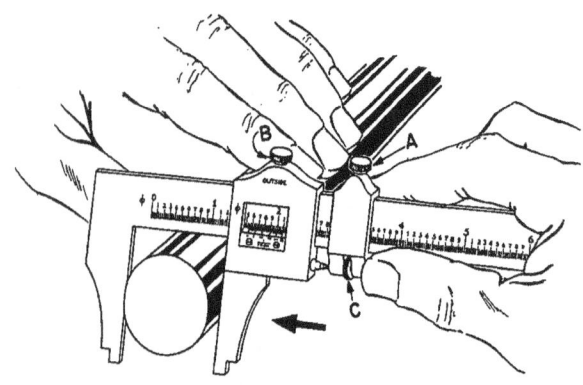

Figure 32.—Measuring an outside diameter with a vernier caliper.

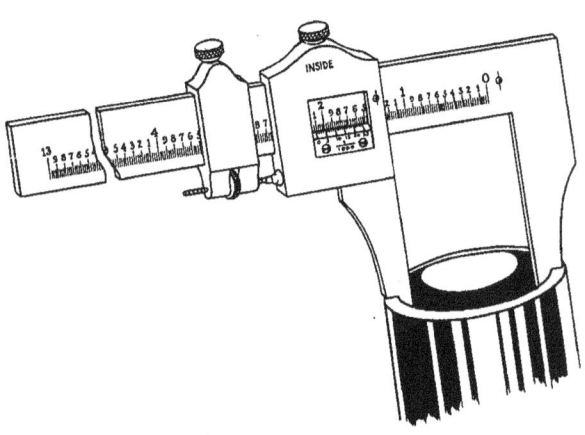

Figure 33.—Measuring an inside diameter with a vernier caliper.

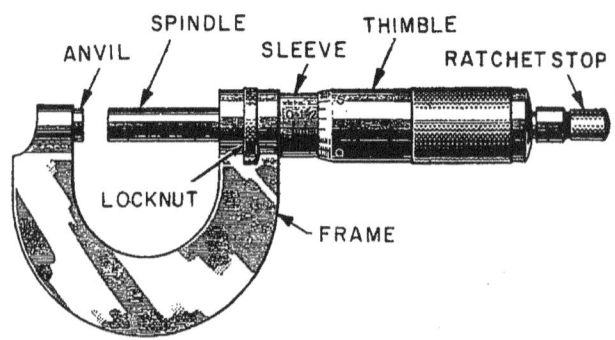

Figure 34.—Nomenclature of an outside micrometer caliper.

screws are at A and B; the horizontal adjusting screw nut is at C. With A and B loose, slide the movable jaw toward the piece being measured until it is almost in contact. Then tighten A to make C operative. With C, adjust the movable jaw to the proper feel and secure the setting with B. The reading can then be taken as explained previously.

Inside Surface Measurements

To measure the distance between inside surfaces, or the inside diameter of a hole, with a vernier caliper, use the scale marked "inside." Figure 33 shows the measuring points in place. Remember that if you are using a vernier caliper with both metric and English scales, the scales appear on opposite sides of the caliper and apply only to outside measurements. Then, to get correct inside measurements, you add to the actual reading the measuring point allowance for the size of caliper you are using. Take this allowance from table 1 or the manufacturer's instructions. The actual measurement in this case is made in the same manner as taking an outside measurement.

CARE OF THE VERNIER CALIPER

The inside faces of the jaws and the outside of the tips must be treated with great care. If they become worn, or the jaws bent, the tool will no longer give accurate readings. The accuracy of vernier calipers should be checked periodically by measuring an object of known dimension. Vernier calipers can be adjusted when they are not accurate, but the manufacturer's recommendations for this adjustment must be followed. Keep vernier calipers lightly oiled to prevent rust and keep them stored away from heavy tools.

IV. MICROMETER

In much wider use than the vernier caliper is the micrometer commonly called the "mike." It is important that a person who is working with machinery or in a machine shop thoroughly understand the mechanical principles, construction, use, and care of the micrometer. Figure 34 shows an outside micrometer caliper with the various parts clearly indicated. Micrometers are used to measure distances to the nearest one thousandth of an inch. The measurement is usually expressed or written as a

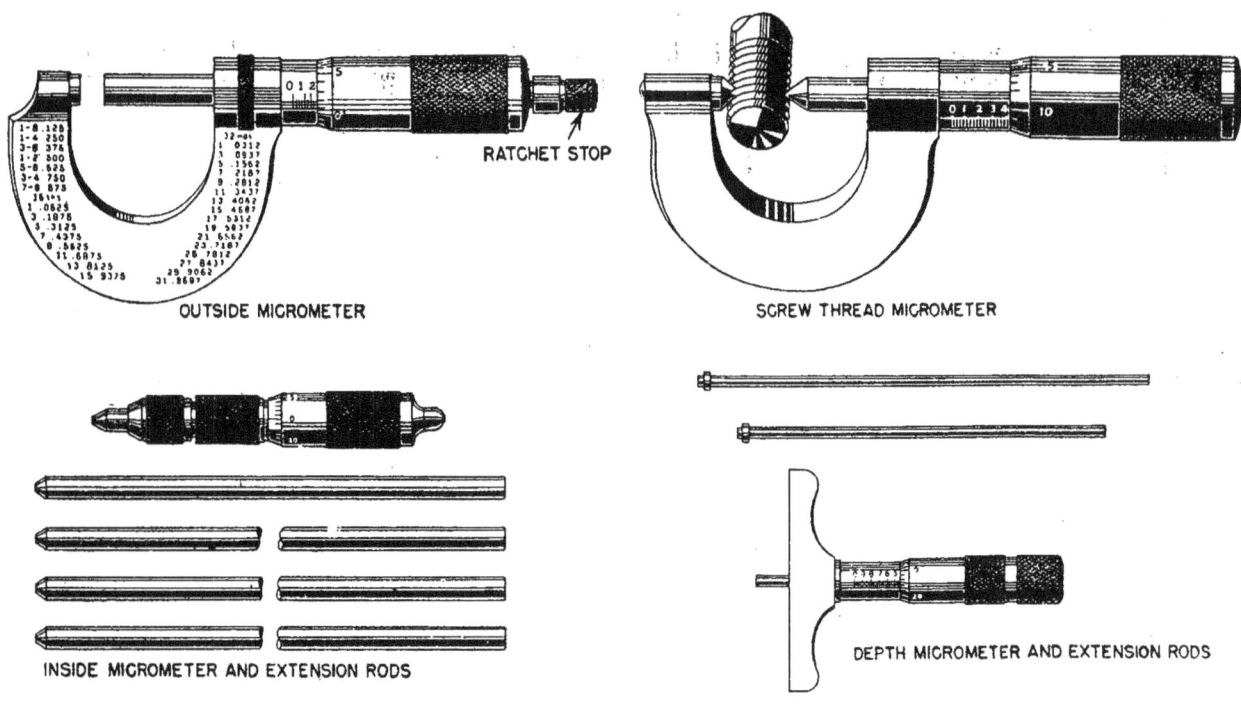

Figure 35.—Common types of micrometers.

decimal; so you must know the method of writing and reading decimals.

TYPES

There are three types of micrometers that are most commonly used:
the outside micrometer caliper (including the screw thread micrometer), the inside micrometer, and the depth micrometer. (See fig. 35.) The outside micrometer is used for measuring outside dimensions, such as the diameter of a piece of round stock. The screw thread micrometer is used to determine the pitch diameter of screws. The inside micrometer is used for measuring inside dimensions, as for example, the inside diameter of a tube or hole, the bore of a cylinder, or the width of a recess. The depth micrometer is used for measuring the depth of holes or recesses.

SELECTING THE PROPER MICROMETER

The types of micrometers commonly used are made so that the longest movement possible between the spindle and the anvil is 1 inch. This movement is called the "range." The frames of micrometers, however, are available in a wide variety of sizes, from 1 inch up to as large as 24 inches. The range of a 1-inch micrometer is from 0 to 1 inch; in other words, it can be used on work where the part to be measured is 1 inch or less. A 2-inch micrometer has a range from 1 inch to 2 inches, and will measure only work between 1 and 2 inches thick; a 6-inch micrometer has a range from 5 to 6 inches, and will measure only work between 5 and 6 inches thick. It is necessary, therefore, that the mechanic in selecting a micrometer first find the approximate size of the work to the nearest inch, and then select a micrometer that will fit it. For example, to find the exact diameter of a piece of round stock; use a rule and find the approximate diameter of the stock. If it is found to be approximately 3 1/4 inches, a micrometer with a 3- to 4-inch range would be required to measure the exact diameter. Similarly, with inside and depth micrometers, rods of suitable lengths must be fitted into the tool to get the approximate dimension within an inch, after which the exact measurement is read by turning the thimble. The size of a micrometer indicates the size of the largest work it will measure.

MEASURING TOOLS AND TECHNIQUES

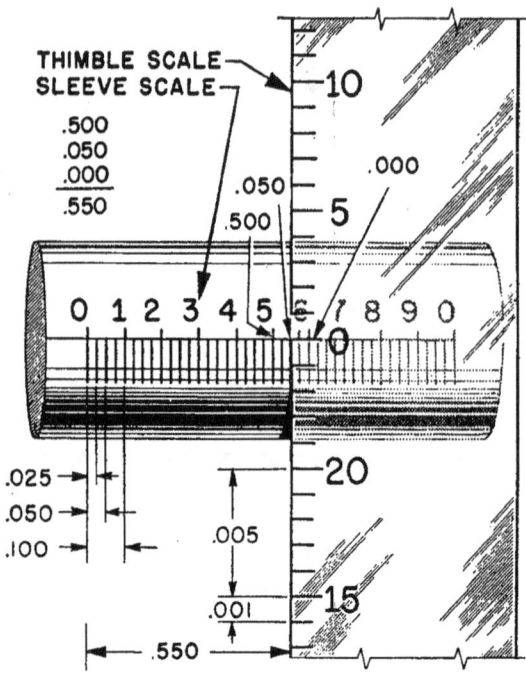

Figure 36.—Sleeve and thimble scales of a micrometer (enlarged).

READING A MICROMETER CALIPER

The sleeve and thimble scales of the micrometer caliper have been enlarged in figure 36. To understand these scales, you need to know that the threaded section on the spindle, which revolves, has 40 threads per inch. Therefore, every time the thimble completes a revolution, the spindle advances or recedes 1/40" (0.025").

Notice that the horizontal line on the sleeve is divided into 40 equal parts per inch. Every fourth graduation is numbered 1, 2, 3, 4, etc., representing 0.100", 0.200", etc. When you turn the thimble so that its edge is over the first sleeve line past the "0" on the thimble scale, the spindle has opened 0.025". If you turn the spindle to the second mark, it has moved 0.025" plus 0.025" or 0.050". You use the scale on the thimble to complete your reading when the edge of the thimble stops between graduated lines. This scale is divided into 25 equal parts, each part representing 1/25 of a turn. And 1/25 of 0.025" is 0.001". As you can see, every fifth line on the thimble scale is marked 5, 10, 15,

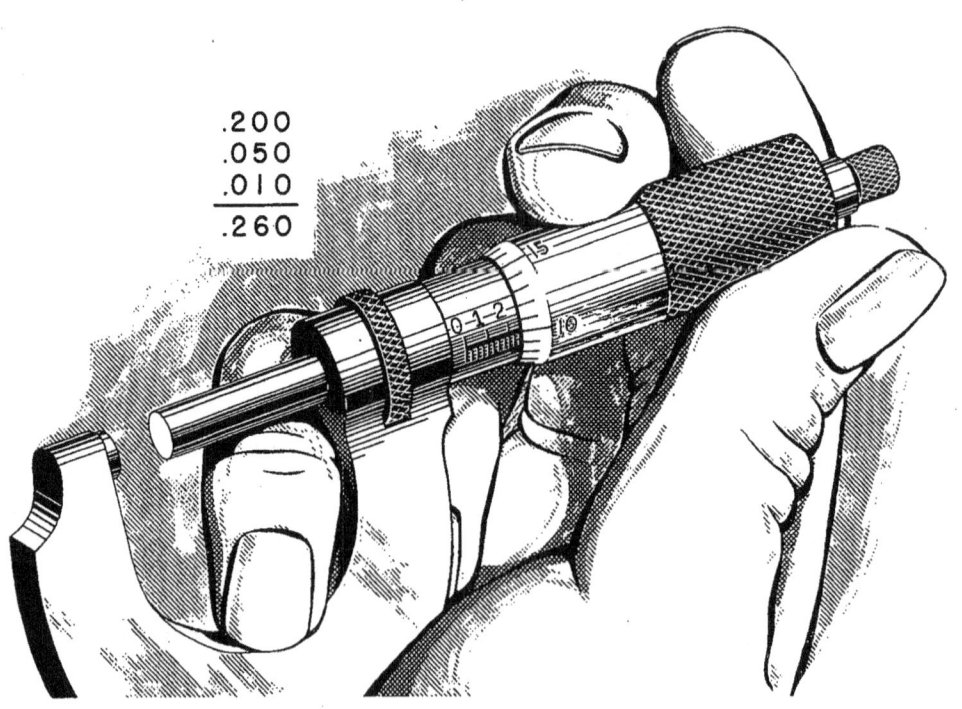

Figure 37.—Read a micrometer caliper.

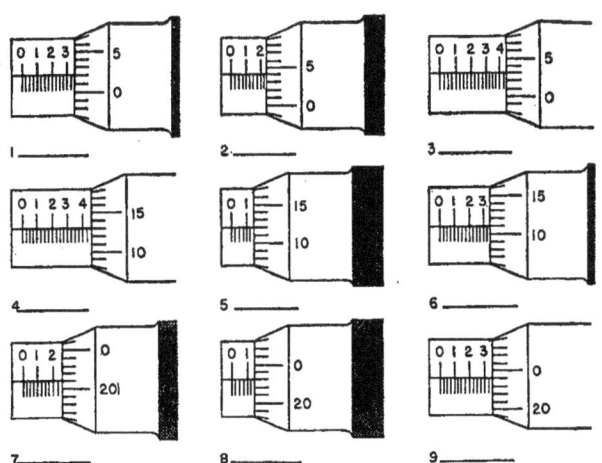

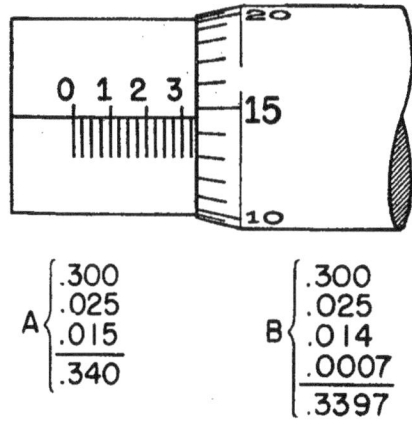

Figure 39.—Interpolating a micrometer reading.

Answers for checking—

1. = 0.327   4. = 0.438   7. = 0.246
2. = 0.229   5. = 0.137   8. = 0.148
3. = 0.428   6. = 0.336   9. = 0.349

Figure 38.—Micrometer-reading exercises.

etc. The thimble scale, therefore, permits you to take very accurate readings to the thousandths of an inch, and, since you can estimate between the divisions on the thimble scale, fairly accurate readings to the ten thousandth of an inch are possible.

The closeup in figure 37 will help you understand how to take a complete micrometer reading. Count the units on the thimble scale and add them to the reading on the sleeve scale. The reading in the figure shows a sleeve reading of 0.250" (the thimble having stopped slightly more than halfway between 2 and 3 on the sleeve) with the 10th line on the thimble scale coinciding with the horizontal sleeve line. Number 10 on this scale means that the spindle has moved away from the anvil an additional 10 x 0.001" or 0.010". Add this amount to the 0.250" sleeve reading, and the total distance is 0.260".

Read each of the micrometer settings in figure 38 so that you can be sure of yourself when you begin to use this tool on the job. The correct readings are given following the figure so that you can check yourself.

Figure 39 shows a reading in which the horizontal line falls between two graduations on the thimble scale and is closer to the 15 graduation than it is to the 14. To read this to THREE decimal places, refer to figure 39 and calculation A. To read it to FOUR decimal places, estimate the number of tenths of the distance between thimble-scale graduations the horizontal line has fallen. Each tenth of this distance equals one ten-thousandth (0.0001) of an inch. Add the ten-thousandths to the reading as shown in the calculations of figure 39B.

READING A VERNIER
MICROMETER CALIPER

Many times you will be required to work to exceptionally precise dimensions. Under these conditions it is better to use a micrometer that is accurate to ten-thousandths of an inch. This degree of accuracy is obtained by the addition of a vernier scale. This scale, shown in figure 40, furnishes the fine readings between the lines on the thimble rather than making you estimate. The 10 spaces on the vernier are equivalent to 9 spaces on the thimble. Therefore, each unit on the vernier scale is equal to 0.0009" and the difference between the sizes of the units on each scale is 0.0001".

When a line on the thimble scale does not coincide with the horizontal sleeve line, you can determine the additional space beyond the readable thimble mark by finding which vernier mark coincides with a line on the thimble scale. Add this number, as that many ten-thousandths of an inch, to the original reading. In figure 41 see how the second line on the vernier scale coincides with a line on the thimble scale.

MEASURING TOOLS AND TECHNIQUES

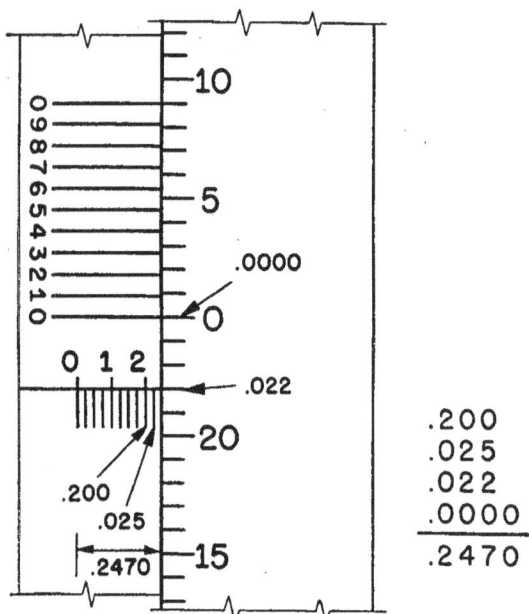

Figure 40.—Vernier scale on a micrometer.

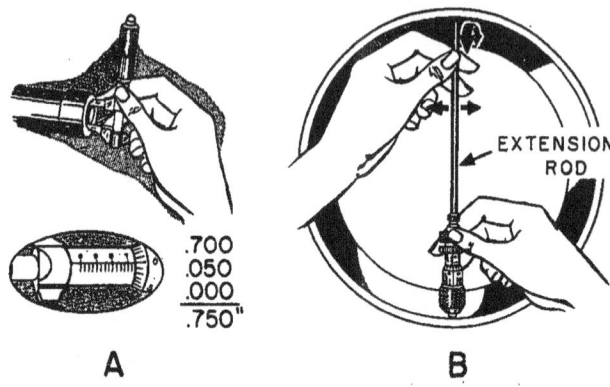

Figure 42.—Measuring an inside diameter with an inside caliper.

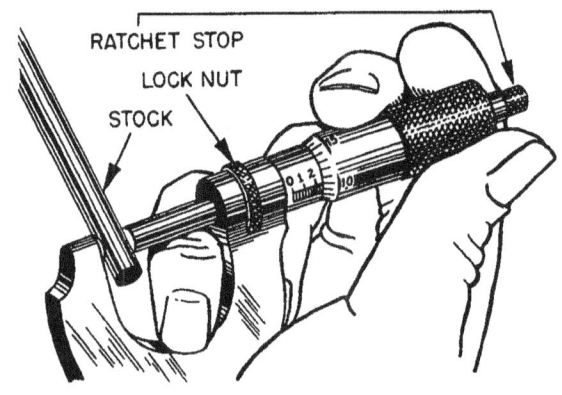

Figure 43.—Measuring round stock with a micrometer caliper.

MEASURING HOLE DIAMETERS WITH AN INSIDE MICROMETER CALIPER

To measure the diameter of small holes from 0.2" to 1" in diameter, an inside micrometer caliper of the jaw type as shown in figure 42A may be used. Note that the figures on both the thimble and the barrel are reversed, increasing in the opposite direction from those on an outside micrometer caliper. This is because this micrometer reads inside measurements. Thus as you turn the thimble clockwise on this micrometer, the measuring surfaces move farther apart and the reading increases. (On an outside micrometer caliper, as you turn the thimble clockwise, the measuring surfaces move closer together and the reading decreases.)

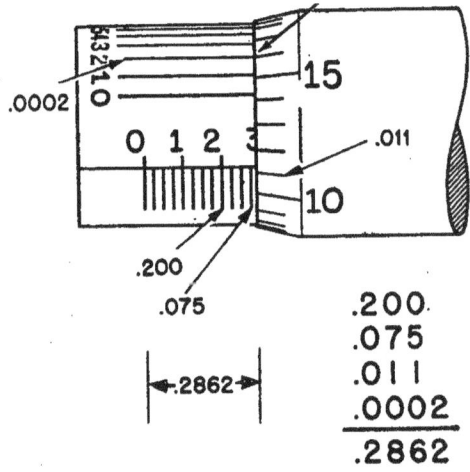

Figure 41.—Read a vernier micrometer caliper.

This means that the 0.011 mark on the thimble scale has been advanced an additional 0.0002" beyond the horizontal sleeve line. When you add this to the other readings, the reading will be 0.200 + 0.075 + 0.011 + 0.0002 or 0.2862", as shown.

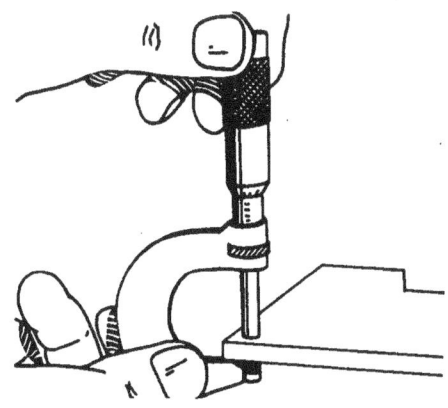

Figure 44.—Measuring flat stock with a micrometer caliper.

For holes from 2" up to several feet in diameter, select the inside micrometer having extension rods whose range includes the required dimension. The extension rod marked "6-7," for example, when inserted into the head of the micrometer, will measure inside diameters from 6" to 7". The shoulder on the rod must seat properly to ensure a correct reading. Figure 42B shows that, for large measurements, both hands are used to set the micrometer for checking a diameter. Hole one end in place with one hand as you "feel" for the maximum possible setting by moving the other end from left to right, and in and out of the hole with the other hand. When no left-to-right movement is possible, and a slight drag is noticed on the in-and-out swing, take the reading.

MEASURING ROUND STOCK

When measuring the diameter of a small piece of round stock, hold the stock to be measured in one hand. Hold the micrometer in the other hand so that the thimble rests between the thumb and the forefinger. (See fig. 43.) The third finger is then in a position to hold the frame against the palm of the hand. The frame is supported in this manner and makes it easy to guide the work over the anvil. The thumb and forefinger are in position to turn the thimble either directly or through the ratchet and bring the spindle over against the surface being measured.

Turn the spindle down to contact by "feel," or else use the ratchet stop. Your feel should produce the same contact pressure and therefore the same reading as that produced when the ratchet stop is used. Develop your "feel" by measuring a certain dimension both with and without the aid of the ratchet stop. When you have the correct feel, you will get the same readings by both methods.

In measuring round stock the feel must be very light because there is only a line contact between the spindle and the stock and the anvil and the stock. Therefore the contact area is exceptionally small, causing a proportionally high contact pressure per unit of area. This tends to give a reading smaller than the true reading unless the light feel is used. Moreover, in measuring a ball from a ball bearing, the contact is at only two points, so the contact area is again very small, which results in a tremendous pressure per unit of area. This condition requires only the lightest possible contact pressure to give a true reading.

Hold the micrometer lightly and for only as long as is necessary to make the measurement. Wrapping the hand around it or holding it for too long a time will cause expansion of the metal and will introduce errors in measurement. Read the setting on the thimble scale (if the object is small) without removing the micrometer caliper from the object.

MEASURING A FLAT SURFACE

When measuring a flat surface with a micrometer caliper, the entire area of both the anvil and the spindle is in contact with the surface being measured. This causes a proportionally low contact pressure per unit of area. Therefore the "feel" should be slightly heavier than when measuring round stock.

On large flat work, it is necessary to have the work stationary and positioned to permit access for the micrometer. The proper method of holding a micrometer when checking a part too large to be held in one hand is shown in figure 44. The frame is held by one hand to position it and to locate it square to the measured surface. The other hand operates the thimble either directly or through the ratchet. A large flat surface should be measured in several places to determine the amount of variation. It is good practice to lock the spindle in place with the locknut before removing the micrometer from the part being measured. After removal of the micrometer the measurement indicated on the thimble scale can then be read.

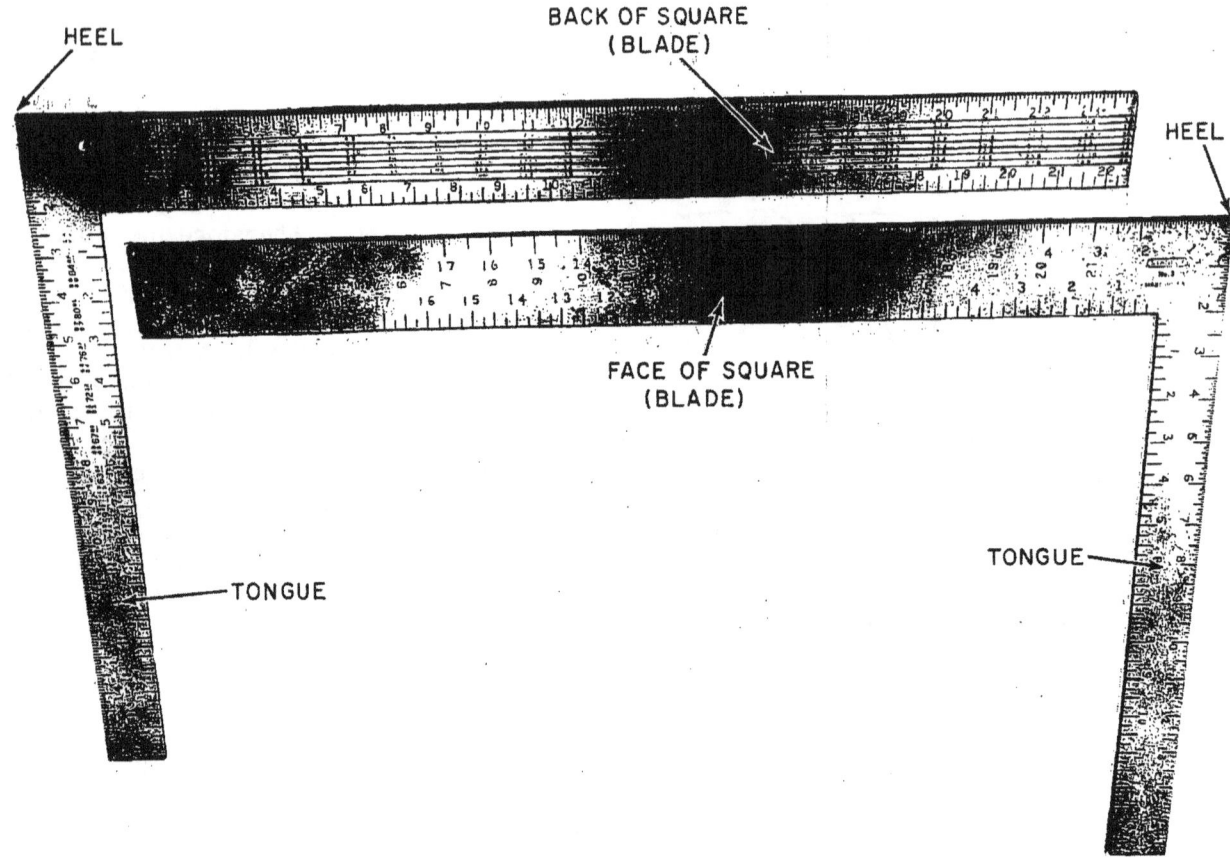

Figure 45.—Carpenter's square.

To retain a particular setting, in cases where several pieces are to be gaged, lock the spindle in place with the locknut. When a piece is "gaged" with a micrometer whose spindle is locked to a particular setting, the piece can quickly be identified as oversize, correct size, or undersize.

CARE OF MICROMETERS

Keep micrometers clean and lightly oiled. Make sure they are placed in a case or box when they are not in use. Anvil faces must be protected from damage and must not be cleaned with emery cloth or other abrasive.

V. SQUARES

Squares are primarily used for testing and checking trueness of an angle or for laying out lines on materials. Most squares have a rule marked on their edge. As a result they may also be used for measuring. There are several types of squares commonly used.

CARPENTER'S SQUARE

The size of a carpenter's steel square (fig. 45) is usually 12 inches x 8 inches, 24 inches x 16 inches, or 24 inches x 18 inches. The flat sides of the blade and the tongue are graduated in inches and fractions of an inch. (The square also contains information that helps to simplify or eliminate the need for computations in many woodworking tasks.) The most common uses for this square are laying out and squaring up large patterns, and for testing the flatness and squareness of large surfaces. Squaring is accomplished by placing the square at right angles to adjacent surfaces and observing if light shows between the work and the square.

One type of carpenter's square (framing) has additional tables engraved on the square. With

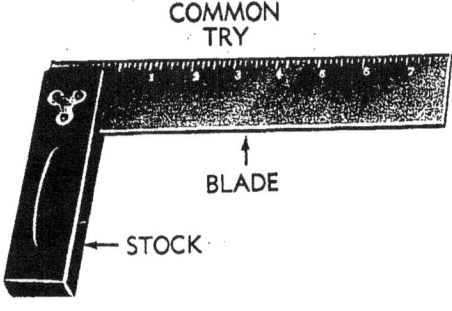

Figure 46.—Common try square.

Figure 47.—Sliding T-bevel.

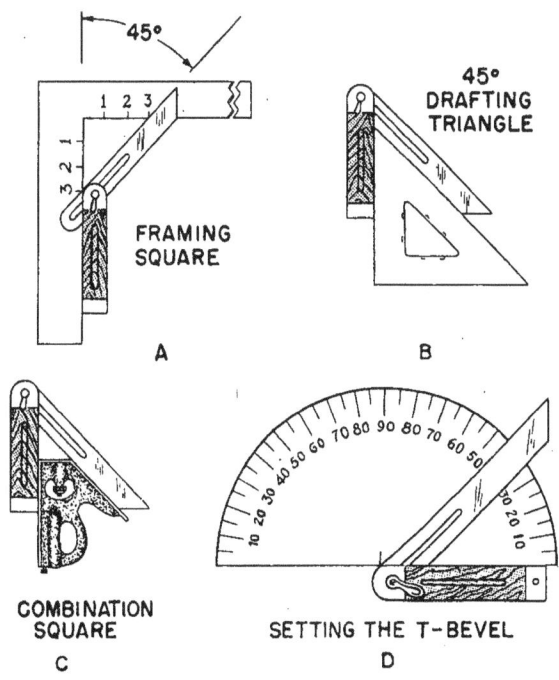

Figure 48.—Adjusting a sliding T-bevel to a desired setting.

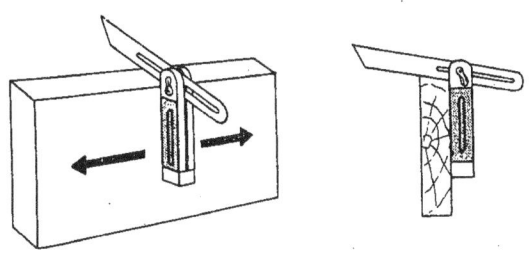

Figure 49.—Testing the trueness of a bevel.

the framing square, the craftsman can perform calculations rapidly and layout rafters, oblique joints and stairs.

TRY SQUARE

The try square (fig. 46) consists of two parts at right angles to each other; a thick wood or iron stock and a thin, steel blade. Most try squares are made with the blades graduated in inches and fractions of an inch. The blade length varies from 2 inches to 12 inches. This square is used for setting or checking lines or surfaces which have to be at right angles to each other.

SLIDING T BEVEL

The sliding T-bevel (fig. 47) is an adjustable try square with a slotted beveled blade. Blades are normally 6 or 8 inches long. The sliding T-bevel is used for laying out angles other than right angles, and for testing constructed angles such as bevels. These squares are made with either wood or metal handles.

Adjustments

To adjust a sliding T-bevel to a desired setting, loosen the blade screw, at the round end of the handle, just enough to permit the blade to slide along its slot and to rotate with slight friction.

To set the blade at a 45° angle, hold the handle against a framing square, as shown in figure 48A, with the blade intersecting equal graduations on the tongue and blade of the square. Or: hold the bevel against the edges of

MEASURING TOOLS AND TECHNIQUES

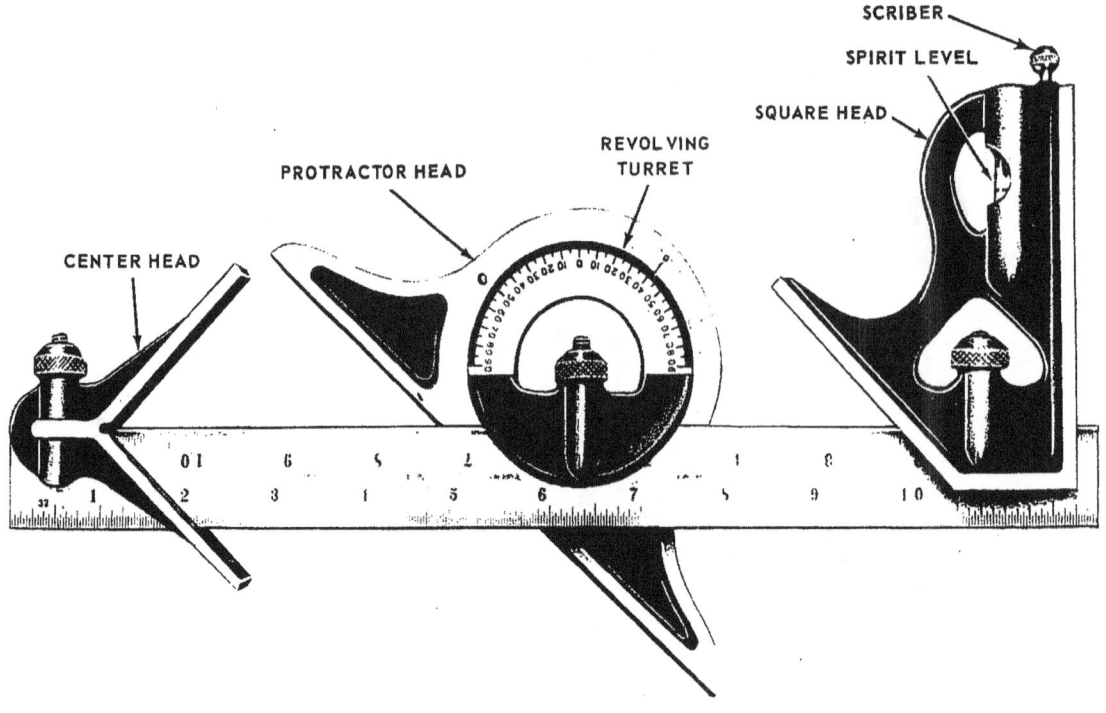

Figure 50.—Combination square set.

a 45° drafting triangle as shown in figure 48B. When using drafting triangles for setting a sliding T-bevel, different size triangles must be used for each different setting. A 45° angle can also be set by using the squaring head of a combination set as shown in figure 48C.

A sliding T-bevel can be set to any desired angle by using a protractor. Loosen the blade screw as before, and hold the bevel with its blade passing through the graduation selected, and the center of the protractor as shown at (D) in figure 48.

Constructed Angle Verification

To test a chamfer or bevel for trueness, set the T-bevel to the required angle, and hold the handle to the working face of the stock being tested. Face a source of light, and with the blade brought into contact with the surface to be tested, pass the blade along the length of the surface. (See fig. 49.) The appearance of light between the blade and the surface of the stock indicates where the angle is not correct. Figure 49 indicates the checking of a bevel, but testing the trueness of a chamfer is accomplished in the same way.

COMBINATION SQUARE

A combination square is equipped with movable heads called a SQUARE HEAD, PROTRACTOR HEAD, and a CENTER HEAD. These combine the functions of several tools, and serve a wide variety of purposes. (See figs. 50 and 51.) Normally, only one head is used at a time.

The SQUARE HEAD may be adjusted to any position along the scale and clamped securely in place. The combination square can thus serve as a depth gage, height gage, or scribing gage. Two of the faces of the head are ground at right angles to each other, and a third face at 45 degrees. A small spirit level is built into the head for checking whether surfaces are plumb, and a small scriber is housed in a hole in the end of the head for marking layout lines.

The CENTER HEAD can be slid on to the blade in place of the square head. This is a V-shaped member so designed that the center of the 90 degree V will lie exactly along one edge of the blade. This attachment is useful when locating the exact center of round stock.

The PROTRACTOR HEAD, commonly called a bevel protractor, can be attached to the scale,

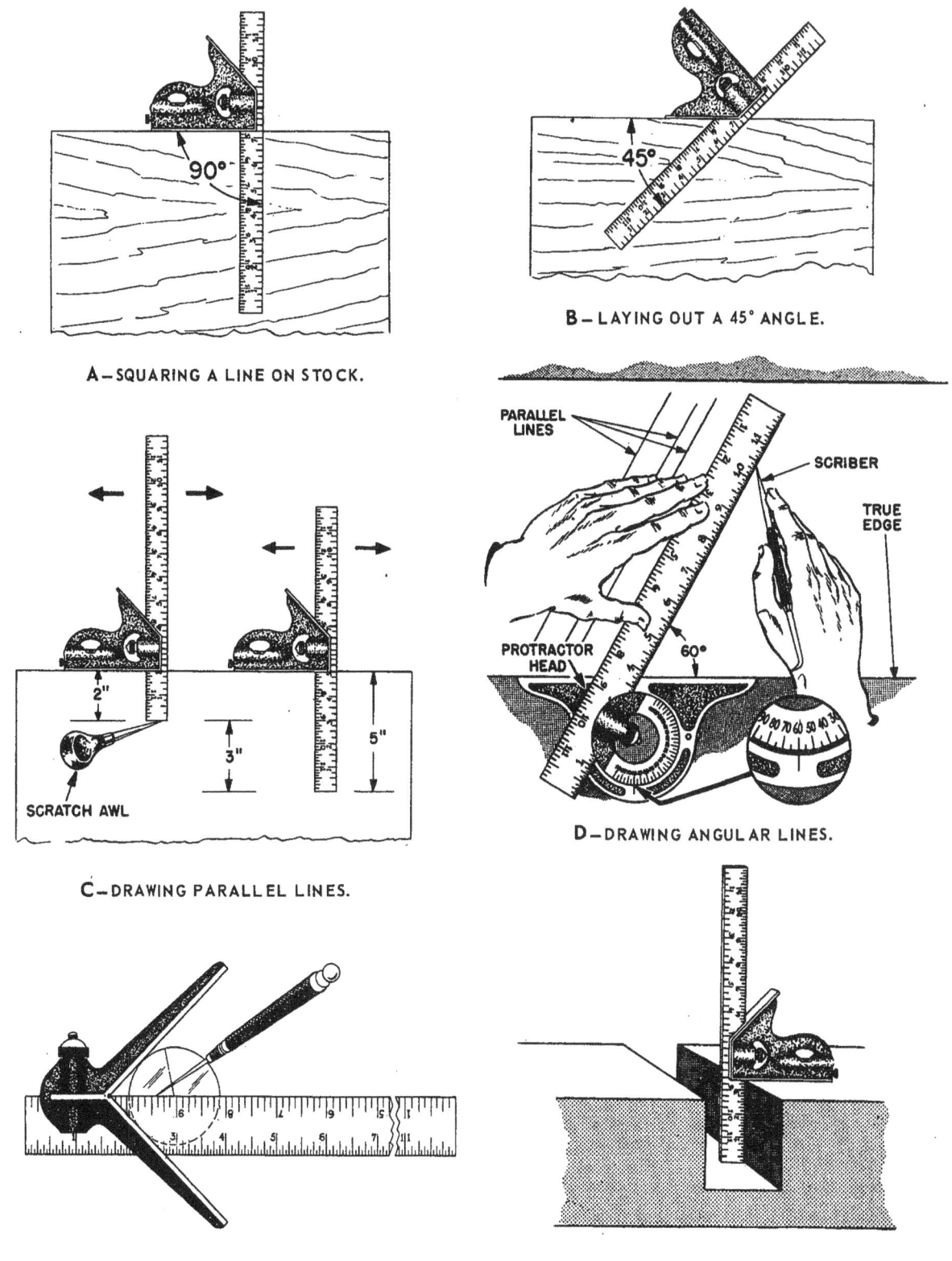

Figure 51.—Combination square applications.

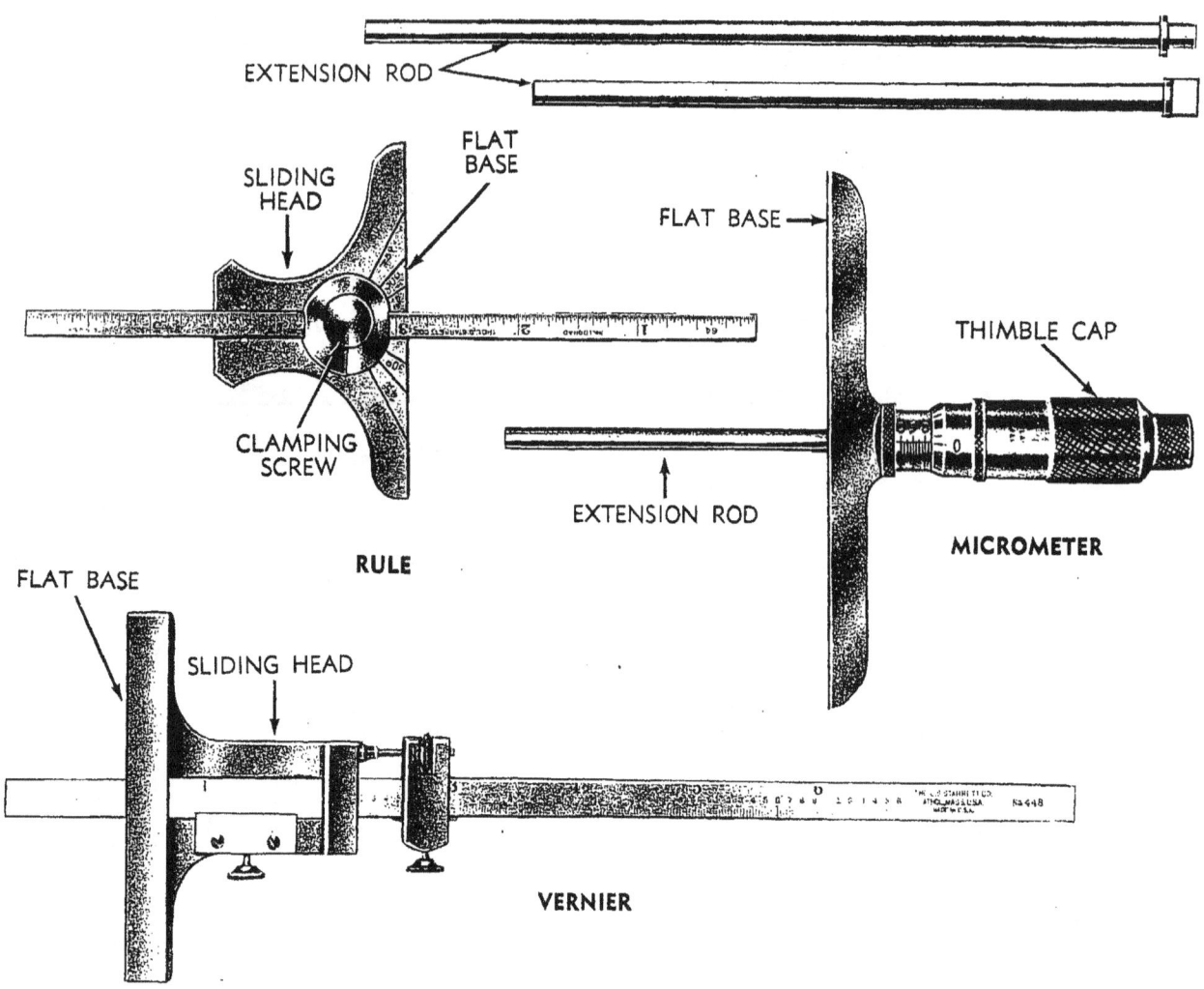

Figure 52.—Types of depth gages.

adjusted to any position on it, and turned and locked at any desired angle. Angular graduations usually read from 0 to 180 degrees both ways, permitting the supplement of the angle to be read. A spirit level may be included on some models forming, in effect, an adjustable level to show any required degree.

Care of Squares

Make certain the blades, heads, dials, and all accessories are clean. Apply a light coat of oil on all metal surfaces to prevent rusting when not in use. Do not use squares for purposes other than those intended. When storing squares or bevels for long periods of time, apply a liberal amount of oil or rust-preventive compound to all surfaces, wrap in oiled paper or cloth, and place in containers or on racks away from other tools.

VI. MISCELLANEOUS GAGES

There are a number of miscellaneous gages. The depth gage, feeler gage, thread gage, telescoping gage, dividers, and plumb bob are among some of the gages that will be discussed here.

DEPTH GAGE

A depth gage is an instrument for measuring the depth of holes, slots, counterbores, recesses,

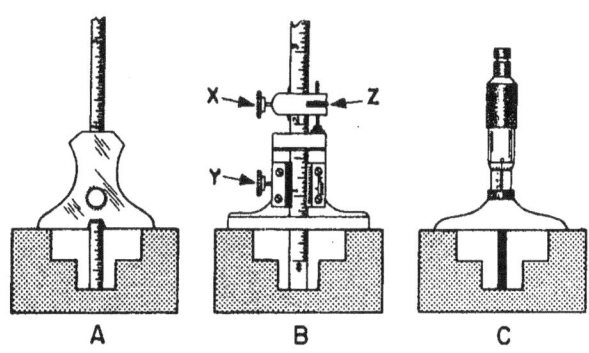

Figure 53.—Using depth gages.

and the distance from a surface to some recessed part. The RULE DEPTH GAGE and the MICROMETER DEPTH GAGE are the most commonly used. (See fig. 52.)

The rule depth gage is a graduated rule with a sliding head designed to bridge a hole or slot, and to hold the rule perpendicular to the surface on which the measurement is taken. This type has a measuring range of 0 to 5 inches. The sliding head has a clamping screw so that it may be clamped in any position. The sliding head has a flat base which is perpendicular to the axis of the rule and ranges in size from 2 to 2 5/8 inches in width and from 1/8 to 1/4 inch in thickness.

The micrometer depth gage consists of a flat base attached to the barrel (sleeve) of a micrometer head. These gages have a range from 0 to 9 inches, depending on the length of extension rod used. The hollow micrometer screw (the threads on which the thimble rotates) itself has a range of either 1/2 or 1 inch. Some are provided with a ratchet stop. The flat base ranges in size from 2 to 6 inches. Several extension rods are normally supplied with this type of gage.

To measure the depth of a hole or slot with reasonable accuracy, use a depth gage as shown in figure 53A. Hold the body of the depth gage against the surface from which the depth is to be measured and extend the scale into the hole or slot. Tighten the setscrew to maintain the setting. Withdraw the tool from the work and read the depth on the scale.

To measure the depth of a hole or slot with more accuracy than is possible with an ordinary depth gage, place a vernier depth gage over the slot as shown in figure 53B. Notice

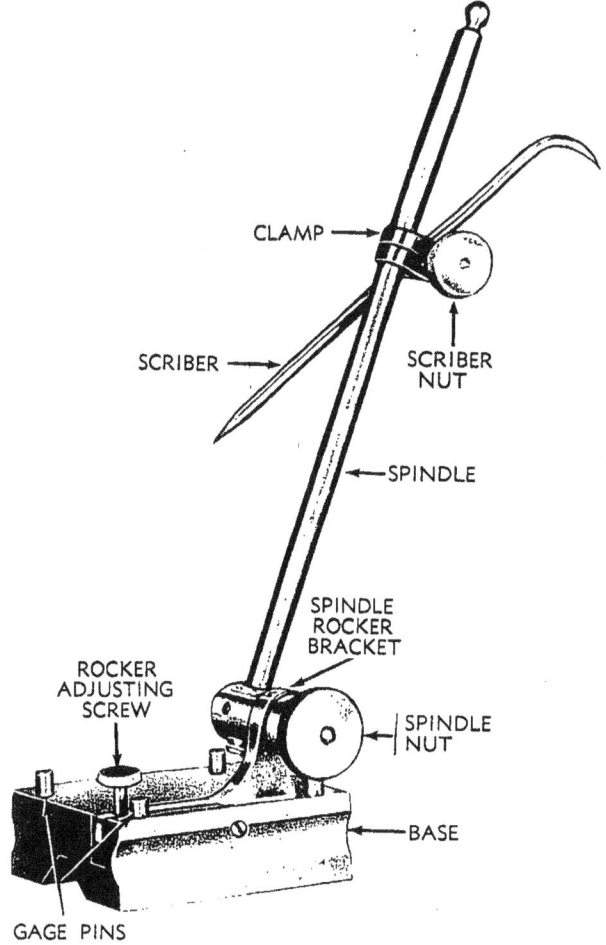

Figure 54.—Surface gage.

the clamping screws are at X and Y; the horizontal adjusting screw nut is at Z. With X and Y loose, slide the scale down into the slot being measured until it is almost in contact. Then tighten X to make Z operative. With Z, adjust the scale to the "proper feel" and secure the setting with Y. By proper feel we mean the adjustment at which you first notice contact between the end of the scale and the bottom of the slot. Then read the setting as described under "Reading a vernier scale."

To set the vernier depth gage to a particular setting, loosen both setscrews at X and at Y and slide the scale through the gage to the approximate setting. Tighten the setscrew at X, turn the knurled nut at Z until the desired setting is made, and tighten the setscrew at Y to hold the setting.

MEASURING TOOLS AND TECHNIQUES

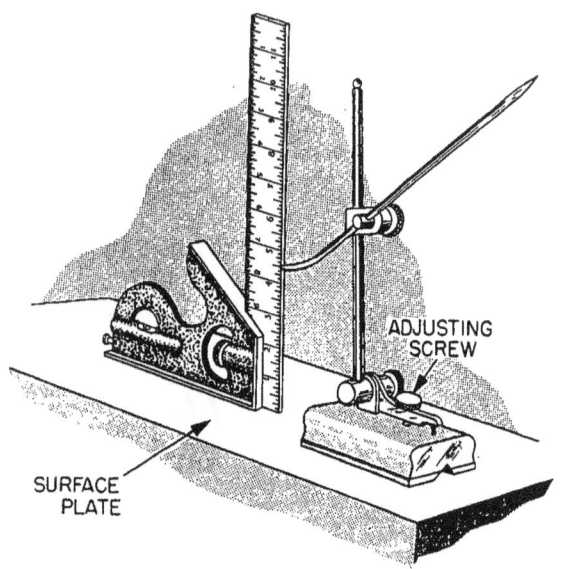

Figure 55.—Setting a surface gage to height.

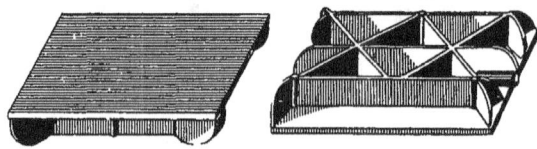

Figure 56.—Surface plate.

To measure the depth of a hole or slot, as shown in figure 53C, with more accuracy than is possible with either an ordinary depth gage or a vernier depth gage, place a micrometer depth gage over the slot and adjust the thimble until the contact of the spindle causes the ratchet stop to slip. Remove the micrometer from the work and read the micrometer. Remember, if extension rods are used, the total depth reading will be the sum of the length of the rods plus the reading on the micrometer.

SURFACE GAGE

A surface gage is a measuring tool generally used to transfer measurements to work by scribing a line, and to indicate the accuracy or parallelism of surfaces.

The surface gage (fig. 54) consists of a base with an adjustable spindle to which may be clamped a scriber or an indicator. Surface gages are made in several sizes and are classified by the length of the spindle, the smallest spindle being 4 inches long, the average 9 or 12 inches long and the largest 18 inches. The scriber is fastened to the spindle with a clamp. The bottom and the front end of the base of the surface gage have deep V-grooves cut in them, which allow the gage to be seated on a cylindrical surface.

The spindle of a surface gage may be adjusted to any position with respect to the base and tightened in place with the spindle nut. The rocket adjusting screw provides for the finer adjustment of the spindle by pivoting the spindle rocker bracket. The scriber can be positioned at any height and in any desired direction on the spindle by tightening the scriber nut. The scriber may also be mounted directly in the spindle nut mounting, in place of the spindle, and used where the working space is limited and the height of the work is within range of the scriber.

To set a surface gage for height, first wipe off the top of a layout table or surface plate and the bottom of the surface gage. Use either a combination square or a rule with rule holder to get the measurement. A rule alone cannot be held securely without wobbling and consequently an error in setting generally results. Because a combination square is generally available, its use for setting a surface gage is explained in this section.

Place the squaring head of a combination square on a flat surface as shown in figure 55, and secure the scale so that the end is in contact with the surface. Move the surface gage into position and set the scriber to the approximate height required, using the adjusting clamp that holds the scriber onto the spindle. Make the final adjustment for the exact height required (4 1/2 inches in this case) with the adjusting screw on the base of the gage.

SURFACE PLATE

A surface plate provides a true, smooth, plane surface. It is a flat-topped steel or cast iron plate that is heavily ribbed and reinforced on the under side. (See fig. 56.) It is often used in conjunction with a surface gage as a level base on which the gage and part to be measured are placed to obtain accurate measurements. The surface plate can also be used for testing parts that must have flat surfaces.

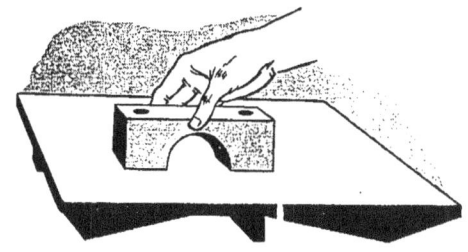

Figure 57.—Testing a surface for flatness.

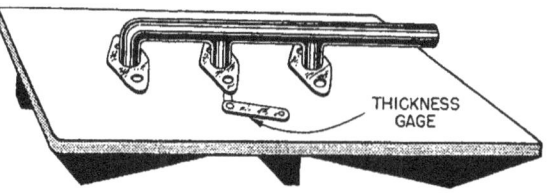

Figure 59.—Checking the conformity of a flat surface.

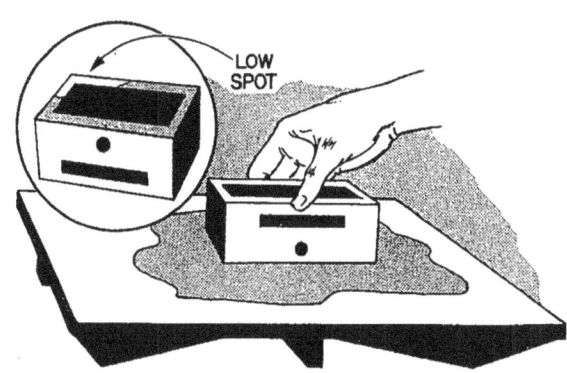

Figure 58.—Using prussian blue to aid in testing a flat surface.

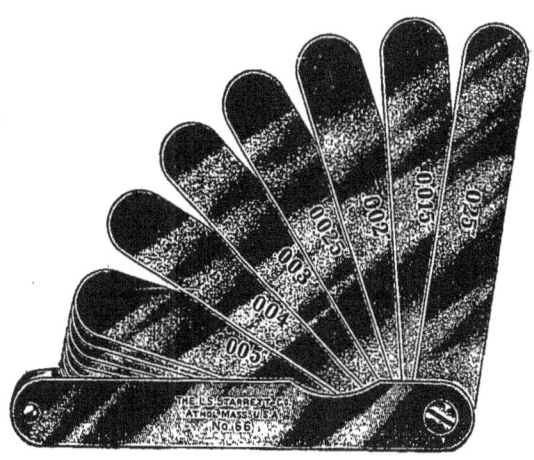

Figure 60.—Thickness gages.

To test a surface for flatness, carefully clean it and remove all burrs. Then place the surface of the object on a flat area such as the surface plate in figure 57. Any rocking motion that is apparent will indicate a variance from flatness of the piece being tested.

For very fine work, lightly coat the surface plate with prussian blue (bearing blue) and move the piece being tested across the blue surface. (See fig. 58.) The low spots on the surface being tested will not take the blue; the high spots will. See insert in figure 58.

To determine how much variation there is from flatness—and where it is—you can insert leaves of a thickness gage to determine the amount of variation of flatness. Remember to add the thickness of all leaves together to get the total variation. (See fig. 59.)

A surface also may be tested for flatness with a straightedge. To do this, clean the surface thoroughly and hold the straightedge on the surface in several places as you look toward a source of light. The light showing between the surface being tested and the straightedge will reveal the low spots.

Care of Surface Plates

The surface plate should be covered when not in use to prevent scratching, nicking, and denting. It must be handled carefully to prevent warping (twisting). Never use the surface plate as an anvil or workbench—except for precision layout work (marking and measuring).

THICKNESS (FEELER) GAGE

Thickness (feeler) gages are used for checking and measuring small openings such as contact point clearances, narrow slots, etc. These gages are made in many shapes and sizes and, as shown in figure 60, thickness gages can be made with multiple blades (usually 2 to 26). Each blade is a specific number of thousandths of an inch thick. This enables the application of one tool to the measurement of a variety of

MEASURING TOOLS AND TECHNIQUES

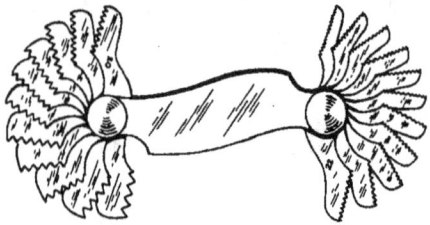

Figure 61.—Screw pitch gage.

GAGING SINGLE PITCH EXTERNAL THREAD

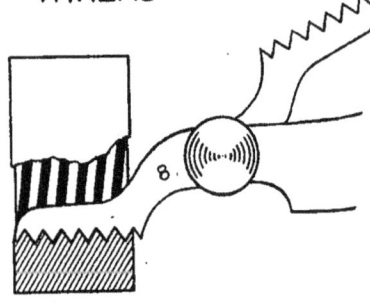

GAGING INTERNAL THREAD

Figure 62.—Using a screw pitch gage.

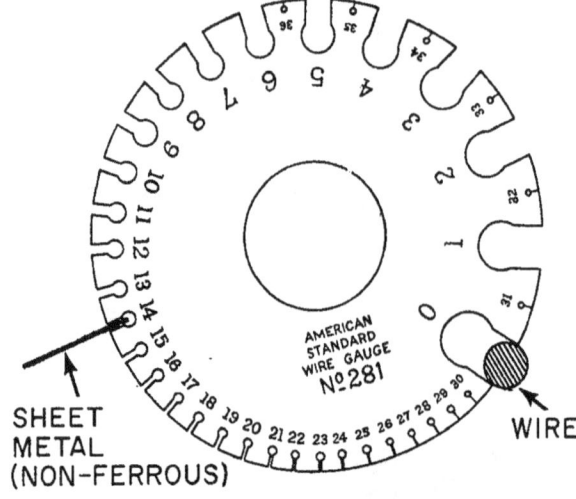

Figure 63.—Using a wire gage to measure wire and sheet metal.

thicknesses. Some thickness gage blades are straight, while others are bent at 45 and 90 degree angles at the end. Thickness gages can also be grouped so that there are several short and several long blades together. Before using a feeler gage, remove any foreign matter from the blades. You cannot get a correct measurement unless the blades are clean.

When using a feeler gage consisting of a number of blades, insert various blades or combinations of blades between two surfaces until a snug fit is obtained. The thickness of the individual blade or the total thickness of ALL THE BLADES USED is the measurement between the surfaces.

Care of Thickness Gages

Handle the blades with care at all times. Keep from forcing the blades into openings that are too small for them. Some blades are very thin and can be bent or kinked easily. Blade edges and polished surfaces are also easy to damage. When not using a thickness gage, keep it closed.

THREAD GAGE

Thread gages (screw-pitch gages) are used to determine the pitch and number of threads per inch of threaded fasteners. (See fig. 61.) They consist of thin leaves whose edges are toothed to correspond to standard thread sections.

To measure the unknown pitch of a thread, compare it with the standards of the screw pitch gage. Hold a gage leaf to the thread being measured (fig. 62), substituting various sizes until you find an exact fit. Look at the fit toward a source of light for best results.

The number of threads per inch is indicated by the numerical value on the blade which is found to fit the unknown threads. Using this

Table 2.—Wire and Sheet Metal Gages

Gage No.	Birmingham wire gage (B.W.G.) or Stubs iron wire gage, for iron wires, hot and cold rolled sheet steel	American wire gage, or Brown & Sharpe (for non-ferrous sheet and wire)	U.S. Standard gage for sheet and plate iron and steel	Steel wire gage, or the W & M (Washburn & Moen) for steel wire
0	.340	.3249	.3125	.3065
1	.300	.2893	.2812	.2830
2	.284	.2576	.2656	.2625
3	.259	.2294	.2500	.2437
4	.238	.2043	.2343	.2253
5	.220	.1819	.2187	.2070
6	.203	.1620	.2031	.1920
7	.180	.1443	.1876	.1770
8	.165	.1285	.1718	.1620
9	.148	.1144	.1562	.1483
10	.134	.1019	.1406	.1350
11	.120	.0907	.1250	.1205
12	.109	.0808	.1093	.1055
13	.095	.0719	.0937	.0915
14	.083	.0640	.0781	.0800
15	.072	.0570	.0703	.0720
16	.065	.0508	.0625	.0625
17	.058	.0452	.0562	.0540
18	.049	.0403	.0500	.0475
19	.042	.0359	.0437	.0410
20	.035	.0319	.0375	.0348
21	.032	.0284	.0343	.0317
22	.028	.0253	.0312	.0286
23	.025	.0225	.0281	.0258
24	.022	.0201	.0250	.0230
25	.020	.0179	.0218	.0204
26	.018	.0159	.0187	.0181
27	.016	.0142	.0171	.0173
28	.014	.0126	.0156	.0162
29	.013	.0112	.0140	.0150
30	.012	.0100	.0125	.0140
31	.010	.0089	.0109	.0132
32	.009	.0079	.0101	.0128
33	.008	.0071	.0093	.0118
34	.007	.0063	.0085	.0104
35	.005	.0056	.0078	.0095
36	.004	.0050	.0070	.0090

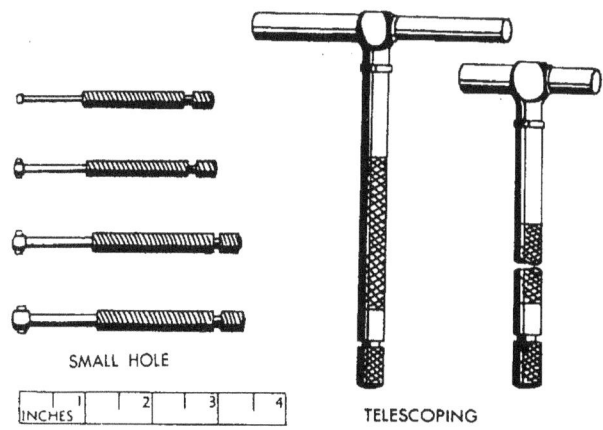

Figure 64.—Small hole and telescoping gages.

value as a basis, correct sizes of nuts, bolts, tap cutters, and die cutters are selected for use.

WIRE GAGE

The wire gage shown in fig. 63, is used for measuring the diameters of wires or the thickness of sheet metal. This gage is circular in shape with cutouts in the outer perimeter. Each cutout gages a different size from No. 0 to No. 36. Examination of the gage will show that the larger the gage number, the smaller the diameter or thickness.

Gages similar to the one shown in figure 63 are available for measuring a variety of wires and sheet metals. The names of some common standard wire gages and their uses are given in the column headings of table 2. The body of this table contains gage numbers and their corresponding equivalents in decimal fractions of an inch.

Wire diameters may also be expressed in mils as well as by gage numbers. One mil equals one thousandth of an inch. Each decimal equivalent in table 2 can be converted to mils by multiplying by 1,000. For example, the circled decimal in the table is equivalent to .0640 x 1000 or 64 mils.

To use table 2, you select from the four gages listed in the table the one that applies to the sheet of metal or wire you want to gage. For instance, column 2 of the table tells you that the American Wire Gage shown in figure 63 is the one to use for nonferrous sheet or wire. Notice that each of the four gages has its own decimal equivalent for a particular gage number.

To measure wire size, apply the gage to the wire as shown in figure 63. Do not force the wire into the slot. Find the slot that refuses to pass the wire without forcing. Then, try the next larger slot until one is found that passes the wire. This is the correct size. Remember, your measurements are taken at the slot portion of the cutout rather than the inner portion of the gage. Now that you have the gage number turn your gage over and read the decimal equivalent for that number.

To measure the gage of a piece of metal, first remove any burr from the place where you

MEASURING TOOLS AND TECHNIQUES

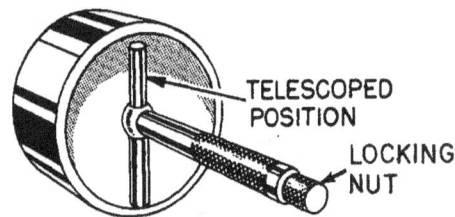

Figure 65.—Using a telescoping gage.

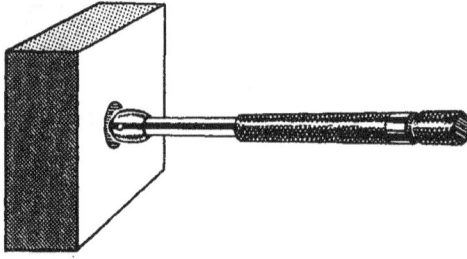

Figure 66.—Measuring the diameter of a hole with a small hole gage.

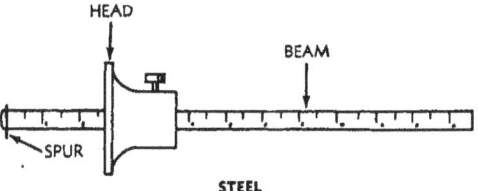

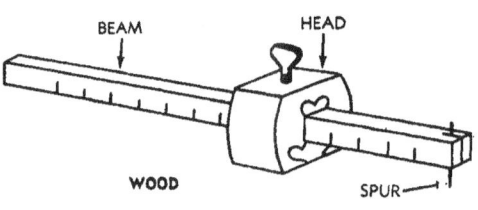

Figure 67.—Marking gages.

intend to apply the gage. Then select the appropriate gage for the metal to be measured.

After the right gage has been selected, apply the gage to the wire, or to the edge of the sheet as shown in figure 63. The number opposite the slot that fits the wire or sheet is its gage number. The decimal equivalent is stamped on the opposite face of the gage.

TELESCOPING GAGE

Telescoping gages are used for measuring the inside size of slots or holes up to 6 inches in width or diameter. They are T-shaped tools in which the shaft of the T is used as a handle, and the crossarm used for measuring. (See fig. 64.) The crossarms telescope into each other and are held out by a light spring. To use the gage the arms are compressed, placed in the hole to be measured, and allowed to expand. A twist of the locknut on top of the handle locks the arms. The tool may then be withdrawn and the distance across the arms measured.

These tools are commonly furnished in sets, the smallest gage for measuring the distances from 5/16 to 1/2 inch, and the largest for distances from 3 1/2 to 6 inches.

To measure the diameter of a hole from 1/2" to 6" in diameter, select from a set of telescoping gages the one whose range includes the size you need. Loosen the knurled nut at the end of the handle, and telescope the adjustable end of the gage to a size slightly smaller than the hole and retighten the nut. Insert the gage into the hole as shown in figure 65, loosen the nut to permit the spring-loaded adjustable end to expand to the hole diameter, and tighten the nut. The spring loaded contact of the adjustable end will assure proper contact. Make sure, however, that the gage is held with the telescoping end at right angles to the axis of the hole to measure the true, maximum diameter. Remove the gage and measure the setting with an outside micrometer caliper.

SMALL HOLE GAGE

For measuring smaller slots or holes than the telescoping gages will measure, small hole gages can be used. These gages come in sets of four or more and will measure distances of approximately 1/8 to 1/2 inch.

The small hole gage (fig. 64) consists of a small, split, ball-shaped member mounted on the end of a handle. The ball is expanded by turning a knurled knob on the handle until the proper feel is obtained (the slight drag of the ball end on the sides of the hole). The gage is then withdrawn (fig. 66) and the size of the ball-shaped member on the end of the gage can be measured with an outside micrometer caliper. On some types of small hole gages, the

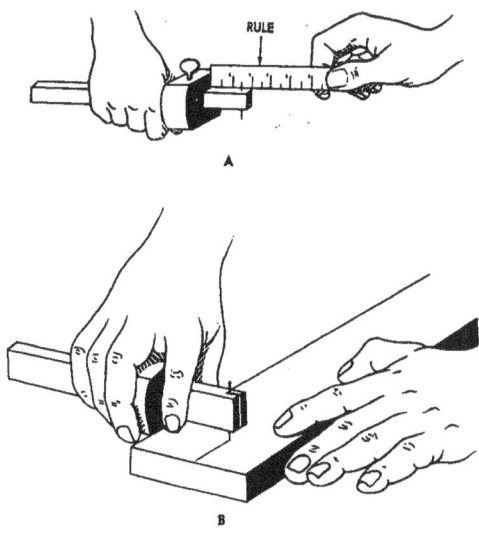

Figure 68.—Using the marking gage.

Figure 70.—Scribing a circle with a divider.

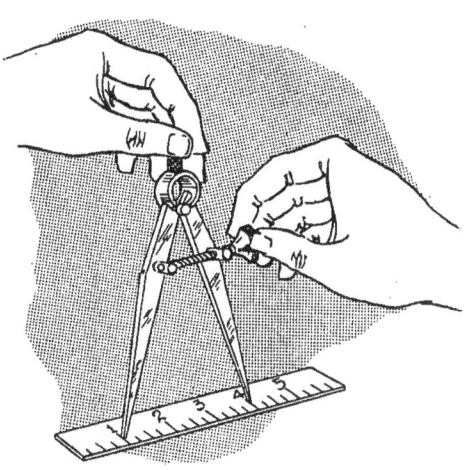

Figure 69.—Setting a divider to a desired radius.

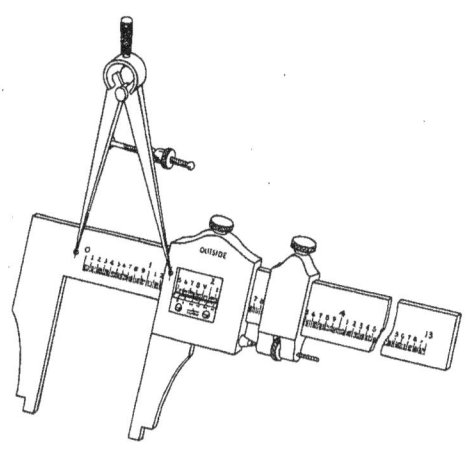

Figure 71.—Setting a divider with a vernier caliper.

the ball is flattened at the bottom near the centerline to permit use in shallow holes and recesses.

MARKING GAGES

A marking gage is used to mark off guidelines parallel to an edge, end, or surface of a piece of wood or metal. It has a sharp spur or pin that does the marking.

Marking gages (fig. 67) are made of wood or steel. They consist of a graduated beam about 8 inches long on which a head slides. The head can be fastened at any point on the beam by means of a thumbscrew. The thumbscrew presses a brass shoe tightly against the beam and locks it firmly in position. The steel pin or spur that does the marking projects from the beam about 1/16 inch.

To draw a line parallel to an edge with a marking gage, first determine the distance the line must be from the edge of the stock. Adjust the marking gage by setting the head the desired distance from the spur. Although the bar of a marking gage is graduated in inches, the spur may work loose or bend. If this occurs, accurate measurement should be made with a

MEASURING TOOLS AND TECHNIQUES

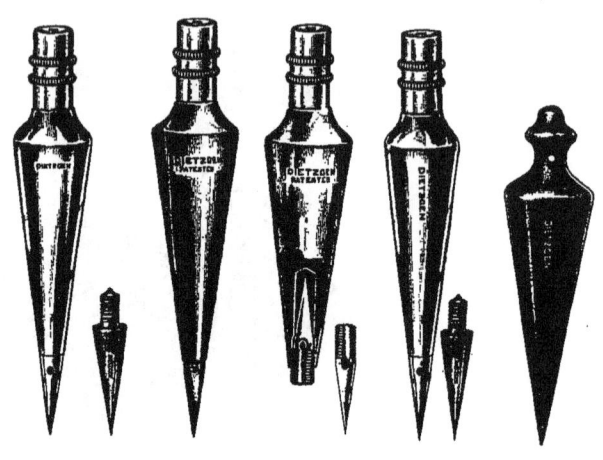

Figure 72.—Plumb bobs.

rule between the head and spur. (See fig. 68A.) To draw a line after setting the gage, grasp the head of the gage with the palm and fingers as shown in figure 68B; extend the thumb along the beam towards the spur. Press the head firmly against the edge of the work to be marked, and with a wrist motion tip the gage forward until the spur touches the work. Push the gage along the edge to mark the work, keeping the head firmly against the edge of the work.

DIVIDERS

Dividers are useful instruments for transferring measurements and are frequently used in scribing arcs and circles in layout work.

To lay out a circle with a divider, set the divider at the desired radius, using a rule as shown in figure 69. Note that the 3-inch radius being set here is being taken at a central portion rather than at the end of the rule. This reduces the chance of error, as each point of the dividers can be set on a graduation.

Place one leg of the divider at the center of the proposed circle, lean the tool in the direction it will be rotated, and rotate it by rolling the knurled handle between your thumb and index finger (fig. 70).

Vernier calipers, which have two center points similar to prick punchmarks are particularly useful in setting a divider to exact dimensions. One center point will be found near the zero end of the scale on the rule. The other point is in line with the first and to the left of the zero on the vernier scale. (See fig. 71.)

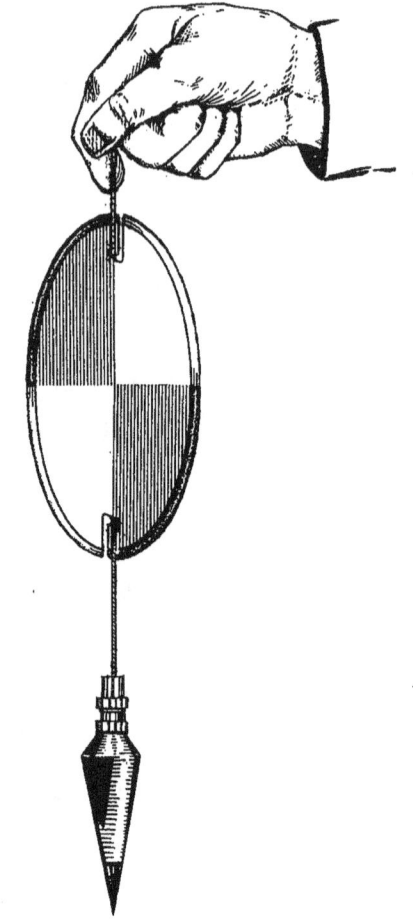

Figure 73.—Plumb bob, cord, and target.

Set and secure the desired setting on the vernier caliper and adjust the divider until both points readily enter the center points on the vernier caliper as shown in figure 71.

PLUMB BOB

A plumb bob (fig. 72) is a pointed, tapered brass or bronze weight which is suspended from a cord for determining the vertical or plumb line to or from a point on the ground. Common weights for plumb bobs are 6, 8, 10, 12, 14, 16, 18, and 24 oz.

A plumb bob is a precision instrument and must be cared for as such. If the tip becomes bent, the cord from which the bob is suspended will not occupy the true plumb line over the point indicated by the tip. A plumb bob usually has a detachable tip, as shown in figure 72, so that if the tip should become damaged it can

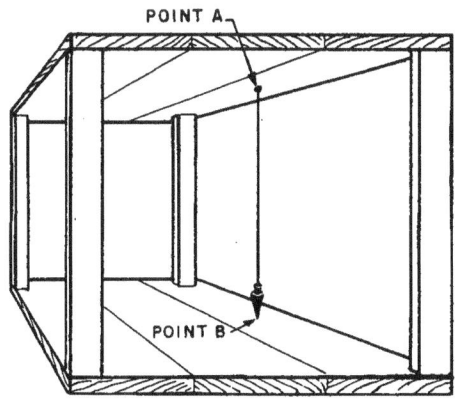

Figure 74.—Locating a point with a plumb bob.

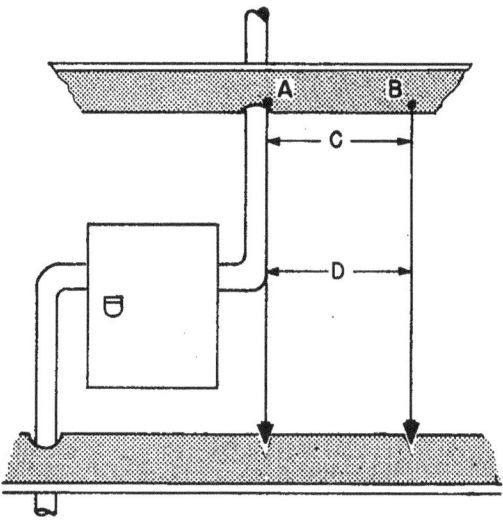

Figure 75.—Plumbing a structural member with a plumb bob.

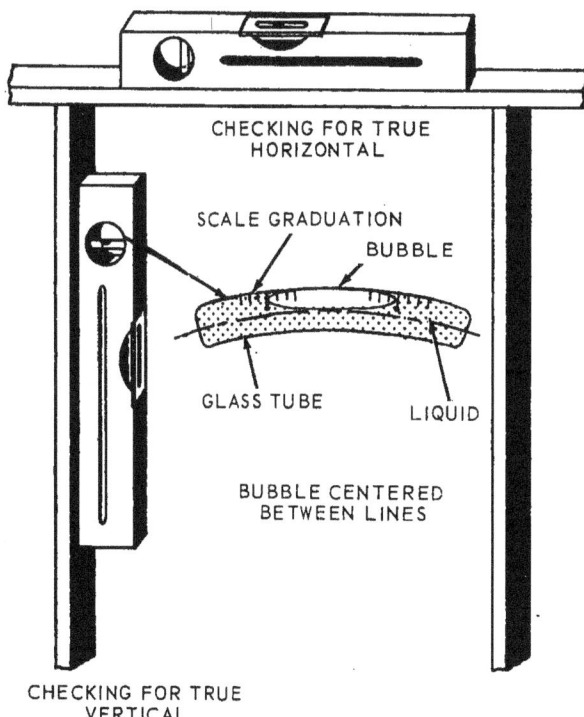

Figure 76.—Horizontal and vertical use of level.

be renewed without replacing the entire instrument.

The cord from a plumb bob can be made more conspicuous, for observation purposes, by attachment of a red-and-white target as shown in figure 73.

The plumb bob is used in carpentry to determine true verticality when erecting vertical uprights and corner posts of framework. Surveyors use it for transferring and lining up points.

To locate a point which is exactly below a particular point in space, when working ashore or on a ship in drydock, secure the plumb bob string to the upper point, such as A in figure 74. When the plumb stops swinging, the point as indicated at B in the illustration, will be exactly below A.

To plumb a structural member, or an electrical conduit, as shown by figure 75, secure the plumb line A so that you can look at both the line and piece behind the line. Then, by sighting, line up the member or conduit with the plumb line.

If this cannot be done, it may be necessary to secure the plumb line at some point such as B, and then measure the offset from the line to the piece at two places so that, for example, C and D in figure 75 are equal. If the distances between C and D are not equal, adjust the structural member or conduit until they are.

LEVELS

Levels are tools designed to prove whether a plane or surface is true horizontal or true vertical. Some precision levels are calibrated so that they will indicate in degrees, minutes, and seconds, the angle inclination of a surface in relation to a horizontal or vertical surface.

MEASURING TOOLS AND TECHNIQUES

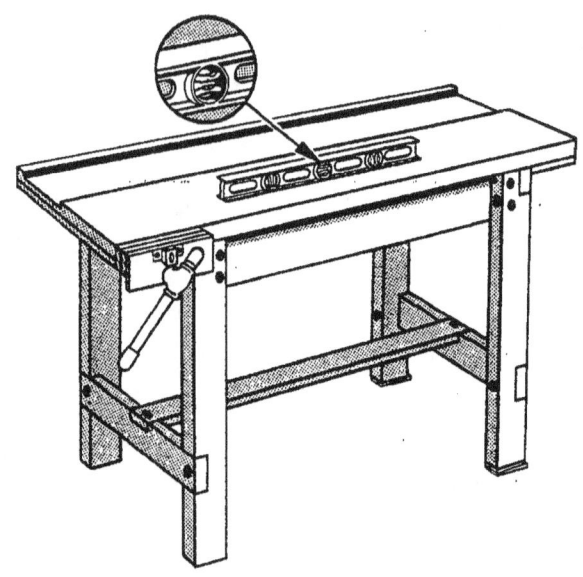

Figure 77.—Leveling a bench.

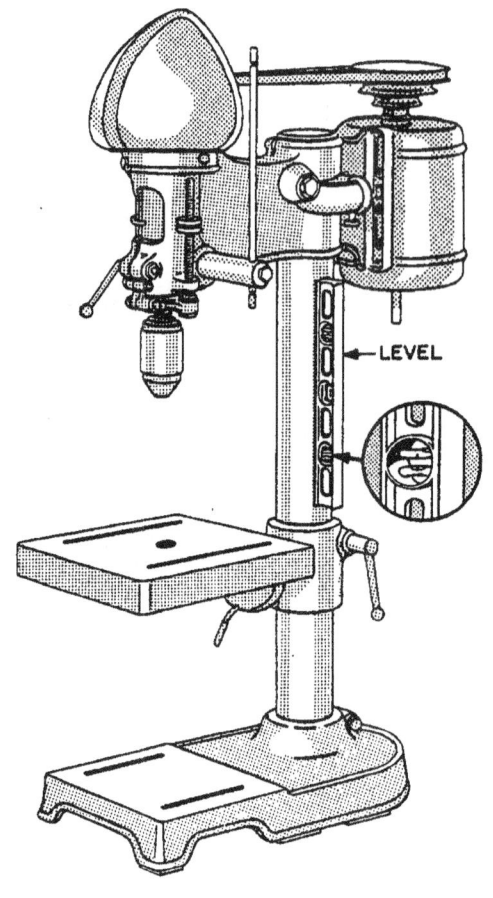

Figure 78.—Plumbing a piece of equipment with a level.

The level is a simple instrument consisting of a liquid, such as alcohol or chloroform, partially filling a glass vial or tube so that a bubble remains. The tube is mounted in a frame which may be aluminum, wood, or iron. Levels are equipped with one, two, or more tubes. One tube is built in the frame at right angles to another (fig. 76). The tube indicated in figure 76 is slightly curved, causing the bubble to seek always the highest point in the tube. On the outside of the tube are two sets of graduation lines separated by a space. Leveling is accomplished when the air bubble is centered between the graduation lines.

To level a piece of equipment, such as the workbench in figure 77, with a carpenter's level, set the level on the bench top parallel to the front edge of the bench. Notice that the level has several pairs of glass vials. Regardless of the position of the level, always watch the bubble in the bottom vial of a horizontal pair. Shim or wedge up the end of the bench that will return that bubble to the center of its vial. Recheck the first position of the level before securing the shims or wedges.

To plumb a piece of equipment, such as the drill press shown in figure 78, place the level on the side and on the front of the main column of the press. Figure 78 shows the level on the side. Use shims as necessary to bring the bubble in the lower vial of either pair of the horizontal vials to the center in each case.

Levels must be checked for accuracy. This is readily accomplished by placing the level on a true horizontal surface and noting the vial indication. Reverse the level end for end. If the bubble appears on one side of the graduations with reference to the operator on the first reading and on the other side for the second reading, the level is out of true and must be adjusted.

Do not drop or handle a level roughly. To prevent damage, store it in a rack or other suitable place when not in use.

GLOSSARY OF METAL WORKING

CONTENTS

	Page
Abrasive ...... Base Metal	1
Bastard ...... Brass	2
Brass Bound ...... Cadmium	3
Calipers ...... Cobolt	4
Cold Chisel ...... Drift	5
Drill Bit ...... Fish Plate	6
Flaring ...... Gunmetal	7
Hacksaw ...... Hollowing Hammer	8
Iron ...... Malleable	9
Mallet ...... Ore	10
Oxidation or Oxidization ...... Post vise	11
Pumice ...... Rust	12
Safe Edge ...... Smooth cut	13
Snap head ...... Steel sheet	14
Stock ...... Tinner's or Tinman's Solder	15
Tinning ...... Wing nut	16
Wiped joint ...... Zinc Chloride	17
Properties of Metals	18
Properties of Alloys	18
Soldering Fluxes	19
Composition of Some Alloys	19

GLOSSARY OF METAL WORKING

A

ABRASIVE
A natural or artificial substance used for grinding, polishing, buffing, lapping or sandblasting. Commonly includes garnet, emery, corundum, diamond, aluminum oxide and silicon carbide.

ACID PICKLE
Diluted acid used for cleaning metal.

AGE HARDEN
The capacity of some metals to get harder as they get older.

ALLOY
A substance having metallic qualities, composed of one or more chemical elements, at least one of which is a metallic element.

ALUMINUM
Lightweight soft white-colored metal, usually alloyed with other metals to increase its hardness and other qualities.

ANGLE IRON
Mild steel. Bars with 90 degree cross-section.

ANNEALING
Treating metal to make it as soft as possible (usually by heating and cooling slowly). The necessary technique varies between metals and alloys.

ANODIZING
Chemical surface treatment for protection and decoration of aluminum and its alloys.

ANTIQUEING
Darkening copper or brass by chemical treatment.

ASBESTOS
Fibrous silicate mineral that is incombustible.

ASH
Springy hard wood used for hammer and mallet handles.

B

BALL PEIN
Hemispherical end of a hammer head.

BASE METAL
At one time, the name for common metals. They are contrast to the "noble" metals which are valuable.

BASTARD
A grade of fairly coarse file.

BEAK OR BICK
Round conical end of an anvil or stake. Also horn.

BELL MOUTH
Spread end of tube.

BICK IRON
Light anvil for sheet metalwork.

BIT
Jaws of tongs. A drill.

BLIND RIVETING
Using tubular rivets on a mandrel with a device for closing each rivet from one side of the metal.

BLOCKING HAMMER
A hammer with two large flat faces.

BLOWLAMP
A torch burning gas, kerosene or other fuel to produce a flame in the form of a jet.

BOLSTER
Block with hole to support work being punched.

BOLT
Screw fastening with a head to take a nut. Only threaded part of its length. If it is threaded fully to its head, it is a metal-threaded screw.

BORAX
Flux for hard soldering and brazing.

BOSS
Center part of a wheel. A locally raised part of sheet metal. The punch used to raise it.

BOSSING MALLET
Wooden mallet with an egg-shaped head for shaping sheet metal.

BOUGE
Knock out dents in raised work over a stake.

BRAKE
Mechanical device for folding sheet metal.

BRASS
An alloy consisting mainly of copper and zinc to which small amounts of other metals may be added. Common brass is yellow.

BRASS-BOUND
   Strengthened with brass straps. Particularly a wooden box or chest.

BRASS SCRIBER
   Pointed brass rod used to mark tinplate.

BRASS TONGS
   Tongs for dipping non-ferrous metals in acid pickles.

BRAZING
   Joining by melting spelter or hard solder.

BRAZING HEARTH
   Trough to hold coke or asbestos and support work while it is brazed.

BRONZE
   Copper alloy with tin and other metals.

BRONZE AGE
   Early period after the Stone Age when primitive man made tools and implements from an early form of copper alloy.

BUFF
   To polish the surface of metal with a powered buffing wheel.

BUFFING WHEEL
   Fabric disks held together, usually by sewing, forming a wheel to be rotated at high speed and used for polishing. Also called a polishing mop.

BURIN
   An engraving tool.

BURNISHER
   Hard steel rubbing tool. Shaping tool used in metal spinning.

BURR
   Turned over edge. Small rotary file.

BUTTERFLY NUT
   A nut to fit on a bolt with projections for hand tightening. Also a wing nut.

BUTT STRAP
   Riveted strip over meeting edges. Also a fish plate.

<u>C</u>

CADMIUM
   Metal used for plating steel to protect it from corrosion.

CALIPERS
Tool with hinged curved jaws for checking thickness and diameters.

CANISTER STAKE
Cylindrical stake with a flat end.

CARBIDE TIP
A very hard tip to make a cutting edge bonded to tool steel, using carbide, which is a compound of carbon with one or more metallic elements.

CARBON
Element added to iron to make steel.

CARRIAGE BOLT
Bolt with a shallow domed head and square neck to prevent it from turning in wood.

CARRIAGE SCREW
A large wood screw with a head to take to wrench.

CASTING
Melting metal and pouring it into molds.

CENTER PUNCH
Pointed punch to make a dot in metal.

CENTIGRADE or CELSIUS
Temperature scale with the freezing point of water 0 degrees and the boiling point 100 degrees.

CHALK LINE
Fine cord that is used with chalk to strike a line.

CHATTER MARKS
Ridges produced by vibration during filing or other work.

CHISEL
An end-cutting tool for wood or metal.

CHROMIUM
Metal that can be alloyed with steel or used for plating.

CHUCK
A holding device for a drill or a lathe. A former for metal spinning.

CIRCUMFERENCE
Distance around a circle or other rounded shape. A similar distance around an angular shape is a perimeter.

COBOLT
Rare metal which can be added to steel to increase its magnetic properties.

COLD CHISEL
　　A tool that is hammered for cutting cold metal.

CORROSION
　　Oxidization of the surface of metal such as rust on iron.

CORRUGATED IRON
　　Sheet iron or steel ridged and grooved regularly across its width. It is usually protected by galvanizing.

COPPER
　　Red colored non-ferrous metal.

COUNTERSINK
　　Bevelled edge of hole. The tool for doing this.

CREASING HAMMER
　　A hammer with two narrow cross peins.

CREASING IRON
　　Stake with grooves across.

CROCUS
　　Fine polishing powder.

CURVE ALLOWANCE
　　Size correction at a bend due to measuring around the neutral axis.

<u>D</u>

DEVELOPMENT
　　Outline of the shape while metal is flat that will give the desired shape after bending.

DIAMETER
　　Distance across a circle.

DIE
　　Tool for cutting a screw thread on a rod. A form into which metal is pressed for shaping.

DIVIDERS
　　Hinged pair of points for scratching a circle or comparing distances

DRAW FILLING
　　Using a file sideways along an edge to remove cross file marks.

DRAWING
　　Pulling metal through holes to form wire.

DRIFT
　　Punch used to draw holes into line.

DRILL BIT
Tool for making a hole by cutting (as distinct from punching).

DRILL PRESS
A machine which uses drill bits to make holes.

E

ELEMENT
Any of about 100 substances that cannot be revolved by chemical means into simpler substances.

EMBOSS
Raise sheet metal, with a hammer, punch or boss from the reverse side.

EMERY
Grit used as abrasive on metal.

ESCUTCHEON
Key hole or the plate around it.

ETCHING
Eating into metal with acid to produce a design, usually a name.

EXCRUDING
Forcing metal through a die to form rods of special section.

EYE BOLT
Bolt with flattened or shaped end with a hole through.

F

FAHRENHEIT
Common temperature scale.

FERROUS
Alloy containing iron.

FERRULE
A tube or cap on a wooden handle to prevent it from splitting.

FILE
Tool with teeth made with grooves cut across it.

FILE CARD
Wire brush for cleaning files.

FISH PLATE
Alternative name for butt strap.

FLARING
Spreading the end of a tube. Giving it a bell mouth.

FLANGE
Folded edge.

FLASH
The movement of solder as it melts around a joint. Excess solder to be removed.

FLUX
Liquid or powder used to help a metal or an alloy to flow in welding, brazing or soldering.

FOCUS
Plural is foci. Point about which a curved shape is generated, The center of a circle is its focus. An ellipse has two foci.

FOLDING BARS
Parallel bars used for bending sheet metal.

G

GALVANIZED IRON
Iron coated with zinc as a protection against rust.

GAUGE
Size, particularly the thickness of sheets or the diameter of wires, according to a recognized scale. The tool for measuring this.

GILDING
Coating with gold leaf.

GILDING METAL
Alloy of copper and zinc with a greater proportion of copper than in brass.

GOLD
One of the rare or noble metals.

GRAVER
Cutting tool with a diamond-shaped cutting point.

GROOVING STAKE
Alternative name for a creasing iron.

GUILLOTINE
Large mechanical shearing machine.

GUNMETAL
Alloy of copper and tin.

H

HACKSAW
Metal-cutting handsaw with its blade tensioned in a frame.

HALF-MOON STAKE
A hatchet stake with a curved edge.

HARD SOLDER
Copper/zinc alloy with other metals added to lower its melting point.

HATCHET SOLDERING IRON
An iron with a copper bit at an angle to the shaft and a straight thin edge.

HATCHET STAKE
Stake with straight sharp edge for bending sheet metal across its top.

HEARTH
Any container for coke or other solid fuel.

HEAT TREATMENT
Heating steel to alter its character. This includes annealing, hardening, tempering and normalizing. Annealing other metals by heating.

HEEL
Opposite end of anvil or bick iron to the beak.

HICKORY
Springy wood used for mallet and hammer handles.

HIDE MALLET
A mallet with a head formed from rolled leather.

HIGH CARBON STEEL
Steel with sufficient carbon to permit hardening and tempering.

HOLD UP
Support one rivet head while the other is formed.

HOLLOW GROUND
A concave bevel on a cutting edge.

HONING
Sharpening or smoothing with a fine abrasive stone.

HORN
Alternative name for beak of anvil or bick iron.

HOLLOWING HAMMER
A hammer with two ball peins.

I

IRON
Silver-white common metal which can be alloyed with carbon to make steel.

IRON AGE
A prehistoric age when man first learned how to make tools and weapons from iron.

J

JAWS
Gripping surfaces of tongs or vise.

JENNY
Hand-operated machine for flanging and wiring sheet metal edges.

K

KILLED SPIRITS
Zinc chloride used as flux when soldering.

L

LEAD
Heavy and soft grey metal. The amount a nut moves forward in one revolution on a threaded rod.

LEG VISE
A strong vise attached to a bench, but with a leg extending to the floor.

LOW CARBON STEEL
Steel that does not contain the proper amount of carbon to permit tempering. Also called mild steel.

M

MACHINIST'S VISE
Vise with a parallel action to mount on a bench.

MAGNESIUM
Very light and combustible metal.

MALACCA
Species of cane used for mallot handles.

MALL OR MAUL
Large two-handed mallet.

MALLEABLE
Capable of being shaped.

MALLET
Type of hammer with wood, rawhide or plastic head.

MANDREL OR MANDRIL
Iron block on which parts are shaped. Particularly a round cone for shaping rings.

MEAN
Average or center. A mean line is the center of the thickness of bent sheet metal.

MILD STEEL
Low-carbon steel which cannot be tempered.

METALLURGY
The science and technology of metals.

MICROMETER
Instrument for making fine measurements using the rotation of a screw.

MUSHROOM STAKE
A round-topped steel anvil.

N

NEUTRAL AXIS
The mean line in the thickness of metal that is neither stretched nor compressed when it is bent.

NIBBLER
Shearing tool that removes particles along a line.

NICKEL
Metal alloyed with steel and used for plating.

NOBLE METALS
At one time the name for valuable metals in contrast with the "base" metals.

NON-FERROUS
Alloy that does not contain iron.

NORMALIZE
Reduce internal stresses after working by heating and allowing to cool slowly in the same way as annealing steel.

O

OFFSET
Double bend to alter alignment of a bar or sheet.

ORE
Solid naturally occurring mineral aggregate from which metal is extracted.

OXIDATION OR OXIDIZATION
: The effect of air on the surface of metal.

P

PATINA
: Colored oxidation on metal surfaces due to long exposure to air particularly on bronze. It can be simulated by chemical action.

PEEN, PEIN or PANE
: The shaped end of a hammer head.

PEENING
: Hollowing with ball peen hammer.

PERIMETER
: Distance around an angular outline. A similar measurement around a curve is a circumference.

PICKLE
: Dilute acid for cleaning metals.

PIERCING
: Cutting internal fretted shapes in sheet metal with a fine saw in a frame.

PITCH
: Composition for supporting repousse work. Distance between holes or the tops of a screw thread.

PLANISHING
: Hammering all over to harden and decorate.

PLANISHING HAMMER
: A hammer with highly polished flat or domed faces.

PLATE
: Alternative name for sheet metal. Usually of the thickert types.

PLATINUM
: Rare and valuable metal used especially in jewelry.

PLIERS
: Small gripping tool with tongs action.

POP RIVETING
: Alternative name for blind riveting.

POST VISE
: Alternative name for a leg vise.

PUMICE
  Volcanic powder used as a fine abrasive.

PUNCH
  Tool intended to be hit with a hammer to make a dent or hole.

Q

QUENCH
  To cool hot metal quickly in a liquid.

R

RADIUS
  Distance from the center to the circumference of a circle.

RAISING
  Making a deep bowl shape by hammering over a stake.

RAISING HAMMER
  A hammer with two cross peins.

RASP
  A coarse file type of tool with teeth individually raised.

RAKE
  Cutting angle of a drill or other tool.

REPOUSSÉ
  Method of raising a pattern from the back of thin metal.

REPOUSSÉ HAMMER
  Light hammer with broad-faced pein.

ROLLING
  Squeezing metal between rollers to form sheets.

ROUGE
  Fine polishing powder.

ROUT
  Cut grooves or hollows.

RULE
  Measuring tool. Not "ruler."

RUST
  Corrosion on iron steel.

S

SAFE EDGE
One edge of a file without teeth. Turned-in edge of sheet metal,

SAND BAG
Leather bag containing sand on which hollowing is done.

SATE
Alternative name for a sett. Used to flatten metal.

SCALLOP
An evenly waved edge.

SCREW
A fastening to take a nut that threaded to the head. If it is only threaded part way, it is a bolt. A screw can cut its own thread in wood or sheet metal.

SCOTS SHEARS
Large snips.

SCRIBE OR SCRIBER
Hard sharp steel point for scratching metal.

SECOND CUT
The grade of file commonly used on edges of sheet metal.

SELF-TAPPING SCREW
Hardened steel screw that cuts its thread in sheet metal.

SET
A hammer-like head on a wooden handle that is hit with a hammer to shape metal.

SET SCREW
Screw used to draw parts together.

SHANK
The neck or part of a tool between the handle and the blade.

SHEAR
Large snips that are often bench mounted with a lever handle.

SILVER SOLDER
Copper/zinc alloy with a small amount of silver included to lower its melting point.

SLEDGE
A large two-handed hammer.

SMOOTH CUT
The finest grade file normally used.

SNAP HEAD
Raised round head on a rivet.

SNIPS
Scissor action shears for cutting sheet metal.

SOFT SOLDER
Low melting point solder. A lead/tin alloy.

SOLDER
Alloy used to fuse into joints. The action of soldering.

SOLDERING IRON
Tool with copper bit that is heated to melt solder.

SPATULA
Iron rod with flattened end that is used to place flux and spelter in brazing or for hard soldering.

SPELTER
Form of brass used in brazing.

SPINNING
Shaping sheet metal in a lathe.

SPRING STEEL
High carbon steel that is similar to tool steel.

SQUARE
As a setting out term, this means at right angles.

STAINLESS STEEL
Steel alloyed with other metals to resist corrosion.

STAKE
Shaped block used as an anvil in sheet metalwork.

STAKE VISE
Alternative name for leg vise.

STEEL
Alloy of iron and carbon.

STEEL PLATE
Steel rolled into sheets more than about three-sixteenths of an inch thick.

STEEL SHEET
Steel rolled thinner than steel plate.

STOCK
  Supply of metal. The body of a tool. One head of a lathe.

STRIKE A LINE
  Draw a line using a chalked cord.

STROP
  Leather strap used in the final stages of tool sharpening.

SULFURIC ACID
  Corrosive fluid used in cleaning metal.

SWAGE BLOCK
  Large block with many hollows and holes.

SWARF
  Filings and other waste removed from metal.

T

TAIL
  Oppposite end of anvil or bick iron to the beak. Also heel.

TANG
  Part of a tool that is driven into a handle.

TAP
  Tool for cutting a screw thread in a hole.

TEMPER
  Reduced full hardened steel to a lesser hardness and less brittle form for a particular use.

TEMPLATE or TEMPLET
  Pattern used for marking around to transfer an outline.

THREE-SQUARE FILE
  A file with a triangular cross section.

TIN
  White metal used in alloys and for coating steel for protection against corrosion.

TINMAN'S or TINNER'S MALLET
  Mallet with a cylindrical wood head.

TINNER
  Worker in tinplate.

TINNER'S or TINMAN'S SOLDER
  Lead/tin alloy. Also called soft solder.

TINNING
    In soldering, coating the bit or the surfaces to be joined with soft solder,

TINPLATE
    Thin sheet steel that is coated with tin.

TINSNIPS
    Small shears for cutting sheet metal.

TINSMITH
    Alternative name for tinner or tinman.

TORCH
    Device for burning gas to produce a forced flame that can be adjusted to size.

TRACER
    Narrow-ended punch used for decorative lines.

TRAMMEL HEADS
    Sliding heads on a bar for use as large compasses or dividers.

TRIPOLI
    A fine polishing compound.

TRUNCATED
    Cut off. Usually applied to part of a cone.

V

VISE
    Two-jawed device with a tightening screw. Attached to bench and used to hold metal being worked on.

VISE GRIP PLIERS
    Pliers that can be locked on to the work.

VISE CLAMPS
    Sheet metal covers that are placed over vise jaws.

W

WELD
    Fuse two pieces of metal together with heat.

WHITING
    Powder used for polishing tinplate.

WING NUT
    Alternative name for butterfly nut.

WIPED JOINT
   Joint between pipes made with plumber's solder.

WIRE EDGE
   Burr on the edge of a sharpened tool.

WIRED EDGE
   Wire enclosed in a rolled sheet metal edge.

WORK HARDEN
   Hardening due to hammering or other work on non-ferrous metals.

WRENCH
   Any tool for levering or twisting. Particularly useful for turning nuts and bolts.

WROUGHT IRON
   Iron with little or no carbon. Produced by the puddling process

Z

ZINC
   Grey/white metal used mainly in alloys and for coating steel

ZINC CHLORIDE
   Chemical used as a flux for soldering.

Properties of Metals

Metal	Chemical symbol	Pounds per cubic in.	Melting Point Degrees F
Aluminum	Al	0.0924	1218
Cadmium	Cd	0.3105	610
Chromium	Cr	0.2347	2939
Cobolt	Co	0.3123	2696
Copper	Cu	0.3184	1981
Gold	Au	0.6975	1945
Iron (wrought)	Fe	0.2834	2750
Lead	Pb	0.4105	621
Magnesium	Mg	0.0628	1204
Nickel	Ni	0.3177	2646
Silver	Ag	0.3802	1761
Tin	Sn	0.2632	449
Zinc	Zn	0.2587	787

Properties of Alloys

Alloy	Composition	Pounds Per Cubic Inch	Melting Point Degrees F
Brass Or	80 copper, 20 zinc	0.3105	1846
Spelter	60 copper, 40 zinc	0.3018	1634
	50 copper, 50 zinc	0.2960	1616
Solder	20 tin, 80 lead	-	532
	40 tin, 60 lead	-	446
	40 tin, 60 lead	-	446
	50 tin, 50 lead	-	401
	60 tin, 40 lead	-	369
	70 tin, 30 lead	-	365
	90 tin, 10 lead	-	419
Steel	-	0.2816	2500

Soldering Fluxes

Prepared fluxes can be purchased, but the following are traditional fluxes for soft soldering. For hand soldering all suitable metals, use borax.

Metal Or Alloy	Flux
Aluminum	Stearin
Brass	Chloride of zinc or resin
Copper	Chloride of zinc or resin
Lead	Tallow or resin
Tinned steel	Chloride of zinc or resin
Galvanized steel	Hydrochloric acid
Zinc	Hydrochloric acid
Pewter	Gallipoli oil
Iron and steel	Chloride of zinc or chloride of ammonia

Composition of Some Alloys

Alloy	copper	lead	tin	zinc	Antimony
Brass	32	-	1.5	10	-
Gunmetal	80	-	10	-	-
Gilding metal	60	-	-	40	-
Bell metal	80	-	20	-	-
Spelter	50	-	-	50	-
Solder	-	60	40	-	-
Britannia metal	2	-	90	-	8
Pewter	2	2	89	-	7
Type metal		50	25	0	25